Philosophical Hermeneutics

Hans-Georg Gadamer

PHILOSOPHICAL HERMENEUTICS

Translated and Edited
by
David E. Linge

UNIVERSITY OF CALIFORNIA PRESS

Berkeley Los Angeles London

UNIVERSITY OF CALIFORNIA PRESS

BERKELEY AND LOS ANGELES, CALIFORNIA

UNIVERSITY OF CALIFORNIA PRESS, LTD.

LONDON, ENGLAND

COPYRIGHT © 1976 BY THE REGENTS OF THE UNIVERSITY OF CALIFORNIA

FIRST PAPERBACK EDITION 1977

ISBN: 0-520-03475-9

LIBRARY OF CONGRESS CATALOG CARD NUMBER: 74-30519

PRINTED IN THE UNITED STATES OF AMERICA

12   13   14   15

THE PAPER USED IN THIS PUBLICATION IS BOTH ACID-FREE AND TOTALLY
CHLORINE-FREE (TCF). IT MEETS THE MINIMUM REQUIREMENTS OF
ANSI/NISO Z39.48-1992 (R 1997) (PERMANENCE OF PAPER). ∞

Contents

Acknowledgments

This book is a collection of translations of essays selected from Hans-Georg Gadamer's *Kleine Schriften,* published in three volumes by J. C. B. Mohr Verlag, Tübingen. "Heidegger's Later Philosophy" first appeared as an introduction to the Reclam edition of Martin Heidegger's *Der Ursprung des Kunstwerkes,* and it is the only essay in the volume not included in the *Kleine Schriften.*

"On the Scope and Function of Hermeneutical Reflection" was translated by G. B. Hess and R. E. Palmer; it first appeared in *Continuum,* Vol. VIII (1970), Copyright © 1970 by Justus George Lawler. "Semantics and Hermeneutics" was translated by P. Christopher Smith. I made only minor alterations in the translations of these two essays in order to bring some of the more technical expressions into line with conventions employed in the rest of the volume. A version of "The Science of the Life-World," translated by Gadamer, appeared in *Analecta Husserliana,* Vol. II (1972). I retranslated this essay from the German for this volume and translated all other essays in this book. In this endeavor I enjoyed the support of a faculty summer research grant from the Graduate School of The University of Tennessee, Knoxville.

I wish to thank Professor Gadamer for his encouragement and for the many hours he spent correcting and improving the translations. Professor John C. Osborne of the University of Tennessee gave unselfishly of his time in reading and checking the translations. In addition, I owe a special word of thanks to Richard Palmer, who suggested important revisions of "The Phenomenological Movement" which improved it substantially.

D. E. L.

Knoxville, Tennessee

Abbreviations

Abbreviations Used in the Footnotes

GS   Wilhelm Dilthey, *Gesammelte Schriften,* 14 vols. Stuttgart: Teubner, 1959-1968.

HB   Martin Heidegger, *Über den Humanismus.* Frankfurt: Klostermann, 1947.

JPPF   Edmund Husserl, et al., ed., *Jahrbuch für Philosophie und phänomenologische Forschung.* Halle: Max Niemeyer, 1913-1930.

K   Edmund Husserl, *Die Krisis der europäischen Wissenschaften und die transzendale Phänomenologie.* The Hague: Nijhoff, 1962. ET: *The Crisis of European Sciences and Transcendental Phenomenology,* trans. David Carr. Evanston, Ill.: Northwestern University Press, 1970.

Krefeld   *Husserl und das Denken der Neuzeit. Second International Phenomenological Colloquium in Krefeld.* The Hague: Nijhoff, 1959.

PG   G. W. F. Hegel, *Phänomenologie des Geistes*.
                            Hamburg: Felix Meiner, 1952. ET: *Phenome-
                            nology of Mind*, trans. J. B. Baillie. London:
                            George Allen & Unwin, 1949.

PhR   Hans-Georg Gadamer, ed., *Philosophische
                            Rundschau*. Tübingen: Mohr, 1953-

PI   Ludwig Wittgenstein, *Philosophical Investiga-
                            tions*, trans. G. E. M. Anscombe. New York:
                            Macmillan, 1953.

Royaumont   *Cahiers de Royaumont*. Paris: Les editions de
                            minuit, 1959.

SuZ   Martin Heidegger, *Sein und Zeit*. Tübingen:
                            Max Niemeyer, 1963. ET: *Being and Time*,
                            trans Macquarrie and Robinson. London:
                            SCM Press, 1962.

T   Ludwig Wittgenstein, *Tractatus Logico-Philos-
                            ophicus*, trans. Pears & McGuinness. London:
                            Routledge & Kegan Paul, 1961.

UhL   Hans Lipps, *Untersuchungen zu einer her-
                            meneutischen Logik*. Frankfurt: Klostermann,
                            1938.

WM   Hans-Georg Gadamer, *Wahrheit und Methode:
                            Grundzüge einer philosophischen Hermeneu-
                            tik*. Tübingen: Mohr, 1960.

Editor's Introduction

The essays contained in this volume continue to develop the philosophical perspective that Gadamer originally set forth in his systematic work, *Truth and Method,* a perspective he has called philosophical hermeneutics. Like the larger work, these essays are not primarily concerned with the methodological questions pertaining to scientific understanding that have been the preoccupation of hermeneutical theory since Schleiermacher's time. Indeed, it is Gadamer's contention that this preoccupation has distorted the hermeneutical phenomenon in its universality by isolating the kind of methical understanding that goes on in the *Geisteswissenschaften* from the broader processes of understanding that occur everywhere in human life beyond the pale of critical interpretation and scientific self-control. The task of philosophical hermeneutics, therefore, is ontological rather than methodological. It seeks to throw light on the fundamental conditions that underlie the phenomenon of understanding in all its modes, scientific and nonscientific alike, and that constitute understanding as an event over which the interpreting subject does not ultimately preside. For philosophical hermeneutics, "the question is not what we do or what we should do, but what happens beyond our willing and doing."[1] The universality of the hermeneutical question can emerge, however, only when

we have freed ourselves from the methodologism that pervades modern thought and from its assumptions regarding
man and tradition.

I

Hermeneutics has its origin in breaches in intersubjectivity.
Its field of application is comprised of all those situations in
which we encounter meanings that are not immediately understandable but require interpretive effort. The earliest situations in which principles of interpretation were worked out
were encounters with religious texts whose meanings were
obscure or whose import was no longer acceptable unless
they could be harmonized with the tenets of the faith.[2] But
this alienation from meaning can just as well occur while
engaging in direct conversation, experiencing a work of art,
or considering historical actions. In all these cases, the hermeneutical has to do with bridging the gap between the familiar
world in which we stand and the strange meaning that resists
assimilation into the horizons of our world. It is vitally
important to recognize that the hermeneutical phenomenon
encompasses both the alien that we strive to understand and
the familiar world that we already understand. The familiar
horizons of the interpreter's world, though perhaps more
difficult to grasp thematically, are as integral a part of the
event of understanding as are the explicit procedures by
which he assimilates the alien object. Such horizons constitute the interpreter's own immediate participation in traditions that are not themselves the object of understanding but
the condition of its occurrence. Yet, this *reflexive* dimension
of understanding has been all but completely ignored by the
"science of hermeneutics" during the last century. The result
has been a distorted and one-sided picture of understanding
and our relationship to tradition.
How did this neglect of the interpreter's situation come
about? In an illuminating discussion of Schleiermacher's hermeneutics, Gadamer observes that Schleiermacher instituted
a subtle shift in the conception of the task of hermeneutics, a shift that has had profound consequences for the

problem of understanding.[3] Before Schleiermacher — for instance, in the hermeneutics of Chladenius or Flacius — the work of hermeneutics arose because of a lack of understanding of the text; the normal situation for them was that of an immediate and unimpeded understanding of the subject matter of the text. Hermeneutics arises as a pedagogical aid in exceptional cases where our understanding of what the text says is blocked for some reason. However, beginning with Schleiermacher, the talk is no longer of "not understanding," but rather of the natural priority of *mis*understanding: "The more lax practice of the art of understanding," declares Schleiermacher, "proceeds on the assumption that understanding arises naturally. . . . The more rigorous practice proceeds on the assumption that misunderstanding arises naturally, and that understanding must be intended and sought at each point."[4] Misunderstanding arises naturally because of the changes in word meanings, world views, and so on that have taken place in the time separating the author from the interpreter. Intervening historical developments are a snare that will inevitably entangle understanding unless their effects are neutralized. For Schleiermacher, therefore, what the text really means is not at all what it "seems" to say to us directly. Rather, its meaning must be recovered by a disciplined reconstruction of the historical situation or life-context in which it originated. Only a critical, methodologically controlled interpretation can reveal the author's meaning to us. Thus the way was cleared for making all valid understanding the product of a discipline.

The far-reaching implications of this identification of understanding with scientific understanding can be seen most clearly in the work of Wilhelm Dilthey, whose aim was to establish hermeneutics as the universal methodological basis of the *Geisteswissenschaften*. Insofar as they adhered to the guidelines of methodical interpretation, the human studies could lay claim to a knowledge of the human world that would be every bit as rigorous as the natural sciences' knowledge of nature. Like Schleiermacher, Dilthey identified the meaning of the text or action with the subjective intention of its author. Starting from the documents, artifacts, actions, and so on that are the content of the historical world, the task of understanding is to recover the original life-world they betoken and to understand the other person (the author or historical agent) as he understood himself. Understanding is essentially a self-transposition or imaginative projection whereby the knower negates the temporal distance that separates him from his object and becomes contemporaneous with it.[5]

It is at this point that the eclipse of the reflexive dimension of the hermeneutical situation that Gadamer attempts to reassert takes place. For Schleiermacher and Dilthey, the knower's own present situation can have only a negative value. As the source of prejudices and distortions that block valid understanding, it is precisely what the interpreter must transcend. Historical understanding, according to this theory, is the action of subjectivity purged of all prejudices, and it is achieved in direct proportion to the knower's ability to set aside his own horizons by means of an effective historical method. Beneath their assertion of the finitude and historicity of man, both Schleiermacher and Dilthey continue to pay homage to the Cartesian and Enlightenment ideal of the autonomous subject who successfully extricates himself from the immediate entanglements of history and the prejudices that come with that entanglement. What the interpreter negates, then, is his own present as a vital extension of the past.

This methodological alienation of the knower from his own historicity is precisely the focus of Gadamer's criticism. Is it the case, Gadamer asks, that the knower can leave his immediate situation in the present merely by adopting an attitude? An ideal of understanding that asks us to overcome our own present is intelligible only on the assumption that our own historicity is an accidental factor. But if it is an *ontological* rather than a merely accidental and subjective condition, then the knower's own present situation is already constitutively involved in any process of understanding. Thus Gadamer takes the knower's boundness to his present horizons and the temporal gulf separating him from his object to be the productive ground of all understanding rather than negative factors or impediments to be overcome. Our prejudices do not cut us off from the past, but initially open it up to us. They are the positive enabling condition of historical understanding commensurate with human finitude. "The historicity of our existence entails that prejudices, in the literal sense of the word, constitute the initial directedness of our whole ability to experience. Prejudices are the biases of our openness to the world."[6] Shaped by the past in an infinity of unexamined ways, the present situation is the "given" in which understanding is rooted, and which reflection can never entirely hold at a critical distance and objectify. This is the meaning of the "hermeneutical situation" as Gadamer employs the term in the essays that follow. The givenness of the hermeneutical situation cannot be dissolved into critical self-knowledge in such fashion that the prejudice-structure of finite understanding might disappear. "To be historical," Gadamer asserts, "means that one is not absorbed into self-knowledge."[7]

It is not surprising that Gadamer's notion of prejudice has been one of the most controversial aspects of his philosophy. More than any other element of his thought, it indicates his determination to acknowledge the unsuspendable finitude and historicity of understanding and to exhibit the positive role they actually play in every human transmission of meaning. For Gadamer, the past has a truly pervasive power in the phenomenon of understanding, and this power was entirely missed by philosophers who dominated the scene before Heidegger. The role of the past cannot be restricted merely to supplying the texts or events that make up the "objects" of interpretation. As prejudice and tradition, the past also defines the ground the interpreter himself occupies when he understands. This fact was overlooked, however, by the Neo-Kantians, whose orientation to the sciences presupposed the essentially situationless, nonhistorical subject of transcendental philosophy. Even the historicism of the late nineteenth and early twentieth centuries, with its affirmation of the historicity and relativity of every human expression and perspective reaching us from the past, stopped short of affirming the interpreter's *own* historicity along with that of his objects.

Despite the many differences between these philosophies, they are one in their commitment to a normative concept of scientific knowledge that prevented them from recognizing the constitutive role of the interpreter's own facticity in all understanding. Only a neutralized, prejudice-free consciousness guarantees the objectivity of knowledge. In "The Universality of the Hermeneutical Problem," Gadamer describes the inevitable result of this orientation as an "experience of alienation" that has distorted what actually takes place in aesthetic and historical interpretation.[8] Here Gadamer's hermeneutics joins Heidegger's attack on the "subjectivism" of Western thought. What Gadamer asks us to see is that the dominant ideal of knowledge and the alienated, self-sufficient consciousness it involves is itself a powerful prejudice that has controlled philosophy since Descartes. By ignoring the intrinsic temporality of human being it also ignores the temporal character of interpretation. This fate has befallen every hermeneutical theory that regards understanding as a repetition or duplication of a past intention — as a reproductive procedure rather than a genuinely productive one that involves the interpreter's own hermeneutical situation.

Over against this dominant ideal, Gadamer develops a conception of understanding that takes the interpreter's present participation in history into account in a central way. *Understanding is not reconstruction but mediation.* We are conveyors of the past into the present. Even in the most careful attempts to grasp the past "in itself," understanding remains essentially a mediation or translation of past meaning into the present situation. Thus Gadamer's specific emphasis is not on the application of a method by a subject, but on the fundamental continuity of history as a medium encompassing every such subjective act and the objects it apprehends. Understanding is an event, a movement of history itself in which neither interpreter nor text can be thought of as autonomous parts. "Understanding itself is not to be thought of so much as an action of subjectivity, but as the entering into an event of transmission in which past and present are constantly mediated. This is what must gain validity in hermeneutical theory, which is much too dominated by the ideal of a procedure, a method."[9]

As mediation or transmission, the interpreter's action belongs to and is of the same nature as the substance of history that fills out the temporal gulf between him and his objects.

The temporal gulf that the older hermeneutics tried to overcome now appears as a continuity of heritage and tradition. It is a process of "presencings," that is, of mediations, through which the past already functions in and shapes the interpreter's present horizon. Thus the past is never simply a collection of objects to be recovered or duplicated by the interpreter, but rather what Gadamer calls an "effective history" (*Wirkungsgeschichte*) that alone makes possible the conversation between each new interpreter and the text or event he seeks to understand. The prejudices and interests that mark out our hermeneutical situation are given to us by the very movement of tradition − of former concretizations that mediate the text to us − and constitute our immediate participation in this effective history. It is not an exaggeration, therefore, to say that for Gadamer prejudices function as a limit to the power of self-consciousness: "It is not so much our judgments as it is our prejudgments that constitute our being."[10]

This open admission of the productive power of prejudice in all understanding seems to place Gadamer in explicit opposition to the scientific ideal of prejudiceless objectivity in interpretation, and his most acrimonious critics have been those who regard his work as jeopardizing the very possibility of scientific understanding.[11] The question of the relation of hermeneutical understanding as Gadamer conceives it to scientific knowledge is always present in his essays and forms the basic theme of the first three essays of Part I. In considering this question, it is helpful to locate the real point of conflict between Gadamer and the science of hermeneutics that has been largely responsible for developing the critical-historical methodology basic to the *Geisteswissenschaften*. What Gadamer's conception of understanding threatens is not our efforts at critical interpretation or what is actually achieved by such efforts, but the self-understanding that has accompanied scientific scholarship during the last two hundred years and the inflated claims it has made on behalf of methodological self-control. Far from excluding the function of prejudice and the continuing standing within tradition that is the mark of historical existence, critical historical scholarship presupposes these things in its actual practice, if not in its theoretical self-justifications. As Gadamer points out to his critics, it is not only ancient texts that betray to the interpreter when and where they were most likely written. Mommsen's *History of Rome* — a veritable masterpiece of critical-historical methodology — gives us just as unequivocal indications of the "hermeneutical situation" in which it was written and proves to be the child of its age rather than the simple result of the application of a method by an anonymous "knowing subject."

To recognize the historicity of the knower does not contest the importance of attempts at critical interpretation, nor does it impair the operation of scientific understanding in the slightest. At the same time, however, Gadamer's insight does give us occasion to question the abstract opposition between knowledge and tradition that has become a dogma in hermeneutical theory and to appreciate the sense in which scientific historical understanding is itself the bearer and continuer of tradition. "Only a naïve and unreflective historicism in hermeneutics would see the historical-hermeneutical sciences as something absolutely new that would do away with the power of 'tradition.' "[12] The aim of Gadamer's philosophical hermeneutics is to illuminate the human context within which scientific understanding occurs and to account for the necessity for repeated attempts at critical understanding. We can indeed gain critical awareness of our prejudices and correct them in our effort to hear what the text says to us. But this correction of prejudices is no longer to be regarded as the transcendence of *all* prejudices in the direction of a prejudice-free apprehension of the text or event "in itself." It is the fact of prejudices as such, and not of one permanent, inflexible set of them, that is symptomatic of our historicity and immersion in effective history. Particular horizons, even if mobile, remain the presupposition of finite understanding. The critical self-consciousness of the interpreter must include an awareness of the continuing power of effective history in his work: "Reflection on a given preunderstanding brings before me something that otherwise happens *'behind my back.'* Something — but not everything, for what I have called the consciousness of effective history is inescapably more being than consciousness, and being is never fully manifest."[13]

Thus for Gadamer the knower's present situation loses its status as a privileged position and becomes instead a fluid and relative moment in the life of effective history, a moment that is indeed productive and disclosive, but one that, like all others before it, will be overcome and fused with future horizons. The event of understanding can now be seen in its genuine productivity. It is the formation of a comprehensive horizon in which the limited horizons of text and interpreter are fused into a common view of the subject matter — the meaning — with which both are concerned.

> In truth, the horizon of the present is conceived in constant formation insofar as we must all constantly test our prejudices. The encounter with the past and the understanding of the tradition out of which we have come is not the last factor in such testing. Hence the horizon of the present does not take shape at all without the past. There is just as little a horizon of the present in itself as there are historical horizons which one would have to attain. Rather, understanding is always a process of the fusing of such alleged horizons existing in themselves.... In the working of tradition such fusion occurs constantly. For there old and new grow together again and again in living value without the one or the other ever being removed explicitly.[14]

The concept of understanding as a "fusion of horizons" provides a more accurate picture of what happens in every transmission of meaning. By revising our conception of the function of the interpreter's present horizons, Gadamer also succeeds in transforming our view of the nature of the past, which now appears as an inexhaustible *source of possibilities of meaning* rather than as a passive object of investigation. Luther's encounter with *Romans* or Heidegger's understanding of Aristotle's *Nichomachean Ethics* might serve as examples of the way a text speaks differently as its meaning finds concretization in a new hermeneutical situation and the interpreter for his part finds his own horizons altered by his appropriation of what the text says. Indeed, as Gadamer tries to show in two fine pieces of phenomenological analysis, the process of understanding that culminates in the fusion of horizons has more in common with a dialogue between persons or with the buoyancy of a game in which the players are absorbed than it has with the traditional model of a methodologically controlled investigation of an object by a subject. This latter model, derived largely from the experimental sciences and never entirely shaken off by earlier hermeneutical theorists, conceals the intrinsically dialectical nature of understanding that transforms both text and interpreter.

Like all genuine dialogue, the hermeneutical conversation between the interpreter and the text involves equality and active reciprocity. It presupposes that both conversational partners are concerned with a common subject matter – a common question – about which they converse, for dialogue is always dialogue *about* something. Unlike the essentially reconstructive hermeneutics of Schleiermacher and Dilthey, which took the language of the text as a cipher for something lying *behind* the text (e.g., the creative personality or the worldview of the author), Gadamer focuses his attention squarely on the subject matter of the text itself, that is, on what it says to successive generations of interpreters. All literary documents possess a certain "ideality of meaning" insofar as what they say to the present is in written form and is thus detached from the psychological and historical peculiarities of their origin. "What we call literature," Gadamer argues, "has acquired its own contemporaneity with every present time. To understand it does not mean primarily referring back to past life, but rather present participation in what is said. It is not really a question of a relation between persons – for instance, between the reader and the author (who is perhaps wholly unknown) – but rather, of a participation in the communication which the text makes to us. Where we understand, the sense of what is said is present entirely independently of whether out of the tradition we can picture the author or whether our concern is the historical interpretation of the tradition as a general source."[15]

The dialogical character of interpretation is subverted when the interpreter concentrates on the other person as such rather than on the subject matter – when he looks *at* the other person, as it were, rather than *with* him at what the other attempts to communicate. Thus the hermeneutical conversation begins when the interpreter genuinely opens himself to the text by listening to it and allowing it to assert its viewpoint. It is precisely in confronting the otherness of the text — in hearing its challenging viewpoint — and not in preliminary methodological self-purgations, that the reader's own prejudices (i.e., his present horizons) are thrown into relief and thus come to critical self-consciousness. This hermeneutical phenomenon is at work in the history of cultures as well as in individuals, for it is in times of intense contact with other cultures (Greece with Persia or Latin Europe with Islam) that a people becomes most acutely aware of the limits and questionableness of its deepest assumptions. Collision with the other's horizons makes us aware of assumptions so deep-seated that they would otherwise remain unnoticed. This awareness of our own historicity and finitude — our consciousness of effective history — brings with it an openness to new possibilities that is the precondition of genuine understanding.

The interpreter must recover and make his own, then, not the personality or the worldview of the author, but the fundamental concern that motivates the text — the question that it seeks to answer and that it poses again and again to its interpreters. This process of grasping the question posed by the text does not lead to the openness of a genuine conversation, however, when it is conceived simply as a scientific isolation of the "original" question, but only when the interpreter is provoked by the subject matter to *question further* in the direction it indicates. Genuine questioning always involves a laying open and holding open of possibilities that suspend the presumed finality of both the text's and the reader's current opinions. We understand the subject matter of the text that addresses us when we locate its question; in our attempt to gain this question we are, in our own questioning, continually transcending the historical horizon of the text and fusing it with our own horizon, and consequently transforming our horizon. To locate the question of the text is not simply to leave it, but to put it again, so that we, the questioners, are ourselves questioned by the subject matter of the text.

The existential and integrative dimension of understanding, which Gadamer ranges over against purely scientific, disinterested interpretation, is evident. Not everyone who

masters the methodology of a discipline becomes a Newton
or a Mommsen. As Gadamer points out, the differentia between methodological sterility and genuine understanding is
imagination, that is, the capacity to see what is questionable
in the subject matter and to formulate questions that question the subject matter further.[16] And the precondition of
this capacity is that one is open to be questioned *by* the text,
to be provoked by it to risk involvement in a dialogue that
carries him beyond his present position. Understanding, then,
does not allow the interpreter to stand beyond the subject
matter which comes to language in the text. In real understanding, as in real dialogue, the interpreter is engaged by the
question, so that text and interpreter are both led by the
subject matter – by the *logos,* as Plato said. We speak,
therefore, of having "gotten into" a discussion, or of being
"caught" in a discussion, and these expressions serve to
indicate the element of buoyancy in understanding that leads
the conversational partners beyond their original horizons
into a process of inquiry that has a life of its own and is often
filled with developments that are unanticipated and unintended. "The real event of understanding," Gadamer contends, "goes continually beyond what can be brought to the
understanding of the other person's words by methodological
effort and critical self-control. It is true of every conversation
that through it something different has come to be." [17]
Plato's dialogues are models of the hermeneutical process in
this dialectical sense, and the unique power of his philosophy
owes much to the sense we have in reading him that we
participate in the very life of understanding as a movement
that bears all participants beyond their initial horizons.

This element of buoyancy – of being borne along by the
subject matter – is illuminated by a second phenomenon that
Gadamer describes in support of his theory of understanding,
the phenomenon of the game or playing. Even more strongly
than the analogy of the conversation, Gadamer's phenomenology of the game suggests the inadequacy of trying to
comprehend understanding from the perspective of the subjectivity of the author or the interpreter. To focus on the
subjective attitude of the player, as Schiller did, for instance,
in his *Letters on the Aesthetic Education of Man,* is a

particularly unfortunate way to pursue the question of the nature of playing. For what reveals itself as most characteristic of the phenomenon of playing is that the individual player is absorbed into the back-and-forth movement of the game, that is, into the definable procedure and rules of the game, and does not hold back in self-awareness as one who is "merely playing." The person who cannot lose himself in full earnest in the game or give himself over to the spirit of the game, but instead stands outside it, is a "spoil sport," one who cannot play. Thus the game cannot be taken as an action of subjectivity. Instead it is precisely a relase from subjectivity and self-possession. The real subject of playing is the game itself. This observation is not contradicted by the fact that one must know the rules of the game and stick to them, or by the fact that the players undergo training and excel in the requisite physical methods of the game. All these things are valuable and "come into play" only for the one who enters the game and gives herself to it. The movement of playing has no goal in which it ceases but constantly renews itself. That is, what is essential to the phenomenon of play is not so much the particular goal it involves but the dynamic back-and-forth movement in which the players are caught up – the movement that itself specifies how the goal will be reached. Thus the game has its own place or space (its *Spielraum*), and its movement and aims are cut off from direct involvement in the world stretching beyond it. The fascination and risk that the player experiences in the game (or in a wider linguistic sense, the fascination experienced by the person who "plays with possibilities," one of which he must choose and carry out) indicate that in the end "all playing is a being-played."

The self-presenting, self-renewing structure of the game helps Gadamer come to terms with one of the most difficult problems of hermeneutics, the problem of meaning and of the fidelity of interpretation to the meaning of the text. The brief comments that follow may help orient the reader to the alternative concept of meaning that is presupposed by Gadamer's theory of understanding. The customary way of defining the meaning of a text has been to identify it with the subjective act of intending of its author. The task of understanding is then construed as the recapturing or repetition of this original intention. Such a theory of meaning has obvious advantages, not the least of which is that it seems to make possible a definitive, canonical interpretation. Because the author intended something specific, the interpretation that recovers and represents that original intention is *the* correct one that banishes all competing interpretations as incorrect. Just as scientific experiments can be repeated exactly any number of times under the same conditions and mathematical problems have but one answer, so the author's intention constitutes a kind of fact, a "meaning-in-itself," which is repeated by the correct interpretation.[18] While there may be varying explications of the *significance* of the text for us, it has only one *meaning,* and that is what the creator meant by his words or by his work of art.

The basic difficulty with this theory is that it subjectifies both meaning and understanding, thus rendering unintelligible the development of tradition that transmits the text or art work to us and influences our reception of it in the present. When meaning is located exclusively in the *mens auctoris,* understanding becomes a transaction between the creative consciousness of the author and the purely reproductive consciousness of the interpreter. The inadequacy of this theory to deal positively with history is perhaps best seen in its inability to explain the host of competing interpretations of texts with which history is replete, and that in fact constitute the substance of tradition. The distinction between meaning and significance is at best difficult to apply to the history of interpretation, for it is indisputably the case that interpreters of Plato, Aristotle, or Scripture in different historical eras differed *in what they thought they saw in the text* and not just in their views of the significance of the "same" textual meaning for themselves. Interpreters of Paul, for instance, have not been arguing all these centuries only over what Paul "means" *pro nobis,* but also over the claim Paul makes regarding the subject matter. Hence agreement on textual meaning, whenever it is achieved, must be accounted for on other grounds than the simple distinction between a supposed meaning-in-itself and its significance for the interpreter. According to this theory, however, disparities in interpretation, which form a part of the substance of spiritual life just as much as agreements in interpretation, must either be reduced to the secondary question of "significance" or, more drastically, to correct and incorrect interpretations. Neither alternative seems entirely adequate. The first does not accord with the phenomenon of interpretation. The second involves a *hubris* regarding our own reality: it denies the role of our own hermeneutical situation and thus exhibits a neglect of the reflexive dimension of understanding that Gadamer has shown to be operative in understanding.

For Gadamer, the meaning of the text cannot be restricted to the *mens auctoris*. Tradition builds upon what he calls the "excess of meaning" that it finds in the text, an excess that goes beyond the author's intention, explicit or implicit, for what he creates.[19]

> Every time will have to understand a text handed down to it in its own way, for it is subject to the whole of the tradition in which it has a material interest and in which it seeks to understand itself. The real meaning of a text as it addresses the interpreter does not just depend on the occasional factors which characterize the author and his original public. For it is also always co-determined by the historical situation of the interpreter and thus by the whole of the objective course of history. . . . The meaning of a text surpasses its author not occasionally, but always. Thus understanding is not a reproductive procedure, but rather always also a productive one. . . . It suffices to say that one understands *differently when one understands at all.*[20]

Underlying these comments is a view of the meaning of the text or the work of art as both eliciting and including in itself the varying interpretations through which it is transmitted, and it is at this point that Gadamer's phenomenology of the game has its bearing on hermeneutical theory. The idea of a self-presenting reality overcomes the isolation of the text as an object over against its interpretations. Neither the historically transmitted text nor the work of art can be regarded as solely dependent on its creator or on its present performer or interpreter, so that by reference to one of these we might get a definitive perception of it "in itself." Like the game, the text or art work lives in its presentations. They are not alien

or secondary to it but are its very being, as possibilities that
flow from it and are included in it as facets of its own
disclosure. The variety of performances or interpretations
are not simply subjective variations of a meaning locked in
subjectivity, but belong instead to the ontological possibility
of the work. Thus there is no canonical interpretation of a
text or art work; rather, they stand open to ever new compre-
hensions.

> The encounter with art belongs within the process of integration
> given to human life which stands within traditions. Indeed, it is even
> a question whether the special contemporaneity of the work of art
> does not consist precisely in this: that it stands open in a limitless
> way for ever new integrations. It may be that the creator of a work
> intends the particular public of his time, but the real being of a work
> is what it is able to say, and that stretches fundamentally out
> beyond every historical limitation.[21]

As the essays in this volume will make clear, Gadamer's
philosophical hermeneutics offers no new canon of interpretation or new methodological proposals for reforming current
hermeneutical practice, but seeks instead to describe what
actually takes place in every event of understanding. The
subjective intention of the author is an inadequate standard
of interpretation because it is nondialectical, while understanding itself, as Gadamer shows, is essentially dialectical —
a new concretization of meaning that is born of the interplay
that goes on continually between the past and the present.
Every interpretation attempts to be transparent to the text,
so that the meaning of the text can speak to ever new
situations. This task does not exclude but absolutely *requires*
the translation of what is transmitted. Thus we can give
Gadamer's insight a paradoxical formulation by saying that
the mediation that occurs in understanding must modify
what is said *so that it can remain the same.* The German
theologian Gerhard Ebeling, who has himself learned much
from Gadamer's philosophical hermeneutics, expresses this
universal characteristic of human understanding as he dis-
covers it within his own field of endeavor: "Actually, both
factors, identity and variability, belong inseparably together

and are linked to one another in the process of interpretation, whose very nature is to say the same thing in a different way and, precisely by virtue of saying it in a different way, to say the same thing. If, by way of pure repetition, we were to say today the same thing that was said 2,000 years ago, we would only be imagining that we were saying the same thing, while actually we would be saying something quite different."[22] The consciousness of effective history is our own consciousness that we are finite, historical beings and that, consequently, the risk of mediation is not optional for us. Critical self-reflection does not remove our historicity, nor do the critical methods we develop change the fact that in our interpretation of the tradition we are "being played" by the movement of tradition itself. At its best, the science of interpretation makes us more honest and more careful in our inevitable playing further of what is transmitted to us. But when it is no longer qualified by the consciousness of the effective power of history, concentration on methods and techniques hides from our vision the noblest achievements of understanding. In his essay "Indirect Language and the Voices of Silence," Maurice Merleau-Ponty points to this deeper achievement of understanding and beautifully confirms Gadamer's hermeneutics in these words:

Husserl has used the fine word *Stiftung* — foundation or establishment — to designate first of all the unlimited fecundity of each present which, precisely because it is singular and passes, can never stop having been and thus being universally; but above all to designate that fecundity of the products of culture which continue to have value after their appearance and which open a field of investigations in which they perpetually come to life again. It is thus that the world as soon as he has seen it, his first attempts at painting, and the whole past of painting all deliver up a tradition to the painter — *that is,* Husserl remarks, *the power to forget origins* and to give to the past not a survival, which is the hypocritical form of forgetfulness, but a new life, which is the noble form of it. . . . The productions of the past, which are the data of our time, themselves once went beyond anterior productions towards a future which we are, and in this sense called for (among others) the metamorphosis which we impose upon them.[23]

II

Gadamer's principal contribution to hermeneutics is to be found in his concerted effort to shift the focus of discussion away from techniques and methods of interpretation, all of which assume understanding to be a deliberate product of self-conscious reflection, to the clarification of understanding as an event that in its very nature is *episodic* and *trans-subjective*. It is episodic in the sense that every particular "act" of understanding is a moment in the life of tradition itself, of which interpreter and text are subordinate parts. It is trans-subjective in that what takes place in understanding is a mediation and transformation of past and present that transcends the knower's manipulative control. If these deeper features of the hermeneutical phenomenon are distorted by concentration on the purely technical aspects of interpretation, they come clearly to light when hermeneutics unfolds as a phenomenology of language. It is no accident that despite their diverse themes, every essay in this volume finally comes to deal with the question of language, for language is the medium in which past and present actually interpenetrate. Understanding as a fusion of horizons is an essentially *linguistic* process; indeed, these two — language and the understanding of transmitted meaning — are not two processes, but are affirmed by Gadamer as one and the same.

We can confirm the convergence of understanding and language by observing that the process of effective history that provides the horizons of our world is concretely present in the language we speak. To say that the horizons of the present are not formed at all without the past is to say that our language bears the stamp of the past and is the life of the past in the present. Thus the prejudices Gadamer identifies as more constitutive of our being than our reflective judgments can now be seen as embedded and passed on in the language we use. Since our horizons are given to us prereflectively in our language, we always possess our world linguistically. Word and subject matter, language and reality, are inseparable, and the limits of our understanding coincide with the limits of our common language. In this sense, there is no "world in itself" beyond its presence as the subject matter of a particular language community. We do not first have an extralinguistic contact with the world and then put this world into the instrumentation of language. To begin by assuming such a schema is to reduce language to the status of a tool, which fails to grasp its all-encompassing, world-constituting significance.

> Language is by no means simply an instrument or a tool. For it belongs to the nature of the tool that we master its use, which is to say we take it in hand and lay it aside when it has done its service. That is not the same as when we take the words of a language, lying ready in the mouth, and with their use let them sink back into the general store of words over which we dispose. Such an analogy is false because we never find ourselves as consciousness over against the world and, as it were, grasp after a tool of understanding in a wordless condition. Rather, in all our knowledge of ourselves and in all knowledge of the world, we are always already encompassed by the language which is our own.[24]

This passage reflects Gadamer's agreement with Heidegger's assertion that language and understanding are inseparable structural aspects of human being-in-the-world, not simply optional functions that man engages in or does not engage in at will. What is given in language is not primarily a relation to this or that object, or even to a field of objects, but rather a relation to the whole of being, a relation that we neither consciously create nor control and objectify as science does its objects. Our possession of language, or better, our possession *by* language, is the ontological condition for our understanding of the texts that address us.

The appearance of particular objects of our concern depends upon a world already having been disclosed to us in the language we use. Our experience of particular objects and our manipulation of them is therefore not self-founding, but presupposes that we are always already oriented to a particular world by means of language. Similarly, our acts of interpretation are not self-founding, as the emphasis on methodology and objective control implies, but rather presuppose our immersion in tradition, which we can now see is given concretely in our total language dependence.

Actually, this affirmation of the world-constituting significance of language is hardly new with Gadamer. That language mediates our relation to reality is the founding insight of linguistic science as it has developed since Wilhelm von Humboldt. "The interdependence of word and idea," Humboldt observed, "shows us clearly that languages are not actually means of representing a truth already known, but rather of discovering the previously unknown. Their diversity is not one of sounds and signs, but a diversity of world perspectives."[25] Gadamer considers this relativistic conviction to be a mistake fostered largely by the tendency of linguistic studies to concentrate on the form or structure of language while overlooking the actual life of language as speaking, that is, as a process of communication that is essentially dialogical. It is just this unreflective life of language as communication — what might be called its *disclosive* function — that is of primary interest to hermeneutics. In "Man and Language," Gadamer points out that in its actual life, language does not draw attention to itself but is transparent to the realities that are manifested through it. Language is profoundly unconscious of itself. Knowing a language, therefore, does not mean knowing rules and structures but rather knowing how to make oneself understood by others regarding the subject matter.[26] The words we speak function precisely by *not* being thematic, but by concretizing and disappearing into the subject matter they open up to the other person. "The more language is a living operation, the less we are aware of it. Thus it follows from the forgetfulness of language that its real being consists in what is said in it. What is said in it constitutes the common world in which we live. . . . The real being of language is that into which we are taken up when we hear it — what is said."[27] Language claims no autonomous being of its own, but instead has its being in its disclosive power. It is on this level that language emerges as the universal medium of understanding.

It is also by reference to the disclosive function of language that hermeneutics dispels the linguistic relativism that has accompanied the investigation of language from Humboldt to Wittgenstein. Just as prejudices are not a prison that isolates us from the new, but a particular starting point from which understanding advances, so to know a language is to be open to participation in a dialogue with others that transforms and broadens the horizons from which we start. Language discloses realities that then react upon language itself as it assimilates what is said. In "Semantics and Hermeneutics," Gadamer shows how language, in its life as conversation, constantly presses against the limits of established conventions and moves between the sedimented meanings and usages that are at its basis and the new that it strives to express. "The fact that one can never depart too far from linguistic conventions is clearly basic to the life of language: he who speaks a private language understood by no one else does not speak at all. But on the other hand, he who only speaks a language in which conventionality has become total in the choice of words, syntax, and in style forfeits the power of address and evocation which comes solely with the individualization of a language's vocabulary and of its means of communication."[28] Thus what we saw in Gadamer's discussion of understanding is now confirmed from the side of language. Understanding is essentially linguistic, but this statement does not mean — as every form of relativism assumes — that understanding is frozen into one static language in such fashion that translation from one language to another is impossible. The constantly self-transcending character of language in its concrete use in conversation is the foundation of the fluid horizons of understanding. Understanding is essentially linguistic, but in such fashion that it transcends the limits of any particular language, thus mediating between the familiar and the alien. The particular language with which we live is not closed off monadically against what is foreign to it. Instead it is porous and open to expansion and absorption of ever new mediated content. "The task of understanding and interpreting," Gadamer says, "always remains meaningful. In this is demonstrated the superior universality with which reason is elevated above the limits of every given system of language. The hermeneutical experience is the corrective through which thinking reason escapes the power of the linguistic even while it is itself linguistically constituted."[29]

The universality and mediating power of language brings us back to the phenomenon of the game, for it is in the playful

give-and-take of the conversation that language has its disclosive function. As dialogue, language is not the possession of
one partner or the other, but the medium of understanding
that lies between them. In conversation, language becomes
individualized, tailored to the situation of speaking. "The
selection of a word," writes Hans Lipps, "is determined by its
'meaning' — but this meaning finds its weight by what is
roused in the other person through the word. It is concretized, unfolded, in the articulation of everything that is
just touched upon in the word. The other person is already
conformed to in the word. The taking up of the word
initiates something. In it, one gives the other person something to understand; what one 'means,' the other person
'should do' in some way. And one tries to bring himself into
the 'vision' of a word when he tries to locate it."[30] The
play-character of language involves a process of natural concept formation that is not simply the employment of pregiven general meanings and rules for their combination.
Rather, the meanings of words depend finally on the concrete circumstances into which they are spoken. On this level,
the logic of language is not simply the formal logic of
Aristotle or that of the positivists, but the "hermeneutical"
logic of question and answer. Conversational language is
therefore not reducible to "propositions" that are understood when their denotations and rules of synthesis are
comprehended. Rather, general word meanings are drawn
into a constant process of concept formation in speaking. As
a result, each word has around it what Hans Lipps has called
the "circle of the unexpressed," which bears directly on the
meaning of the language.[31] In every moment of dialogue, the
speaker holds together what is said and addressed to the
other person with the "infinity of the unsaid."[32] It is this
infinity of the unsaid — this relation to the whole of being
that is disclosed in what *is* said — into which the one who
understands is drawn.

The whole of being that is mirrored and disclosed in
language — including the language of texts — gives interpretation its continuing task. The infinity of the unsaid that is
essential to language cannot be reduced to propositions, that
is, to the merely present-at-hand, for every new interpreta-

tion brings with it a new "circle of the unexpressed." Thus what is disclosed in language poses ever new questions to its interpreters and gives new answers to those who are challenged by it and play its meaning further within the dialectic of question and answer. Every conversation has an inner infinity and no end. "One breaks it off because it seems that enough has been said or that there is nothing more to say. But every such break has an intrinsic relation to the resumption of the dialogue."[33] Similarly, a tradition has an inner relation to every new horizon of interpretation for which it mirrors and discloses a whole of being. The conversation with the text is in this sense resumed anew by each succeeding horizon that takes it up, applying it and bringing it to language within the present situation.

III

The emphasis Gadamer places on interpersonal communication as the locus for the real determination of meaning seems to bring his concept of language into close relation to the "ordinary language" philosophy of the later Wittgenstein and his followers. In several places, Gadamer alludes to the convergence he sees occurring between Wittgenstein's approach and the phenomenological tradition out of which his own work comes.[34] But the careful reader of these essays may well wonder whether Gadamer has explored the differences between his position and Wittgenstein's as well as he might.

In his later writings, Wittgenstein launches an attack on his former allies, the positivists, and abandons his own epoch-making *Tractatus Logico-Philosophicus.* In comparing the *Tractatus* with his later position, one might say that Wittgenstein has changed his mind as radically as he has changed his style. His approach to the subject of language is more cautious and empirical in his later writings than it was in the *Tractatus.* If we want to know what meaning is and how our words acquire meaning, we must start by seeing how words are actually used in ordinary discourse. We cannot begin, as the *Tractatus* did, by assuming that all words have one purpose and can all get their meaning in one way — a way that can be stated in terms of a logical calculus. In the *Tractatus,* Wittgenstein could contend that meaning arose when the logical simples of language were combined in such fashion as to correspond to ("picture") nonverbal facts. One understands a sentence when one understands its constituent parts.[35] However, in his later philosophy Wittgenstein argues that what appears to be the meaning of a word in one context does not necessarily carry over into its use in another. This fact causes Wittgenstein to abandon his earlier belief that words and sentences have clear and precise meanings that can be seen *in abstracto.* The meaning of a word is precisely its use. "The sentence," Wittgenstein remarks, "gets its significance from the system of signs, from the language to which it belongs. Roughly: understanding a sentence means understanding a language."[36] There is no single definition of a word that covers all the uses we give it in ordinary discourse. When we are asked the precise definitions for common words we cannot give them, simply because they *have* no precise meaning. We can perhaps suggest several definitions that, taken together, roughly correspond to the uses of a common word. In other cases a word may be used in dozens of different ways that gradually merge into one another. We cannot give a universal rule for its use. There may be "family resemblances" in the various usages, but no single, normative meaning is to be found. Ordinary words have "blurred edges." In order to clarify these edges, we do not have recourse to an ideal logic but rather look to the specific context of their use in order to discover the "grammar" actually assigned to them in social intercourse. "Don't think," says Wittgenstein, "but look!"[37]

In contrast to the transcendental grammar of the positivists, Wittgenstein contends that the uses that specify the meaning of words in common discourse are inexhaustibly flexible and various. Wittgenstein's concept of "language games" thus replaces the ideal of a universal grammar. It indicates that language owes its form primarily to the use people make of it, that is, to the way the words they use in social intercourse are connected with and facilitate specific actions and expectations of actions. The rules immanent in the particular language game are the rules of a life form, that is, of a socially induced and instituted form of behavior. For Wittgenstein, therefore, to learn a language is to be able to participate in (i.e., to know how to use the rules of) the form of life the language depends on and is itself instrumental in specifying and perpetuating. "The learning of a language," he declares, "is no explanation, but training."[38] The grammars of language games contain rules according to which children are trained up into existing life-forms: they are "didactic rules for linguistic instruction." And when children learn such games by training, they are in fact introduced to *a priori* ways of seeing the world.

Wittgenstein's idea of the language game is thus in certain respects similar to Gadamer's own concept of prejudice structures. In fact, what Wittgenstein has formulated in the concept of language games is not unlike what Heidegger and Gadamer call an "understanding of being," which is also not simply the product of the individual's "inner experience," but has intersubjective validity, going before and along with all empirical experience, and yet is preontological (preconceptual). "In language," says Heidegger, "as a way things have been expressed or spoken out, there is hidden a way in which the understanding has been interpreted."[39]

What Gadamer and Wittgenstein share in common, therefore, is the affirmation of the unity of linguisticality and institutionalized, intersubjectively valid ways of seeing. Furthermore, and more significantly, both of them stress that the rules of a language game are discovered only by observing its concrete use in interpersonal communication. For both, the concrete meaning of a piece of language therefore involves as an essential element how others respond to the words spoken to them. This dimension of use transcends a merely formal logic and in effect introduces a kind of hermeneutics into the clarification of language. In Wittgenstein's case, however, the development of this hermeneutical aspect is hampered by his understanding of the task of philosophy as well as by certain features of his conception of language games themselves.

For Wittgenstein, the multifarious uses that we discover in analyzing ordinary language are irreducible. Because their rules are immanent, the clarification of a language game must be made "from within" rather than "from without." There are indeed "family resemblances" between language games, but there is no common structure that philosophical analysis can uncover and employ as a basis for mediating between these various games, which consequently stand in apparent isolation from each other. To protest against this seeming fragmentation of language and to argue that there *must* be such universal factors is to "think" and not to "look." Such a metaphysic of language would be another game, and one with a queer grammar. To conceive of philosophy as supplying a transcendental grammar, that is, as responsible somehow for developing and justifying norms common to all language games, is to deny Wittgenstein's fundamental argument that norms are in fact indigenous to the language games themselves and do not constitute a transcendental grammar. Wittgenstein even repudiates a purely descriptive task for philosophy. Philosophy is for him a kind of linguistic therapy, which ends when the philosopher exposes mistaken applications of linguistic rules. At this point, the Wittgenstein of the *Philosophical Investigations* is still in agreement with the Wittgenstein of the *Tractatus:* philosophy has no position of its own over against the positive sciences, and thus no positive task of its own beyond the immanent clarification of grammar.

Because Wittgenstein does not allow for mediation between language games, he is left with a multitude of hermetically sealed usages and corresponding life forms. The horizons of the user (and analyzer) of language are closed. Working against the background of his own *Tractatus* and other excesses of linguistic positivism, Wittgenstein seems to regard *any* mediation that breaks down the absolute autonomy of the grammar of individual language games as a return to the transcendental rules of a universal language. *Either* one must settle for a plurality of relative games, *or* one has a metalanguage that does violence to the empirical richness of usages and life forms.

Wittgenstein's worry about the autonomy of language games and his desire to avoid a transcendental position from which the plurality of games might be reduced to the rules of one transcendental game led him to overlook precisely the assimilative power of language as a constant mediation and translation. Wittgenstein never clarifies the position occupied by the one who views various games in their autonomy and uncovers their rules. Ironically, this lack of clarification leads to a dilemma similar to that of romantic hermeneutics, which believed the one who understands abandons his own horizons and simply steps into the historical horizons of his subject matter. As already noted, Gadamer's critique of this approach to understanding sought to show that the present hermeneutical situation is always already constitutively involved so that the achievement of understanding has an essentially mediating or integrative character, transcending the old horizons marked out by the text and the interpreter's own initial position. The analyzer of language games is himself involved in an integration or fusing of language games, not in the form of one transcendental game, but in a finite form appropriate to all human reflection, namely, as insight into how language games, in their actual playing, grow and absorb each other. "Perhaps the field of language is not only the place of reduction for all philosophical ignorance, but rather itself an actual whole of interpretation which, from the days of Plato and Aristotle till today, requires not only to be accepted, but to be thought through to the end again and again."[40]

The inadequacy of Wittgenstein's monadic isolation of language games also becomes apparent when we consider language games in their immediate use, for the integrative task of philosophy is a reflection of what Gadamer takes to be the self-transcending character of language itself. Consider, for example, the question of how we learn new language games. The close connection of language and practice means that we cannot learn a language, or clarify difficulties in one we know, by reference to an ideal grammar or a lexicon. We achieve these ends only by actual use, that is, by recalling the situation of training in which we learned the language. Accordingly, to learn a new language game, one must virtually repeat the socialization process of the persons who use it. "In such a difficulty," Wittgenstein advises, "always ask yourself: How did we learn the meaning of this word? From what sort of examples? In what language games?"[41]

We must ask, however, if one ever undergoes more than

once a training or socialization such as children undergo. Learning our first language and learning subsequent ones are not the same thing. The latter always presupposes the mastery of at least one language, and in learning the first language, we acquire the basis for altering it and fusing it with other language games. In the learning of the mother tongue we learn not only its particular grammar but also the way to make other languages intelligible. That is the hermeneutical dimension of language that Wittgenstein ignores: with the learning of our native language we have at the same time learned how one learns languages in general. Thus, we can never again undergo training in the original sense. We already possess all other language games in principle, not by a new socialization, but through mediation, translation. For Gadamer, to learn a new language involves using it, but we never learn the new game in a vacuum. Instead, we bring our native language along, so that learning is not a new socialization, but an expansion of the horizons with which we began. By virtue of learning our first language, then, we acquire a position that at one and the same time is the basis for understanding and yet can itself be transformed by particular acts of understanding. To know a language is to have horizons from which we enter into a subject matter that broadens those very horizons. Commerce between language games goes on constantly, not as a new "training" that abandons our present game and places us "within" the new game (and form of life), but as a mediation of the new with the old. And this mediation is always achieved in particular, finite acts of language that are episodic and open to new mediations.

One certainly does not get the impression from reading Wittgenstein that he wishes to deny the growing, self-transforming character of language games. Quite the contrary: his analysis bears witness to the almost uncontrollable inventiveness of language use. However, missing from his later work is any explanation for this inventiveness comparable to the one Gadamer gives by relating the dynamic character of language to the subject matter that communication discloses and interprets without ever exhausting.[42] In the dialectic of question and answer, form and content (language and subject matter) interact, so that *what* is understood can affect the form or rules that compose one's horizons. The subject matter opened up by the rules of language can call those rules into question and provoke new rules — or rather, new applications of the rules — and consequently, new modes of perception and action. Thus the particular, finite act of interpretation in language affects human life-forms and makes historical development possible. In this sense, language itself makes possible ever new concretizations of its subject matter and functions as the universal medium of understanding.

These observations do not diminish the substantial affinities between Wittgenstein's later philosophy and the view of language Gadamer sets forth in these essays, but they do point to an Hegelian influence on Gadamer that is missing in Wittgenstein. This influence is evident in Gadamer's refusal to leave language games in unmediated isolation from each other. Hegel's dialectic of the limit has its hermeneutical application. As Hegel pointed out in opposition to Kant's doctrine of the Understanding, limitations only exist dialectically for reason, for to posit a limit is already to be beyond it.[43] Thus Gadamer rejects any absolutizing of the horizons that distinguish the present from the past, or any individual structure of meaning from our own. So far as any alien horizon is a transmission of articulate meaning, it is open to assimilation by understanding. The concept of language as something within which men are bound and frozen is an illusion, because it contains only half the truth. Whoever has language "has" the world in that he is free from the restrictions of an animal's environment and thus is open to the truth of every linguistic world. Worlds given in language are not mutually exclusive entities; it is the power of language that such "mutually exclusive" worlds can merge in understanding. "The other world," Gadamer says, "that stands over against us is not only a foreign, but a relatively other world. It does not have its own truth simply *for itself* but also its truth *for us.*"[44]

It was Hegel who saw that knowledge is a dialectical process in which both the apprehending consciousness and its objects are altered. In the *Phenomenology of Spirit* Hegel sought to show that every new achievement of knowledge is a mediation or refocusing of the past within a new and ex-

panded context. This dynamic and self-transcending character of knowledge is at the center of Gadamer's concept of
understanding as a concrete fusing of horizons. The event of
understanding is "the elevation to a higher universality which
overcomes not only one's own particularity but also that of
the other person."[45] For Gadamer, however, this "higher
universality" remains finite and surpassable and is not to be
equated with Hegel's absolute knowledge in concepts. Gadamer draws mainly on the empirical or phenomenological side
of Hegel's thought. It is not absolute knowledge, but the
moving, dialectical life of reason that finds expression in
Gadamer's description of what takes place in the "fusion of
horizons." As Hegel demonstrated in the *Phenomenology*,
every experience passes over into another experience. Understanding has this same dialectical character. We can now
recognize that in its life as dialogue language is the medium in
which understanding occurs. Language makes possible agreements that broaden and transform the horizons of those who
use it. But every dialogue relates to the "infinity of the
unsaid," which presents understanding with its ongoing task.

IV

The essays in Part II are devoted largely to Gadamer's
interpretation and assessment of the immediate background
of his thought in the phenomenological movement of the
1920s and 1930s and in Martin Heidegger's philosophy. They
provide an enormously valuable and illuminating insight into
the genesis of some of the major themes and problems of
German philosophy in the twentieth century. Indeed, one is
tempted to say that these essays constitute something of a
philosophical memoir. Gadamer was born in 1900, and in the
1920s was a student of philosophy and classical philology at
Marburg and Freiburg. There he witnessed the struggle between the philosophical and theological perspectives that
antedated World War I (Neo-Kantianism and 'liberal' theology) and the radical new tendencies of the postwar period
whose supporters were launching a frontal attack on the
cherished assumptions of established thought. On the one

hand was the assertion of the finitude and the situational character of human existence – the determination to explore the limits of human experience and control that marks the work of Jaspers and Heidegger and dialectical theology – and on the other was the epistemological orientation of philosophy to the sciences and the confident assumption of cultural progress.

The first essay in this section makes it clear that Gadamer considers the philosophical foundations of the twentieth century to be intimately connected with the triumph of these new tendencies. The principal philosophical development of the twentieth century is the thoroughgoing attack on the subjectivism of modern thought with its foundation in self-conscious reflection and on the corresponding reduction of the world to an object of scientific investigation and control. The influence of this subjectivism is hardly limited to academic philosophy. It functions much more pervasively as the assumption behind society's faith in the rational control of the future: "Society clings with bewildered obedience to scientific expertise, and the ideal of conscious planning and precisely functioning administration dominates every sphere of life even down to the level of the molding of public opinion."[46] Since the 1920s, philosophy has mercilessly exposed the naïveté of "subjective consciousness" and its ideal of objectifying knowledge. Wittgenstein exposed the difficulties involved in treating language as a logically perfect artificial system that we "apply," and he recognized the priority of the ordinary language within which we live. Existentialism, following Nietzsche (and Freud), unmasked the naïveté of reflective consciousness and penetrated the explicit intentions of reflection to the hidden sources and the finitude of reason. Phenomenology undermined the subjectivism of earlier epistemology, which had confined consciousness to its own contents and then had sought to construct the world out of such abstractions as "sense data" and pure judgments. These movements and others participate in the fundamental task of contemporary philosophy, which Gadamer identifies as the overcoming of the alienation of the "subject" from a world that was reduced to "objects" of experience and reflection. The philosophical foundations of the twentieth century are found, therefore, in the effort to situate consciousness and to define the limits of objectifying knowledge.

In "The Phenomenological Movement," Gadamer credits Edmund Husserl with initiating the drive to penetrate the absolutizing of the world of science that had taken place in the philosophy of his day to the phenomena themselves as given to immediately living consciousness. The phenomenological slogan, "To the things themselves! " expresses this desire to gain access to the prereflective givenness of things in a way that would not be distorted by theories or "anticipatory ideas of any kind," and especially (as Husserl came to see in his last great work, *The Crisis of European Sciences and Transcendental Phenomenology*) not by the pervasive objectivism that had dominated European thought since Galileo and Descartes.[47] Actually, this movement to recover the life-world that precedes theoretical objectifications had begun even earlier with the "philosophy of life" that is associated with the names of Nietzsche, Bergson, Simmel, and Dilthey. In connection with Dilthey's work in particular, hermeneutics began to emerge as the philosophical investigation of "understanding" in a new and comprehensive sense — as a "hermeneutics of life" that attempted to grasp the "lived experience" of self and world and to trace out the origin of the reflective forms in which lived experience is ultimately stabilized and communicated. But Dilthey's hermeneutics opened up a diversity of prereflective experience and world-orientations that philosophy seemed powerless to unify. Indeed, Dilthey contended that all efforts of reflection to systemize or unify the worldviews that issue from lived experience can only lead to the onesidedness of yet another world-orientation, thus compounding the problem of relativism rather than solving it. Dilthey's hermeneutical enterprise remained trapped, therefore, in historicism and went no further than a typology of divergent worldviews in their actuality.[48]

Husserl's approach was entirely different. Dissatisfied and irritated by the increasing "irrationalism" and relativism of the time, he followed the basic ideas of the Neo-Kantian school, but with the special claim that he had grounded his philosophy in a careful descriptive analysis of the "phenomena." In this way he intended to put philosophical knowledge for the first time on a rigorously scientific footing that would avoid both the scientism and the historicism rampant in the first decades of this century. In this context he developed the strategy of transcendental phenomenology.[49] By suspending the general positing function of consciousness, that is, by bracketing the affirmation of the actual existence of the world, Husserl restricted the task of philosophy to the correlation of phenomena in their essential nature with corresponding acts of consciousness in which they are constituted in their objectivity. The ultimate foundation of objectivity (and thus of the positive sciences and ordinary experience) is the transcendental ego, from which the essential validity of everything existing can be derived by constitutional analysis.

Husserl's writings in the 1920s seek to elaborate and perfect this program by means of a transcendental reduction that would bring all being within the scope of the transcendental ego. Husserl saw these efforts threatened not only by his opponents, who followed the naïve realism of the sciences and remained in the "natural attitude," but also by his own students, who failed to hold to the task of transcendental phenomenology he had marked out. Moreover, two difficulties seemed to threaten the transcendental reduction from within and to indicate fatal limits to the entire enterprise of transcendental phenomenology — the problem of intersubjectivity and that of the life-world.

The problem of the life-world is the focus of Gadamer's interpretation of Husserl in both "The Phenomenological Movement" and "The Science of the Life-World." These essays are a valuable contribution to the current discussion of Husserl's late philosophy. In them, Gadamer defends the continuity and integrity of Husserl's transcendental approach against the interpretations of Jean Wahl, Eugen Fink, and Ludwig Landgrebe, among the many who find in Husserl's treatment of the life-world a break with his transcendental phenomenology and an abandonment of the transcendental ego.[50] At the same time, the concept of the life-world is undoubtedly the closest point of contact with Gadamer's own philosophical concerns, and it marks the transition from Husserl's transcendentalism to Heidegger's philosophy.

The concept of the life-world calls attention to the original, taken-for-granted horizon of lived meanings that is anterior to all those levels of experience that Husserl had sought to embrace by his transcendental reduction. How could the validity of the life-world — or rather, of the bewildering multiplicity of subjective-relative life-worlds — be reduced and legitimated by constitutional analysis? In the *Crisis* Husserl recognizes the new and universal task that the life-world poses:

> ... there opens up to us, to our growing astonishment, an infinity of ever new phenomena belonging to a new dimension, coming to light only through consistent penetration into meaning-and-validity-implications of what was thus taken for granted — an infinity, because continued penetration shows that every phenomenon attained through this unfolding of meaning, given at first in the life-world as obviously existing, itself contains meaning-and validity-implications whose exposition leads again to new phenomena, and so on.[51]

The life-world was overlooked by constitutional analysis as Husserl had practiced it, for while the transcendental reduction aimed at explicit objects of consciousness, the life-world functioned precisely as the horizon of intentional objects without ever becoming thematic itself. How could the phenomenologist's own enterprise avoid presupposing the self-evident validity of a life-world in which his praxis had its meaning?[52] Indeed, this life-world, present as a nonobjectified horizon of meaning, seems to encompass transcendental subjectivity itself and in this sense threatens to displace it as the absolute foundation of experience. The ego at this point appears to be "in" the life-world.

The point of Gadamer's argument in both essays on Husserl is to show that Husserl did not relinquish the priority of the transcendental ago, but saw the reduction of the life-world itself as the final task that would complete the program of transcendental phenomenology. The purpose of the *Crisis* is to investigate the essential structure of the life-world (the *eidos* "life-world") and to deal with the relativity of life-worlds as variations of that structure. If his transcendental program founders on the nonobjectifiable horizon of the life-world (and Gadamer believes it does), Husserl himself never recognized his failure, but believed himself to be master of the difficulty.

It is curious that Gadamer, who stands at some considerable distance from Husserlian phenomenology, is able to argue convincingly that the *Crisis* represents Husserl's *rebuttal* of Heidegger, while those closer to Husserl consider him in effect to have at least partially abandoned the foundations of his life-long program in the face of Heidegger's *Being and Time*. The temptation to interpret Husserl's last work in terms of Heidegger is as futile in the last analysis as the effort to understand *Being and Time* as a simple continuation of Husserl's transcendental phenomenology.

In Heidegger's philosophy we encounter a more radical critique of the foundations of Western metaphysical thinking, one that in its unfolding undercuts the concept of the transcendental ego as completely as it does the traditional notion of being as substance. But the full implications of this critique were not at once apparent when *Being and Time* first appeared in 1927; to many, Heidegger did indeed seem to be continuing Husserl's line of inquiry, even if in a way that was not sanctioned by Husserl. Concentrating on the nonobjectifying modes of disclosure in which Dasein is directly engaged in its world rather than reflecting upon it, Heidegger's *Being and Time* seemed to represent an effort to deal with the prereflective human experience of the life-world to which Husserl himself had already pointed in *Ideas II* (1920), but did not consider in detail until after *Being and Time* had had its impact. In *Being and Time,* the life-world is disclosed by Dasein not as a realm of neutral things or objects – as present-at-hand (*vorhanden*) – but rather as the referential totality of Dasein's own direct involvement, as a realm of possibilities upon which it has already projected itself. The entities of Dasein's world manifest themselves initially as tool-like in character (*zuhanden*) and deteriorate into mere "objects" only when they fall out of Dasein's own projects. Closely connected with this, Heidegger's analysis shows that this disclosure of the world is also Dasein's *self*-disclosure, but no longer in the idealist sense of the objectification of infinite spirit or in Husserl's implied sense of the life-world as disclosive of the constitutive accomplishments of the transcendental ego. Rather, Dasein comes upon itself as radically finite and temporal "being-in-the-world." Thus the effect of Heidegger's analytic of Dasein was to render unsuspendable precisely the life-world Husserl intended to reduce and to replace the transcendental ego with the being whose facticity reflection could not set aside. Dasein has its essence, paradoxically, in its existence.

In the last analysis, however, both the continuities and discontinuities between Heidegger and Husserl become clear only when we recognize the fundamental question that motivates Heidegger's thought from the very beginning: what is the meaning of being? The purpose of *Being and Time* is to recover the experience of being that lies concealed behind the dominant modes of Western thought. The recovery begins as an investigation of the structures of Dasein's mode of being insofar as Dasein constitutes a unique entree to the meaning of being as such. The existential analysis of Dasein that Heidegger presents in *Being and Time* is therefore not conceived by him as being a "regional ontology" in Husserl's sense of the term. "Philosophy is universal phenomenological ontology, and takes its departure from the hermeneutic of Dasein, which, as an analytic of *existence,* has made fast the guiding-line for all philosophical inquiry at the point where it *arises* and to which it *returns.*"[53]

This statement gives the direction of Heidegger's answer to the phenomenological problem of access, and the appearance of the term "hermeneutic of Dasein" indicates the central, ontological role that understanding and hermeneutics play in his early thought. Hermeneutics no longer refers to the science of interpretation, but rather to the process of interpretation that is an essential characteristic of Dasein.[54] "Dasein," says Heidegger, "is an entity which, in its very being, comports itself understandingly towards that being."[55] Dasein is open to beings because it has already construed being in some way as the horizon against which they appear. The mode of access to being is through this understanding of being that

Dasein already has.— the understanding of being in light of which it discloses the beings with which it is directly involved. An understanding of being is ingredient, therefore, in the human situation, not as the *theory* of being, arrived at by contemplation or inductive generalization from the beings actually encountered, but as the precondition of their meaningful disclosure. The sense of understanding as one kind of cognition among others (e.g., explaining, hypothesizing) is derivative from the primary understanding that Dasein always already has.

Heidegger's discovery of the *ontological* significance of understanding is a major turning point in hermeneutical theory, and Gadamer's work can be conceived as an attempt to work out the implications of the new starting point Heidegger provides. All deliberate interpretation takes place on the basis of Dasein's historicity, that is, on the basis of a prereflective understanding of being from within a concrete situation that has intrinsic relation to the interpreter's past and future. It is the meaning of Heidegger's description of Dasein as "thrown projection," a description that is of fundamental significance for Gadamer. As projective, understanding is intrinsically related to the future into which Dasein continually projects itself. Similarly, understanding is thrown, that is, situated by the past as a heritage of funded meanings that Dasein takes over from its community. Thus Heidegger shows that every interpretation — even scientific interpretation — is governed by the concrete situation of the interpreter. There is no presuppositionless, "prejudiceless" interpretation, for while the interpreter may free himself from this or that situation, he cannot free himself from his own facticity, from the *ontological* condition of always already having a finite temporal situation as the horizon within which the beings he understands have their initial meaning for him. In this way Heidegger ends the long struggle of German philosophy to overcome historicism and relativism by means of ever more refined methodological reflections that would neutralize the knower's own immediate participation in history. Every apprehension of meaning is a *finite* apprehension from within the pretheoretical givenness of man's historical situation.

Certainly no long discussion is required to demonstrate the influence of Heidegger's analysis of facticity on the conception of interpretation Gadamer advances in these essays. It offers Gadamer a powerful means of overcoming the initial isolation of the knower from tradition that was axiomatic to earlier hermeneutical theory. The projective character of understanding as the appropriation or "repetition" of meanings as possibilities of Dasein's own existence, finds expression in Gadamer's insistence that interpretation is mediation rather than contemplative reconstruction. And the "thrownness" of Dasein is elaborated by Gadamer in his conception of the interpreter's inevitable involvement in "effective history."

As deeply as these connections show *Being and Time* to have affected Gadamer, however, it is nonetheless true that the decisive impact of Heidegger's thought on Gadamer comes with the *Kehre* — the "turn" that distinguishes the fundamental ontology of *Being and Time* from the more explicit, even if often more enigmatic, reflection on being that is the dominant theme of Heidegger's later philosophy. In concluding, therefore, we must consider Gadamer's interpretation of the "turn" in Heidegger's thinking and assess its influence on Gadamer's philosophical hermeneutics.

All of Heidegger's writings, including *Being and Time,* reflect his consistent effort to conceive the meaning of being in a way that is not distorted by the objectifying categories of Western metaphysics. Given the historicity of all thinking, which Heidegger affirms, this effort to "overcome" metaphysics can only take place as a probing of the inherited meanings that compose the "hermeneutical situation" in which present thinking stands. In this sense, Heidegger's effort to overcome the tradition begins, as Gadamer shows, from within the tradition itself. Thus *Being and Time* attempts to interpret the "everyday" understanding of being that Dasein already has, and the writings after 1927 constitute an ever-deepening dialogue with the history of metaphysical thinking. Both approaches seek to recover the original possibilities for understanding the meaning of being that are latent in the tradition.[56]

The basic error of the metaphysical tradition, according to Heidegger, is that it transformed the question of being into that of the "being of beings" — that is, into the question of beings considered with respect to their universal characteristics. By concentrating on the beings that are disclosed to its gaze, metaphysical thinking forgot being itself as the event of disclosure or openness that allows beings to come forward into unconcealedness.

> Metaphysics thinks about beings as beings. Wherever the question is asked what beings are, beings as such are in sight. Metaphysical representation owes this sight to the light of Being. The light itself, i.e., that which such thinking experiences as light, does not come within the range of metaphysical thinking; for metaphysics always represents beings only as beings.[57]

This forgetting of being (of what Heidegger calls the ontological difference) opens the way to conceiving being in static, thing-like terms — as the underlying permanent substance of things, or their uncaused cause, eternal ground, and so on.

Hand in hand with this substantive rendering of being comes the "humanization" of being in Western thought. Since being itself is not a thing that can appear, it is neglected by man. According to Heidegger, this process begins with Plato, who identifies the permanent form (the idea) of things that the mind apprehends with what most truly *is*. Thus reality is conceived as the stable world that appears to man's outlook or viewpoint, and man's vision and thinking become determinative of truth and being. What happens with Descartes, and in modern thought generally, is therefore only the working out in a more radical fashion of what was prepared in earlier metaphysics. Now in the modern era man guarantees truth and being by the intrinsic clarity of his own vision. With Descartes, man the subject grasps beings in his representations, and the conditions for the clarity and distinctness of his vision, that is, the conditions for his certitude, are *eo ipso* the foundation of beings themselves. The world becomes the object or field of objects in proportion as man, the thinking subject, becomes the center, guarantor, and calculator of beings. "The basic process of modern times," Heidegger contends, "is the conquest of the world as picture. The world 'view' now means the product of representational building. In it man fights for the position in which he can be that being which sets the standard for all beings and draws the guiding principles for them."[58] This dominance of the human subject and its calculating techniques and methods over the world considered as a realm of things is most characteristic of modern thinking.

In *Being and Time,* Heidegger described this humanization of being as the mistaken priority of the "apophantic as" over the "hermeneutical-existential as" — the interpretive "as" of judgments and propositions over the "as" of the life-world discovery and disclosure of beings from which it is originally derived.[59] As the locus of truth, judgments or representations no longer serve truth as disclosive, that is, they do not point beyond themselves so that beings can shine forth. Rather, they become ends in themselves, objects of the mind's attention, and truth becomes the adjustment of the entity "judgment" to the entity "object" — *adequatio intellectus et reium.* Truth is transformed from an event of disclosure ($\dot{\alpha}\lambda\dot{\eta}\theta\epsilon\iota\alpha$ — unconcealment) in which beings stand out to information residing in the adequate representation of beings. Small wonder that thinking concentrates increasingly on the question of proper intellectual "vision" and the techniques for securing and guaranteeing certitude of vision. Here we can recall Gadamer's indictment of the "naïvete of assertions" in "The Philosophical Foundations of the Twentieth Century."

Difficulties in interpreting Heidegger's philosophy begin with determining the relation of his own *magnum opus* to this critique of Western thought, for *Being and Time* seems to represent precisely the radical subjectivism and "humanism" Heidegger is attacking. Heidegger's determination to interpret Dasein's mode of being out of itself and to make its finitude — its temporality — the horizon for the question of being and truth is, as Walter Schulz has skillfully argued, [60] itself the culmination of Western metaphysics as subjectivism: Being and truth seem to have their final ground in the horizon of Dasein's finite projects. Hence Heidegger can say, "Of course only as long as Dasein *is* (that is, only as long as an understanding of Being is ontically possible) 'is there' Being."[61] Is not this Dasein-relativity a radical undercutting

of the *transcendence* of being (i.e., of the ontological difference) quite comparable to Descartes's *res cogitans* or Kant's
transcendental ego? Does not the analytic of Dasein — and
more specifically, Dasein's "self-understanding" — function
as the transcendental condition for the question of being, so
that Heidegger's later assertion of the priority of being over
Dasein must appear as a *reversal* (indeed, as a contradiction)
of his position in *Being and Time*?

In his essays, as in *Truth and Method,* Gadamer argues that
despite the inadequacies of Heidegger's language, there is a
consistent development throughout Heidegger's thinking, and
that the "turn" after *Being and Time* serves to draw out and
clarify the basic insight into the relation of being and
human-being that was present from the beginning of Heidegger's work. What appears in *Being and Time* as subjectivism is
Heidegger's designation of Dasein as hermeneutical, but
Heidegger's analysis there had already made it clear that
Dasein's self-understanding does not objectify being or make
it the product of Dasein's conscious reflection. Repeatedly in
these essays, Gadamer calls our attention to Heidegger's distinction between objectifying reflection (*actus signatus*) and
a direct, non-objectifying awareness (*actus exercitus*) from
within existence itself, in order to demonstrate that "self-
understanding" as Heidegger used it had already broken de-
cisively with transcendental reflection in the idealistic sense.

> In *Being and Time* the real question is not in what way being can be
> understood, but in what way understanding *is* being, for the under-
> standing of being represents the existential distinction of Dasein.
> Already at this point Heidegger does not understand being to be the
> result of the objective operation of consciousness, as was still the
> case in Husserl's phenomenology. Rather, the question of being, as
> Heidegger poses it, breaks into an entirely different dimension by
> focusing on the being of Dasein which understands itself. And this is
> where the transcendental schema must finally founder. The infinite
> contrast between the transcendental ego and its objects is finally
> taken up into the ontological question. In this sense, *Being and Time*
> already begins to counteract the forgetfulness of being which
> Heidegger was later to designate as the essence of metaphysics. What
> he calls the 'turn' is only his recognition that it is impossible to
> overcome the forgetfulness of being within the framework of tran-
> scendental reflection.[62]

The historicity and temporality of Dasein in *Being and Time* meant that Dasein's grasp of being is not the result of the neutral, free-floating activity of self-consciousness. Rather, determinate thinking of any kind can go on only because being has already been understood in some specific way — and in this sense *it is not we who grasp being, but being that grasps us.* Heidegger's emphasis on Dasein as being-disclosing leads to the centrality of Dasein as the "place" or "clearing" where disclosure occurs; his emphasis on the finitude and givenness of Dasein leads to the affirmation of the priority and initiative of being and to Dasein's role as the "servant" or "instrument" of being. Far from being contradictory, these two points of emphasis are in fact complementary; the "turn" in Heidegger's thought is in fact the turning of his attention from the former to the latter of these interrelated insights.

How does Heidegger formulate his insight into the priority of being? In "Heidegger's Later Philosophy," Gadamer takes up this question by referring to Heidegger's 1935 lecture, "The Origin of the Work of Art." In this lecture, Heidegger begins to depart from the Dasein-centered terminology of *Being and Time* and to point to resistance or hiddenness as well as unconcealedness as essential to being. Because being is concealedness as well as unconcealment, earth as well as world, beings can stand in themselves and withhold themselves from man. This more *dialectical* structure of being is most apparent in the work of art. The art work and the disclosure that occurs in it can be comprehended neither in terms of the being of the thing or object (*Vorhandensein*) nor as a tool used by Dasein (*Zuhandensein*). The peasant's shoes in Van Gogh's painting, for example, are not simply objects we contemplate nor are they of any conceivable use to us in controlling things in our world. By standing in itself and withholding itself, the art work "changes our usual relations to world and earth and henceforth stops our customary acting and valuing, knowing and observing."[63] Out of its hiddenness, the work can be the revelation of a world: the hopes and fears, the sufferings and travail of the peasant's world open up to us and are preserved in it. Being as event involves concealment as well as disclosure, obstinateness as

well as openness. Thus according to Gadamer, Heidegger's
analysis of the work of art strengthens his concept of the
eventful nature of being by protecting beings against the total
disclosure that is the aim of objectification.

> The conflict between revealment and concealment is not the truth of
> the work of art alone, but the truth of every being, for as unhidden-
> ness, truth is always such an *opposition of revealment and conceal-
> ment.* The two belong necessarily together. This obviously means
> that truth is not simply the mere presence of a being, so that it
> stands, as it were, over against its correct representation. Such a
> concept of being unhidden would presuppose the subjectivity of the
> Dasein which represents beings. But beings are not correctly defined
> in their being if they are defined merely as objects of possible
> representation. Rather, it belongs just as much to their being that
> they withhold themselves. As unhidden, truth contains in itself an
> inner tension and ambiguity.[64]

   In Heidegger's later thought, the decisional language of
Being and Time, seen most clearly perhaps in the key concepts of resolute decision and authentic and inauthentic
existence, give way to the notion of thinking as a response to
the disposing power of being. Here Heidegger's thought becomes truly historical in a way that is reminiscent of Hegel,
for the disposing power of being finds concrete expression in
how being reveals and conceals itself in the fateful thinking
of each historical epoch. The initiative of being illuminates
history (*Geschichte*) as "fate" (*Geschick*).[65] "That being
itself and how being itself concerns thinking," says Heidegger, "does not depend initially or ever entirely on thinking.
That and how being itself affects thinking brings thinking to
the point at which it arises from being itself in order that it
corresponds to being as such."[66] It is just this enigmatic
interinvolvement of disclosure and concealment, of the giving
and withdrawing of being, that Gadamer seizes upon and
develops in his own thought. While Heidegger's reflection has
concentrated more and more on the poet and the philosopher, seemingly abandoning the humanistic disciplines to
technology, Gadamer's aim, as these essays demonstrate, is to
bring Heidegger's later philosophy to bear on the whole range

of interpretive disciplines that constitute the humanistic and social sciences. "It seems to me," Gadamer declares, "that it is possible to bring to expression within the hermeneutical consciousness itself Heidegger's statements concerning 'being' and the line of inquiry he developed out of the experience of the 'turn,' and I have carried out this attempt in *Truth and Method.*"[67]

The reader of these essays and of *Truth and Method* will find a close parallel between the relation of being and thinking in Heidegger's later writings and Gadamer's conception of the relation of tradition and understanding. Like Heidegger's notion of being, tradition is not a thing existing somehow behind its disclosures. As we have already seen, tradition *is* precisely its happening, its continuing self-manifestations, much as Heidegger defines being as eventful, i.e., as disclosive rather than substantive. Now we can recognize the further affinity between the hiddenness of being and the inexhaustibleness of tradition that preserves it in the face of every investigation and prevents it from becoming a mere totality of objects. For Gadamer, the ontological difference preserves tradition as the inexhaustible reservoir of possibilities of meaning.

The priority and initiative Heidegger claims for being in its relation to thinking has a further implication that is of great importance to Gadamer: it drives the concept of self-understanding — indeed, the entire notion of selfhood — from its central position in Western philosophy. Man is not to be defined prior to or independently of the event of being which thinking essentially serves. Not only is man not primary in his relation to being: man *is* at all only insofar as he is addressed by being and, in his thinking, participates in the event of being. Thus, for Heidegger, the basic relation is not man's relation to himself (i.e., his "self-consciousness," his subjectivity) but his relation to and immersion in the event of being in which beings manifest themselves. Thinking is the place where being clears itself and shines forth. "Standing within the illumination of being," Heidegger says, "is what I call the ek-sistence of man. . . . Man *is* in such fashion that he is the 'there,' i.e., the illumination of being. This 'being' of the

there, and only this, has the basic character of ek-sistence,
i.e., of the ecstatic standing-within the truth of being." [68]
What fascinates Heidegger about thinking is not its character
as a deliberate action of a subject, but its ontological role
within the occurrence of disclosure in which it is used by
being. Man's thinking is the place – the "there" – where
being discloses itself. The most accurate characterization of
thinking, therefore, is not as the achievement or work of man
but as the achievement of being. *Thinking has an ontological
status transcending human intentionality and purpose.* For
both Heidegger and Gadamer, this statement is the corollary
of the assertion that being (tradition) has primacy rather than
man.

Students of the later Heidegger will find the strongest
confirmation of the parallel between Heidegger's conception
of being and Gadamer's conception of tradition in the central
role language plays in both thinkers. We have already seen the
emphasis Gadamer places on the disclosing and concealing
power of language as it functions in living conversation. In
what we say and in what is said to us, beings disclose
themselves, but they withdraw from us as well and are never
fully manifest, for what is spoken has about it the circle of
the unsaid. For Heidegger and Gadamer alike, man not only
uses language to express "himself," but, more basically, he
listens to it and hence to the subject matter that comes to
him in it. The words and concepts of a particular language
reveal an initiative of being: the language of a time is not so
much chosen by the persons who use it as it is their historical
fate – the way being has revealed itself to and concealed
itself from them as their starting point. The universal task of
hermeneutical reflection, as Gadamer conceives it in these
essays, is to hearken to and bring to language the possibilities
that are suggested but remain unspoken in what the tradition
speaks to us. This task is not only universal – present wherever language is present – but it is also never finished. This is
the mark of our finitude. Every historical situation elicits
new attempts to render the world into language. Each makes
its contribution to the tradition, but is itself inevitably
charged with new unspoken possibilities that drive our think-

ing further and constitute the radical creativity of tradition. As Heidegger has said, we are therefore always "on the way to language."

NOTES

1. *WM*, p. xiv.
2. Cf. "On the Problem of Self-Understanding" and Dilthey's instructive essay "Die Entstehung der Hermeneutik," in *GS*, vol. 5, pp. 317-338, esp. pp. 321-326.
3. Cf. pp. 7, 98-99.
4. Schleiermacher, *Hermeneutik*, trans. H. Kimmerle (Heidelberg: Karl Winter, 1959), p. 86.
5. For Dilthey's theory of understanding, cf. *GS*, vol. 7, pp. 200-220.
6. P. 9, also cf. *WM*, p. 261.
7. *WM*, p. 285.
8. Pp. 4-9.
9. *WM*, pp. 274-275.
10. *WM*, p. 261.
11. Cf. esp. Emilio Betti, *Die Hermeneutik als allgemeine Auslegungstheorie* (Tübingen: Mohr, 1962) and Eric Hirsch, Jr., *Validity in Interpretation* (New Haven: Yale University Press, 1967), pp. 245-264. Jürgen Habermas's *Zur Logik der Sozialwissenschaften* (*PhR*, Beiheft 5; Tübingen: Mohr, 1967), though generally more sympathetic to Gadamer's position, shares this criticism. Cf. esp. pp. 272-276.
12. P. 29.
13. P. 38, also cf. "Semantics and Hermeneutics."
14. *WM*, p. 289.
15. *WM*, 369.
16. Cf. esp. "The Universality of the Hermeneutical Problem."
17. P. 58.
18. Cf. Hirsch, *Validity in Interpretation*, chap. 2.
19. Cf. p. 209. Although the *mens auctoris* provides no positive standard for interpretation, it has the important *negative* function of excluding anachronistic interpretations, etc. Cf. also "Aesthetics and Hermeneutics."
20. *WM*, p. 280.
21. P. 96.
22. Gerhard Ebeling, *The Problem of Historicity* (Philadelphia: Fortress Press, 1967), p. 26.
23. Maurice Merleau-Ponty, *Signs* (Evanston, Ill.: Northwestern University Press, 1964), p. 59.
24. P. 62.

25. Wilhelm von Humboldt, *Werke* (Darmstadt: Wissenschaftliche Buchgesellschaft, 1963), vol. 3, pp. 19-20.

26. Cf. *WM*, p. 418.

27. P. 65. Cf. also "The Philosophical Foundations of the Twentieth Century.

28. Pp. 85-86.

29. *WM*, p. 380.

30. *UhL*, p. 86. Cf. *WM*, p. 405.

31. *UhL*, p. 71.

32. Cf. *WM*, pp. 443-444.

33. P. 67.

34. Pp. 126-127.

35. *T*, 4.024.

36. Wittgenstein, *The Blue Book* (Oxford; Blackwell, 1960), p. 5.

37. *PI*, I, 66.

38. *PI*, I, 5; cf. *The Blue Book*, p. 17.

39. *SuZ*, pp. 167-168.

40. P. 177.

41. *PI*, I, 77; also cf. *PI*, I, 7.

42. Cf. *PI*, I, 219: "When I obey a rule, I do not choose. I obey the rule *blindly*." Cf. also *PI*, I, 198, 206, 217.

43. Cf. Hegel, *The Science of Logic* (London: George Allen & Unwin, 1951), vol. 1, pp. 36-37, 67 ff., and *PG*, p. 44 (ET, pp. 111-112).

44. *WM*, p. 418.

45. *WM*, p. 288.

46. P. 111.

47. Cf. *K*, pt. 2.

48. Cf. the essays in *GS*, vol. 8, *WM*, pp. 204-228, and my essay "Dilthey and Gadamer: Two Theories of Historical Understanding," in *The Journal of the American Academy of Religion*, vol. 41 (1973), pp. 536-553.

49. Husserl states his intentions clearly in the famous *Logos* article of 1911, "Philosophie als strenge Wissenschaft." Two years later *Ideas I* appeared and began to implement the program of transcendental phenomenology.

50. A clear statement of the interpretation Gadamer is opposing is found in Ludwig Landgrebe, "Husserls Abschied vom Cartesianismus " *PhR*, IX (1962), pp. 133-177.

51. *K*, p. 114 (ET, p. 112).

52. Cf. *K*, pp. 140-145 (ET, pp. 137-141), where Husserl raises this radical question of the possible self-referential character of phenomenology in dealing with the life-world.

53. *SuZ*, p. 38.

54. Heidegger, *Unterwegs zur Sprache* (Pfullingen: Neske, 1959), pp. 97-98 (ET: *On the Way to Language* [New York: Harper & Row, 1971], pp. 9-10).

55. *SuZ*, pp. 52-53.

56. Cf. *SuZ*, pp. 41-49, esp. p. 44.

57. Heidegger, *Was Ist Metaphysik?* (Frankfurt: Klostermann, 1965), pp. 7-8.

58. Heidegger, *Holzwege* (Frankfurt: Klostermann, 1950), p. 87.

59. *SuZ*, pp. 158-159, 359-360, and Heidegger, *Vom Wesen des Grundes* (Frankfurt: Klostermann, 1955), pp. 12-16.

60. Cf. Walter Schulz, "Über den philosophiegeschichtlichen Ort Martin Heideggers," *PhR*, I (1953-54), pp. 65-93, 211-232, and esp. pp. 69-79.

61. *SuZ*, p. 212.

62. Pp. 49-50, and *WM*, pp. 241-243.

63. Heidegger, *Holzwege*, p. 54.

64. P. 226.

65. Cf. *HB*, p. 46.

66. Heidegger, *Was Ist Metaphysik?*, p. 10.

67. P. 50.

68. *HB*, pp. 13, 15, and *Identität und Differenz* (Pfullingen: Neske, 1957), p. 22.

Part I:
The Scope of
Hermeneutical Reflection

1
The Universality of the Hermeneutical Problem (1966)

Why has the problem of language come to occupy the same central position in current philosophical discussions that the concept of thought, or "thought thinking itself," held in philosophy a century and a half ago? By answering this question, I shall try to give an answer indirectly to the central question of the modern age — a question posed for us by the existence of modern science. It is the question of how our natural view of the world — the experience of the world that we have as we simply live out our lives — is related to the unassailable and anonymous authority that confronts us in the pronouncements of science. Since the seventeenth century, the real task of philosophy has been to mediate this new employment of man's cognitive and constructive capacities with the totality of our experience of life. This task has found expression in a variety of ways, including our own generation's attempt to bring the topic of language to the center of philosophical concern. Language is the fundamental mode of operation of our being-in-the-world and the all-embracing form of the constitution of the world. Hence we always have in view the pronouncements of the sciences, which are fixed in nonverbal signs. And our task is to reconnect the objective world of technology, which the sciences place at our disposal and discretion, with those fundamental

3

orders of our being that are neither arbitrary nor manipulable by us, but rather simply demand our respect.

I want to elucidate several phenomena in which the universality of this question becomes evident. I have called the point of view involved in this theme "hermeneutical," a term developed by Heidegger. Heidegger was continuing a perspective stemming originally from Protestant theology and transmitted into our own century by Wilhelm Dilthey.

What is hermeneutics? I would like to start from two experiences of alienation that we encounter in our concrete existence: the experience of alienation of the aesthetic consciousness and the experience of alienation of the historical consciousness. In both cases what I mean can be stated in a few words. The aesthetic consciousness realizes a possibility that as such we can neither deny nor diminish in its value, namely, that we relate ourselves, either negatively or affirmatively, to the quality of an artistic form. This statement means we are related in such a way that the judgment we make decides in the end regarding the expressive power and validity of what we judge. What we reject has nothing to say to us — or we reject it because it has nothing to say to us. This characterizes our relation to art in the broadest sense of the word, a sense that, as Hegel has shown, includes the entire religious world of the ancient Greeks, whose religion of beauty experienced the divine in concrete works of art that man creates in response to the gods. When it loses its original and unquestioned authority, this whole world of experience becomes alienated into an object of aesthetic judgment. At the same time, however, we must admit that the world of artistic tradition — the splendid contemporaneousness that we gain through art with so many human worlds — is more than a mere object of our free acceptance or rejection. Is it not true that when a work of art has seized us it no longer leaves us the freedom to push it away from us once again and to accept or reject it on our own terms? And is it not also true that these artistic creations, which come down through the millennia, were not created for such aesthetic acceptance or rejection? No artist of the religiously vital cultures of the past ever produced his work of art with any other intention then that his creation should be received in terms of what it says and presents and that it should have its place in the world where men live together. The consciousness of art — the aesthetic consciousness — is always secondary to the immediate truth-claim that proceeds from the work of art itself. To this extent, when we judge a work of art on the basis of its aesthetic quality, something that is really much more intimately familiar to us is alienated. This alienation into aesthetic judgment always takes place when we have withdrawn ourselves and are no longer open to the immediate claim of that which grasps us. Thus one point of departure for my reflections in *Truth and Method* was that the aesthetic sovereignty that claims its rights in the experience of art represents an alienation when compared to the authentic experience that confronts us in the form of art itself.

About thirty years ago, this problem cropped up in a particularly distorted form when National Socialist politics of art, as a means to its own ends, tried to criticize formalism by arguing that art is bound to a people. Despite its misuse by the National Socialists, we cannot deny that the idea of art being bound to a people involves a real insight. A genuine artistic creation stands within a particular community, and such a community is always distinguishable from the cultured society that is informed and terrorized by art criticism.

The second mode of the experience of alienation is the historical consciousness — the noble and slowly perfected art of holding ourselves at a critical distance in dealing with witnesses to past life. Ranke's celebrated description of this idea as the extinguishing of the individual provided a popular formula for the ideal of historical thinking: the historical consciousness has the task of understanding all the witnesses of a past time out of the spirit of that time, of extricating them from the preoccupations of our own present life, and of knowing, without moral smugness, the past as a human phenomenon. In his well-known essay *The Use and Abuse of History,* Nietzsche formulated the contradiction between this historical distancing and the immediate will to shape things that always cleaves to the present. And at the same time he exposed many of the consequences of what he called the "Alexandrian," weakened form of the will, which is found in modern historical science. We might recall his indictment of the weakness of evaluation that has befallen the modern mind because it has become so accustomed to considering things in ever different and changing lights that it is blinded and incapable of arriving at an opinion of its own regarding the objects it studies. It is unable to determine its own position vis-à-vis what confronts it. Nietzsche traces the value-blindness of historical objectivism back to the conflict between the alienated historical world and the life-powers of the present.

To be sure, Nietzsche is an ecstatic witness. But our actual experience of the historical consciousness in the last one hundred years has taught us most emphatically that there are serious difficulties involved in its claim to historical objectivity. Even in those masterworks of historical scholarship that seem to be the very consummation of the extinguishing of the individual demanded by Ranke, it is still an unquestioned principle of our scientific experience that we can classify these works with unfailing accuracy in terms of the political tendencies of the time in which they were written. When we read Mommsen's *History of Rome,* we know who alone could have written it, that is, we can identify the political situation in which this historian organized the voices of the past in a meaningful way. We know it too in the case of Treitschke or of Sybel, to choose only a few prominent names from Prussian historiography. This clearly means, first of all, that the whole reality of historical experience does not find expression in the mastery of historical method. No one disputes the fact that controlling the prejudices of our own present to such an extent that we do not misunderstand the witnesses of the past is a valid aim, but obviously such control does not completely fulfill the task of understanding the past and its transmissions. Indeed, it could very well be that only *insignificant* things in historical scholarship permit us to approximate this ideal of totally extinguishing individuality, while the great productive achievements of scholarship always preserve something of the splendid magic of immediately mirroring the present in the past and the past in the present. Historical science, the second experience from which I begin, expresses only one part of our actual experience —

our actual encounter with historical tradition – and it knows only an alienated form of this historical tradition.

We can contrast the hermeneutical consciousness with these examples of alienation as a more comprehensive possibility that we must develop. But, in the case of this hermeneutical consciousness also, our initial task must be to overcome the epistemological truncation by which the traditional "science of hermeneutics" has been absorbed into the idea of modern science. If we consider Schleiermacher's hermeneutics, for instance, we find his view of this discipline peculiarly restricted by the modern idea of science. Schleiermacher's hermeneutics shows him to be a leading voice of historical romanticism. But at the same time, he kept the concern of the Christian theologian clearly in mind, intending his hermeneutics, as a general doctrine of the art of understanding, to be of value in the special work of interpreting Scripture. Schleiermacher defined hermeneutics as the art of avoiding misunderstanding. To exclude by controlled, methodical consideration whatever is alien and leads to misunderstanding – misunderstanding suggested to us by distance in time, change in linguistic usages, or in the meanings of words and modes of thinking – that is certainly far from an absurd description of the hermeneutical endeavor. But the question also arises as to whether the phenomenon of understanding is defined appropriately when we say that to understand is to avoid misunderstanding. Is it not, in fact, the case that every misunderstanding presupposes a "deep common accord"?

I am trying to call attention here to a common experience. We say, for instance, that understanding and misunderstanding take place between I and thou. But the formulation "I and thou" already betrays an enormous alienation. There is nothing like an "I and thou" at all – there is neither the I nor the thou as isolated, substantial realities. I may say "thou" and I may refer to myself over against a thou, but a common understanding [*Verständigung*] always precedes these situations. We all know that to say "thou" to someone presupposes a deep common accord [*tiefes Einverständnis*]. Something enduring is already present when this word is spoken. When we try to reach agreement on a matter on which we have different opinions, this deeper factor always comes into play, even if we are seldom aware of it. Now the science of hermeneutics would have us believe that the opinion we have to understand is something alien that seeks to lure us into misunderstanding, and our task is to exclude every element through which a misunderstanding can creep in. We accomplish this task by a controlled procedure of historical training, by historical criticism, and by a controllable method in connection with powers of psychological empathy. It seems to me that this description is valid in one respect, but yet it is only a partial description of a comprehensive life-phenomenon that constitutes the "we" that we all are. Our task, it seems to me, is to transcend the prejudices that underlie the aesthetic consciousness, the historical consciousness, and the hermeneutical consciousness that has been restricted to a technique for avoiding misunderstandings and to overcome the alienations present in them all.

What is it, then, in these three experiences that seemed to us to have been left out, and what makes us so sensitive to the distinctiveness of these experiences? What is the *aesthetic* consciousness when compared to the fullness of what has already addressed us — what we call "classical" in art? Is it not always already determined in this way what will be expressive for us and what we will find significant? Whenever we say with an instinctive, even if perhaps erroneous, certainty (but a certainty that is initially valid for our consciousness) "this is classical; it will endure," what we are speaking of has already preformed our possibility for aesthetic judgment. There are no purely formal criteria that can claim to judge and sanction the formative level simply on the basis of its artistic virtuosity. Rather, our sensitive-spiritual existence is an aesthetic resonance chamber that resonates with the voices that are constantly reaching us, preceding all explicit aesthetic judgment.

The situation is similar with the historical consciousness. Here, too, we must certainly admit that there are innumerable tasks of historical scholarship that have no relation to our own present and to the depths of its historical consciousness. But it seems to me there can be no doubt that the great horizon of the past, out of which our culture and our present live, influences us in everything we want, hope for, or fear in the future. History is only present to us in light of our futurity. Here we have all learned from Heidegger, for he exhibited precisely the primacy of futurity for our possible recollection and retention, and for the whole of our history.

Heidegger worked out this primacy in his doctrine of the productivity of the hermeneutical circle. I have given the following formulation to this insight: It is not so much our judgments as it is our prejudices that constitute our being.* This is a provocative formulation, for I am using it to restore to its rightful place a positive concept of prejudice that was driven out of our linquistic usage by the French and the English Enlightenment. It can be shown that the concept of prejudice did not originally have the meaning we have attached to it. Prejudices are not necessarily unjustified and erroneous, so that they inevitably distort the truth. In fact, the historicity of our existence entails that prejudices, in the literal sense of the word, constitute the initial directedness of our whole ability to experience. Prejudices are biases of our openness to the world. They are simply conditions whereby we experience something — whereby what we encounter says something to us. This formulation certainly does not mean that we are enclosed within a wall of prejudices and only let through the narrow portals those things that can produce a pass saying, "Nothing new will be said here." Instead we welcome just that guest who promises something new to our curiosity. But how do we know the guest whom we admit is one who has something *new* to say to us? Is not our expectation and our readiness to hear the new also necessarily determined by the old that has already taken possession of us? The concept of prejudice is closely connected to the concept of authority, and the above image makes it clear that it is in need of hermeneutical rehabilitation. Like every image, however, this one too is misleading. The nature of the hermeneutical experience is not that something is outside and desires admission. Rather, we are possessed by something and precisely by means of it we are opened up for the new, the different, the true. Plato made this clear in his beautiful

*Cf. *WM*, p. 261.

comparison of bodily foods with spiritual nourishment: while we can refuse the former (e.g., on the advice of a physician), we have always taken the latter into ourselves already.

But now the question arises as to how we can legitimate this hermeneutical conditionedness of our being in the face of modern science, which stands or falls with the principle of being unbiased and prejudiceless. We will certainly not accomplish this legitimation by making prescriptions for science and recommending that it toe the line — quite aside from the fact that such pronouncements always have something comical about them. Science will not do us this favor. It will continue along its own path with an inner necessity beyond its control, and it will produce more and more breathtaking knowledge and controlling power. It can be no other way. It is senseless, for instance, to hinder a genetic researcher because such research threatens to breed a superman. Hence the problem cannot appear as one in which our human consciousness ranges itself over against the world of science and presumes to develop a kind of antiscience. Nevertheless, we cannot avoid the question of whether what we are aware of in such apparently harmless examples as the aesthetic consciousness and the historical consciousness does not represent a problem that is also present in modern natural science and our technological attitude toward the world. If modern science enables us to erect a new world of technological purposes that transforms everything around us, we are not thereby suggesting that the researcher who gained the knowledge decisive for this state of affairs even considered technical applications. The genuine researcher is motivated by a desire for knowledge and by nothing else. And yet, over against the whole of our civilization that is founded on modern science, we must ask repeatedly if something has not been omitted. If the presuppositions of these possibilities for knowing and making remain half in the dark, cannot the result be that the hand applying this knowledge will be destructive?

The problem is really universal. The hermeneutical question, as I have characterized it, is not restricted to the areas from which I began in my own investigations. My only concern there was to secure a theoretical basis that would enable us to deal with the basic factor of contemporary culture, namely, science and its industrial, technological utilization. Statistics provide us with a useful example of how the hermeneutical dimension encompasses the entire procedure of science. It is an extreme example, but it shows us that science always stands under definite conditions of methodological abstraction and that the successes of modern sciences rest on the fact that other possibilities for questioning are concealed by abstraction. This fact comes out clearly in the case of statistics, for the anticipatory character of the questions statistics answer make it particularly suitable for propaganda purposes. Indeed, effective propaganda must always try to influence initially the judgment of the person addressed and to restrict his possibilities of judgment. Thus what is established by statistics seems to be a language of facts, but which questions these facts answer and which facts would begin to speak if other questions were asked are hermeneutical questions. Only a hermeneutical inquiry would legitimate the meaning of these facts and thus the consequences that follow from them.

But I am anticipating, and have inadvertently used the phrase, "which answers to which questions fit the facts." This phrase is in fact the hermeneutical *Urphänomen*: No assertion is possible that cannot be understood as an answer to a question, and assertions can only be understood in this way. It does not impair the impressive methodology of modern science in the least. Whoever wants to learn a science has to learn to master its methodology. But we also know that methodology as such does not guarantee in any way the productivity of its application. Any experience of life can confirm the fact that there is such a thing as methodological sterility, that is, the application of a method to something not really worth knowing, to something that has not been made an object of investigation on the basis of a genuine question.

The methodological self-consciousness of modern science certainly stands in opposition to this argument. A historian, for example, will say in reply: It is all very nice to talk about the historical tradition in which alone the voices of the past gain their meaning and through which the prejudices that determine the present are inspired. But the situation is completely different in questions of serious historical research. How could one seriously mean, for example, that the clarification of the taxation practices of fifteenth-century cities or of the marital customs of Eskimos somehow first receive their meaning from the consciousness of the present and its anticipations? These are questions of historical knowledge that we take up as tasks quite independently of any relation to the present.

In answering this objection, one can say that the extremity of this point of view would be similar to what we find in certain large industrial research facilities, above all in America and Russia. I mean the so-called random experiment in which one simply covers the material without concern for waste or cost, taking the chance that some day one measurement among the thousands of measurements will finally yield an interesting finding; that is, it will turn out to be the answer to a question from which someone can progress. No doubt modern research in the humanities also works this way to some extent. One thinks, for instance, of the great editions and especially of the ever more perfect indexes. It must remain an open question, of course, whether by such procedures modern historical research increases the chances of actually noticing the interesting fact and thus gaining from it the corresponding enrichment of our knowledge. But even if they do, one might ask: Is this an ideal, that countless research projects (i.e., determinations of the connection of facts) are extracted from a thousand historians, so that the 1001st historian can find something interesting? Of course I am drawing a caricature of genuine scholarship. But in every caricature there is an element of truth, and this one contains an indirect answer to the question of what it is that really makes the productive scholar. That he has learned the methods? The person who never produces anything new has also done that. It is imagination [*Phantasie*] that is the decisive function of the scholar. Imagination naturally has a hermeneutical function and serves the sense for what is questionable. It serves the ability to expose real, productive questions, something in which, generally speaking, only he who masters all the methods of his science succeeds.

As a student of Plato, I particularly love those scenes in

which Socrates gets into a dispute with the Sophist virtuosi and drives them to despair by his questions. Eventually they can endure his questions no longer and claim for themselves the apparently preferable role of the questioner. And what happens? They can think of nothing at all to ask. Nothing at all occurs to them that is worth while going into and trying to answer.

I draw the following inference from this observation. The real power of hermeneutical consciousness is our ability to see what is questionable. Now if what we have before our eyes is not only the artistic tradition of a people, or historical tradition, or the principle of modern science in its hermeneutical preconditions but rather the whole of our experience, then we have succeeded, I think, in joining the experience of science to our own universal and human experience of life. For we have now reached the fundamental level that we can call (with Johannes Lohmann) the "linguistic constitution of the world."[1] It presents itself as the consciousness that is effected by history [*wirkungsgeschichtliches Bewusstsein*] and that provides an initial schematization for all our possibilities of knowing. I leave out of account the fact that the scholar — even the natural scientist — is perhaps not completely free of custom and society and from all possible factors in his environment. What I mean is that precisely *within* his scientific experience it is not so much the "laws of ironclad inference" (Helmholz) that present fruitful ideas to him, but rather unforseen constellations that kindle the spark of scientific inspiration (e.g., Newton's falling apple or some other incidental observation).

The consciousness that is effected by history has its fulfillment in what is linquistic. We can learn from the sensitive student of language that language, in its life and occurrence, must not be thought of as merely changing, but rather as something that has a teleology operating within it. This means that the words that are formed, the means of expression that appear in a language in order to say certain things, are not accidentally fixed, since they do not once again fall altogether into disuse. Instead, a definite articulation of the world is built up — a process that works as if guided and one that we can always observe in children who are learning to speak.

We can illustrate this by considering a passage in Aristotle's *Posterior Analytics* that ingeniously describes one definite aspect of language formation.[2] The passage treats what Aristotle calls the *epagoge,* that is, the formation of the universal. How does one arrive at a universal? In philosophy we say: how do we arrive at a general concept, but even words in this sense are obviously general. How does it happen that they are "words," that is, that they have a general meaning? In his first apperception, a sensuously equipped being finds himself in a surging sea of stimuli, and finally one day he begins, as we say, to know something. Clearly we do not mean that he was previously blind. Rather, when we say "to know" [*erkennen*] we mean "to recognize" [*wiedererkennen*], that is, to pick something out [*herauserkennen*] of the stream of images flowing past as being identical. What is picked out in this fashion is clearly retained. But how? When does a child know its mother for the first time? When it sees her for the first time? No. Then when? How does it take place? Can we really say at all that there is a single event in which a first knowing extricates the child from the darkness of not knowing? It seems obvious to me that we cannot. Aristotle has described this wonderfully. He says it is the same as when an army is in flight, driven by panic, until at last someone stops and looks around to see whether the foe is still dangerously close behind. We cannot say that the army stops when one soldier has stopped. But then another stops. The army does not stop by virtue of the fact that two soldiers stop. When does it actually stop, then? Suddenly it stands its ground again. Suddenly it obeys the command once again. A subtle pun in involved in Aristotle's description, for in Greek "command" means *arche,* that is, *principium.* When is the principle present as a principle? Through what capacity? This question is in fact the question of the occurrence of the universal.

If I have not misunderstood Johannes Lohmann's exposition, precisely this same teleology operates constantly in the life of language. When Lohmann speaks of linguistic tendencies as the real agents of history in which specific forms expand, he knows of course that it occurs in these forms of realization, of "coming to a stand" [*Zum-Stehen-Kommen*], as the beautiful German word says. What is manifest here, I contend, is the real mode of operation of our whole human experience of the world. Learning to speak is surely a phase of special productivity, and in the course of time we have all transformed the genius of the three-year-old into a poor and meager talent. But in the utilization of the linguistic interpretation of the world that finally comes about, something of the productivity of our beginnings remains alive. We are all acquainted with this, for instance, in the attempt to translate, in practical life or in literature or wherever; that is, we are familiar with the strange, uncomfortable, and tortuous feeling we have as long as we do not have the right word. When we have found the right expression (it need not always be one word), when we are certain that we have it, then it "stands," then something has come to a "stand." Once again we have a halt in the midst of the rush of the foreign language, whose endless variation makes us lose our orientation. What I am describing is the mode of the whole human experience of the world. I call this experience hermeneutical, for the process we are describing is repeated continually throughout our familiar experience. There is always a world already interpreted, already organized in its basic relations, into which experience steps as something new, upsetting what has led our expectations and undergoing reorganization itself in the upheaval. Misunderstanding and strangeness are not the first factors, so that avoiding misunderstanding can be regarded as the specific task of hermeneutics. Just the reverse is the case. Only the support of familiar and common understanding makes possible the venture into the alien, the lifting up of something out of the alien, and thus the broadening and enrichment of our own experience of the world.

This discussion shows how the claim to universality that is appropriate to the hermeneutical dimension is to be understood. Understanding is language-bound. But this assertion does not lead us into any kind of linguistic relativism. It is indeed true that we live within a language, but language is not a system of signals that we send off with the aid of a telegraphic key when we enter the office or transmission station. That is not speaking, for it does not have the infinity of the act that is linguistically creative and world experiencing. While we live wholly within a language, the fact that we do so does not constitute linguistic relativism because there is absolutely no captivity within a language – not even within our native language. We all experience this when we learn a foreign language, especially on journeys insofar as we master the foreign language to some extent. To master the foreign language means precisely that when we engage in speaking it in the foreign land, we do not constantly consult inwardly our own world and its vocabulary. The better we know the language, the less such a side glance at our native language is perceptible, and only because we never know foreign languages well enough do we always have something of this feeling. But it is nevertheless already speaking, even if perhaps a stammering speaking, for stammering is the obstruction of a desire to speak and is thus opened into the infinite realm of possible expression. Any language in which we live is infinite in this sense, and it is completely mistaken to infer that reason is fragmented because there are various languages. Just the opposite is the case. Precisely through our finitude, the particularity of our being, which is evident even in the variety of languages, the infinite dialogue is opened in the direction of the truth that we are.

If this is correct, then the relation of our modern industrial world, founded by science, which we described at the outset, is mirrored above all on the level of language. We live in an epoch in which an increasing leveling of all life-forms is taking place – that is the rationally necessary requirement for maintaining life on our planet. The food problem of mankind, for example, can only be overcome by the surrender of the lavish wastefulness that has covered the earth. Unavoidably, the mechanical, industrial world is expanding within the life of the individual as a sort of sphere of technical perfection. When we hear modern lovers talking to each other, we often wonder if they are communicating with words or with advertising labels and technical terms from the sign language of the modern industrial world. It is inevitable that the leveled life-forms of the industrial age also affect language, and in fact the impoverishment of the vocabulary of language is making enormous progress, thus bringing about an approximation of language to a technical sign-system. Leveling tendencies of this kind are irresistible. Yet in spite of them the simultaneous building up of our own world in language still persists whenever we want to say something to each other. The result is the actual relationship of men to each other. Each one is at first a kind of linguistic circle, and these linguistic circles come into contact with each other, merging more and more. Language occurs once again, in vocabulary and grammar as always, and never without the inner infinity of the dialogue that is in progress between every speaker and his partner. That is the fundamental dimension of hermeneutics. Genuine speaking, which has something to say and hence does not give prearranged signals, but rather seeks words through which one reaches the other person, is the universal human task — but it is a special task for the theologian, to whom is commissioned the saying-further (*Weitersagen*) of a message that stands written.

NOTES

1. Cf. Johannes Lohmann, *Philosophie und Sprachwissenschaft* (Berlin: Duncker & Humbolt, 1963).
2. Aristotle, *Posterior Analytics,* 100a 11-13.

2
On the Scope and Function of Hermeneutical Reflection (1967)

(Translated by G. B. Hess and R. E. Palmer)

Introduction

Philosophical hermeneutics takes as its task the opening up of the hermeneutical dimension in its full scope, showing its fundamental significance for our entire understanding of the world and thus for all the various forms in which this under-standing manifests itself: from interhuman communication to manipulation of society; from personal experience by the individual in society to the way in which he encounters society; and from the tradition as it is built of religion and law, art and philosophy, to the revolutionary consciousness that unhinges the tradition through emancipatory reflection.

Despite this vast scope and significance, however, individual explorations necessarily start from the very limited experiences and fields of experience. My own effort, for instance, went back to Dilthey's philosophical development of the heritage of German romanticism, in that I too made the theory of the *Geisteswissenschaften* (humanistic sciences and social sciences) my theme. But I hope to have placed it on a new and much broader footing linguistically, ontologically, and aesthetically; for the experience of art can answer the prevailing presumption of historical alienation in the human-istic disciplines, I believe, with its own overriding and victori-ous claim to contemporaneousness, a claim that lies in its

18

very essence. It should be evident already from the essential linguisticality of all human experience of the world, which has as its own way of fulfillment a constantly self-renewing contemporaneousness. I maintain that precisely this contemporaneousness and this linguisticality point to a truth that goes questioningly behind all knowledge and anticipatingly before it.

And so it was unavoidable that in my analysis of the universal linguisticality of man's relation to the world, the limitations of the fields of experience from which the investigation took its start would unwittingly predetermine the result. Indeed, it paralleled what happened in the historical development of the hermeneutical problem. It came into being in encounter with the written tradition that demanded translation, for the tradition had become estranged from the present as a result of such factors as temporal distance, the fixity of writing, and the sheer inertia of permanence. Thus it was that the many-layered problem of translation became for me the model for the linguisticality of all human behavior in the world. From the structure of translation was indicated the general problem of making what is alien our own. Yet further reflection on the universality of hermeneutics eventually made clear that the model of translation does not, as such, fully come to grips with the manifoldness of what language means in man's existence.[1] Certainly in translation one finds the tension and release that structure all understanding and understandability, but it ultimately derives from the universality of the hermeneutical problem. It is important to realize that this phenomenon is not secondary in human existence, and hermeneutics is not to be viewed as a mere subordinate discipline within the arena of the *Geisteswissenschaften.*

The universal phenomenon of human linguisticality also unfolds in other dimensions than those which would appear to be directly concerned with the hermeneutical problem, for hermeneutics reaches into all the contexts that determine and condition the linguisticality of the human experience of the world. Some of those have been touched upon in my *Truth and Method;* for instance, the *wirkungsgeschichtliches Bewusstsein* (consciousness of effective history, or the consciousness in which history is ever at work) was presented in a conscious effort to shed light on the idea of language in some phases of its history. And of course linguisticality extends into many different dimensions not mentioned in *Truth and Method*.[2]

In rhetoric, linguisticality is attested to in a truly universal form, one that is essentially prior to the hermeneutical and almost represents something like the "positive" as over against the "negative" of linguistic interpretation. And in this connection the relationship between rhetoric and hermeneutics is a matter of great interest.[3] In the social sciences, one finds linguisticality deeply woven into the sociality of human existence, so that the theorists of the social sciences are now becoming interested in the hermeneutical approach. Preeminently, Jürgen Habermas has recently established a relationship between philosophical hermeneutics and the logic of the social sciences in his significant contribution to the *Philosophische Rundschau*,[4] evaluating this relationship from within the epistemological interests of the social sciences. This relationship too raises important questions as to the proper interests and purposes of hermeneutical reflection as compared with those characteristic of the sciences and social sciences.

It seems advisable, then, if not imperative, to take up the question of the interdependence of rhetoric, hermeneutics, and sociology as regards the universalities that run through all three, and to try to shed some light on the various kinds of legitimacy possessed by these elements. This endeavor is the more important in view of the fact that the claim to being strictly a science is in all three cases rendered rather ambiguous because of an obvious relationship to praxis. Of course this relationship applies most openly and clearly to rhetoric and hermeneutics; but it also applies to sociology, as we shall see presently.

For it is clear that rhetoric is not mere theory of forms of speech and persuasion; rather, it can develop out of a native talent for practical mastery, without any theoretical reflection about ways and means. Likewise, the art of understanding, whatever its ways and means may be, is not dependent on an explicit awareness of the rules that guide and govern it. It builds, as does rhetoric, on a natural power that everyone possesses to some degree. It is a skill in which one gifted person may surpass all others, and theory can at best only tell us why. In both rhetoric and hermeneutics, then, theory is subsequent to that out of which it is abstracted; that is, to praxis.

Historically it is worthy of note that while rhetoric belongs to the earliest Greek philosophy, hermeneutics came to flower in the Romantic era as a consequence of the modern dissolution of firm bonds with tradition. Of course, hermeneutics occurs in earlier times and forms, but even in these it represents an effort to grasp something vanishing and hold it up in the light of consciousness. Therefore, it occurs only in later stages of cultural evolution, like later Jewish religion, Alexandrian philology, Christianity as inheriting the Jewish gospel, or Lutheran theology as refuting an old tradition of Christian dogmatics. The history-embracing and history-preserving element runs deep in hermeneutics, in sharp contrast to sociological interest in reflection as basically a means of emancipation from authority and tradition. Reflection in rhetoric, like that in hermeneutics, is a meditation about a praxis that is in itself already a natural and sophisticated one. I should like to recall something of the early history of both rhetoric and hermeneutics in order to characterize and compare the scope and functions of the two fields.

Rhetoric and Hermeneutics

The first history of rhetoric was written by Aristotle, and we now possess only fragments of it. It is clear, however, that basically Aristotle's theory of rhetoric was developed to carry out a program originally projected by Plato. Plato, going back behind all the shallow claims put forward by the contemporary teachers of rhetoric, had discovered a genuine foundation for rhetoric that only the philosopher, the dialectician, could carry out: the task is to master the faculty of speaking in such an effectively persuasive way that the arguments brought forward are always appropriate to the specific receptivity of the souls to which they are directed. Certainly this statement of the task of rhetoric is theoretically enlightening,

but implicit in it are two Platonic assumptions: first, that
only he who has a grasp of the truth (i.e., the ideas) can
unerringly devise the probable *pseudos* of a rhetorical argument; second, that one must have a profound knowledge of
the souls of those one wishes to persuade. Aristotelian rhetoric is preeminently an expansion of the latter theme. In it is
fulfilled the theory of the mutual accommodation of speech
and soul demanded by Plato in the *Phaedrus,* now in the
form of an anthropological foundation for the art of speech.

Rhetorical theory was a long prepared-for, result, of a
controversy that represented the breaking into Greek culture
of an intoxicating and frightening new art of speaking and a
new idea of education itself: that of the Sophists. At that
time an uncanny new skill in standing everything on its head,
the Sicilian art of oratory, flowed in on the strait-laced but
easily influenced youths of Athens. Now it became para-
mountly necessary to teach this new power (this great ruler,
as Gorgias had called oratory) its proper limits — to discipline
it. From Protagoras to Isocrates, the masters of rhetoric
claimed not only to teach speaking, but also the formation of
a civic consciousness that bore the promise of political success. But it was Plato who first created the foundations out
of which a new and all-shattering art of speaking (Aristophanes has depicted it for us blatantly enough) could find its
limits and legitimate place.

The history of understanding is no less ancient and venera-
ble. If one acknowledges hermeneutics to exist wherever a
genuine art of understanding manifests itself, one must begin
if not with Nestor in the *Iliad,* then at least with Odysseus.
One can point out that the new philosophical movement
represented by the Sophists was concerned with the interpretation of sayings by famous poets and depicted them very
artfully as pedagogical examples. Certainly this was a form of
hermeneutics. Over against this, one can place the Socratic
hermeneutics.[5] Still, it is far from a full-fledged theory of
understanding. It seems, rather, to be generally characteristic
of the emergence of the "hermeneutical" problem that something *distant* has to be brought close, a certain strangeness
overcome, a bridge built between the once and the now. Thus
hermeneutics, as a general attitude over against the world,

came into its own in modern times, which had become aware
of the temporal distance separating us from antiquity and of
the relativity of the life-worlds of different cultural traditions. Something of this awareness was contained in the
theological claim of Reformation biblical exegesis (in the
principle of *sola scriptura*), but its true unfolding only came
about when a "historical consciousness" arose in the Enlightenment (although it was influenced by the novel insights of
Jesuit chronological information) and matured in the romantic period to establish a relationship (however broken) to our
entire inheritance from the past.

Because of this historical development of hermeneutics
hermeneutical theory oriented itself to the task of interpreting expressions of life that are fixed in writing, although
Schleiermacher's theoretical working out of hermeneutics
included understanding as it takes place in the oral exchange
of conversation. Rhetoric, on the other hand, concerned
itself with the impact of *speaking* in all its immediacy. It did
of course also enter into the realm of effective *writing,* and
thus it developed a body of teaching on style and styles.
Nevertheless, it achieved its authentic realization not in the
act of reading but in speaking. The phenomenon of the orally
read speech occupies an in-between, a hybrid, position: already it displays a tendency to base the art of speaking on
the techniques of expression inherent in the medium of
writing, and thus it begins to abstract itself from the original
situation of speaking. Thus begins the transformation into
poetics, whose linguistic objects are so wholly and completely art that their transformation from the oral sphere into
writing and back is accomplished without loss or damage.

Rhetoric as such, however, is tied to the immediacy of its
effect. Now the arousing of emotions, which is clearly the
essence of the orator's task,[6] is effectual to a vastly diminished degree in written expression, which is the traditional
object of hermeneutical investigation. And this is precisely
the difference that matters: the orator carries his listeners
away with him; the convincing power of his arguments over-
whelms the listener. While under the persuasive spell of
speech, the listener for the moment cannot and ought not to
indulge in critical examination. On the other hand, the read-

ing and interpreting of what is written is so distanced and detached from its author — from his mood, intentions, and unexpressed tendencies — that the grasping of the meaning of the text takes on something of the character of an independent productive act, one that resembles more the art of the orator than the process of mere listening. Thus it is easy to understand why the theoretical tools of the art of interpretation (hermeneutics) have been to a large extent borrowed from rhetoric.[7]

Where, indeed, but to rhetoric should the theoretical examination of interpretation turn? Rhetoric from oldest tradition has been the only advocate of a claim to truth that defends the probable, the *eikós* (verisimile), and that which is convincing to the ordinary reason, against the claim of science to accept as true only what can be demonstrated and tested! Convincing and persuading, without being able to prove — these are obviously as much the aim and measure of understanding and interpretation as they are the aim and measure of the art of oration and persuasion. And this whole wide realm of convincing "persuasions" and generally reigning views has not been gradually narrowed by the progress of science, however great it has been; rather, this realm extends to take in every new product of scientific endeavor, claiming it for itself and bringing it within its scope.

The ubiquity of rhetoric, indeed, is unlimited. Only through it is science a sociological factor of life, for all the representations of science that are directed beyond the mere narrow circle of specialists (and, perhaps one should say, insofar as they are not limited in their impact to a very small circle of initiates) owe their effectiveness to the rhetorical element they contain. Even Descartes, that great and passionate advocate of method and certainty, is in all his writings an author who uses the means of rhetoric in a magnificent fashion.[8] There can be no doubt, then, about the fundamental function of rhetoric within social life. But one may go further, in view of the ubiquity of rhetoric, to defend the primordial claims of rhetoric over against modern science, remembering that all science that would wish to be of practical usefulness at all is dependent on it.

No less universal is the function of hermeneutics. The lack

of immediate understandability of texts handed down to us historically or their proneness to be misunderstood is really only a special case of what is to be met in all human orientation to the world as the *atopon* (the strange), that which does not "fit" into the customary order of our expectation based on experience. Hermeneutics has only called our attention to this phenomenon. Just as when we progress in understanding the *mirabilia* lose their strangeness, so every successful appropriation of tradition is dissolved into a new and distinct familiarity in which it belongs to us and we to it. They both flow together into one owned and shared world, which encompasses past and present and which receives its linguistic articulation in the speaking of man with man.

The phenomenon of understanding, then, shows the universality of human linguisticality as a limitless medium that carries *everything* within it — not only the "culture" that has been handed down to us through language, but absolutely everything — because everything (in the world and out of it) is included in the realm of "understandings" and understandability in which we move. Plato was right when he asserted that whoever regards things in the mirror of speech becomes aware of them in their full and undiminished truth. And he was profoundly correct when he taught that all cognition is only what it is as re-cognition, for a "first cognition" is as little possible as a first word. In fact, a cognition in the very recent past, one whose consequences appear as yet unforeseeable, becomes what it truly is for us only when it has unfolded into its consequences and into the medium of intersubjective understanding.

And so we see that the rhetorical and hermeneutical aspects of human linguisticality completely interpenetrate each other. There would be no speaker and no art of speaking if understanding and consent were not in question, were not underlying elements; there would be no hermeneutical task if there were no mutual understanding that has been disturbed and that those involved in a conversation must search for and find again together. It is a symptom of our failure to realize this and evidence of the increasing self-alienation of human life in our modern epoch when we think in terms of organizing a perfect and perfectly manipulated information — a turn modern rhetoric seems to have taken. In this case, the sense of mutual interpenetration of rhetoric and hermeneutics fades away and hermeneutics is on its own.

Hermeneutics and the Social Sciences

It is in keeping with the universality of the hermeneutical approach that hermeneutics must be taken into account with regard to the logic of the social sciences, and especially in relation to the intentional alienation and distancing present in sociological methodology. Jürgen Habermas in his article on the subject worked with my analysis of the *wirkungs-geschichtliches Bewusstsein* and the model of translation as both were given in *Truth and Method* with the hope that they could help to overcome the positivistic ossification of sociological logic and move sociological theory beyond its historical failure to reflect upon its linguistic foundations. Now Habermas's use of hermeneutics stands on the premise that it shall serve the methodology of the social sciences. But this premise is, in itself, a prior decision of greatest significance, for the purpose of sociological method as emancipating one from tradition places it at the outset very far from the traditional purpose and starting point of the hermeneutical problematic with all its bridge building and recovery of the best in the past.

Admittedly the methodical alienation that comprises the very essence of modern science is indeed to be found also in the *Geisteswissenschaften,* and the title of *Truth and Method* never intended that the antithesis it implies should be mutually exclusive.[9] But the *Geisteswissenschaften* were the starting point of my analysis in *Truth and Method* precisely because they related to experiences that have nothing to do with method and science but lie beyond science — like the experience of art and the experience of culture that bears the imprint of its historical tradition. The hermeneutical experience as it is operative in all these cases is not in itself the object of methodical alienation but is directed against alienation. The hermeneutical experience is prior to all methodical alienation because it is the matrix out of which arise the questions that it then directs to science. The modern social scientists, on the other hand, insofar as they recognize hermeneutical reflection as unavoidable, nevertheless advance the claim (as Habermas has formulated it) of raising understanding up out of a prescientific exercise to the rank of a self-reflecting activity by "controlled alienation" — that is, through "methodical development of intelligence."[10]

It has been the way of science from its earliest stages to achieve through teachable and controllable ways of proceeding what individual intelligence would also occasionally attain, but in unsure and uncheckable ways. But is this way to be absolutized and idolized? Is it right that social scientists should believe that through it they attain human personal judging and practice? What kind of understanding does one achieve through "controlled alienation"? Is it not likely to be an alienated understanding? Is it not the case that many social scientists are more interested in using the sedimented truisms inherent in linguisticality (so as to grasp "scientifically" the "real" structures, as they define them, of society) than in really understanding social life? Hermeneutical reflection will not, however, allow a restriction of itself to this function that is immanent in the sciences. And most especially it will not be deterred from applying hermeneutical reflection anew to the methodical alienation of understanding practiced by the social sciences, even though it exposes itself to positivistic detraction.

But let us examine first how the hermeneutical problematic applies within social scientific theory and how it would be seen from that vantage point. Habermas sees in its analysis of historicity one of the principal values of hermeneutics for social theory. So it is the claim of hermeneutics that the idea of *Wirkungsgeschichte* (effective history) furnishes a means of access to the realm of objects treated by sociology. The *wirkungsgeschichtliches Bewusstsein* (consciousness of effective history) seeks to be aware of its prejudgments and to control its own preunderstanding; and thus it does away with that naïve objectivism that falsifies not only the positivistic theory of science but also any project of laying either a phenomenological or language-analytical foundation for sociology.

Yet the question arises as to what hermeneutical reflection

really does. Habermas answers this question in reference to universal history, a goal that unavoidably lifts itself out of the multiple goals and conceptions of goal in social actions. He asserts that if hermeneutical reflection were simply satisfied with general considerations, such as that nobody is able to reach beyond the limitedness of his own standpoint, then it would be ineffectual. The claim to a material philosophy of history may be contested by such a consideration, but historical consciousness nevertheless constantly will project an anticipated universal history. What is the good, after all, Habermas asks, of knowing merely that a projected futurity cannot be other than preliminary and essentially provisional? So, where it is effective and operational, what does hermeneutical reflection do? In what relationship to the tradition of which it becomes conscious does this "historically operative" reflection stand?

My thesis is — and I think it is the necessary consequence of recognizing the operativeness of history in our conditionedness and finitude — that the thing which hermeneutics teaches us is to see through the dogmatism of asserting an opposition and separation between the ongoing, natural "tradition" and the reflective appropriation of it. For behind this assertion stands a dogmatic objectivism that distorts the very concept of hermeneutical reflection itself. In this objectivism the understander is seen — even in the so-called sciences of understanding like history — not in relationship to the hermeneutical situation and the constant operativeness of history in his own consciousness, but in such a way as to imply that his own understanding does not enter into the event.

But this is simply not the case. Actually, the historian even the one who treats history as a "critical science," is so little separated from the ongoing traditions (for example, those of his nation) that he is really *himself engaged in* contributing to the growth and development of the national state. He is one of the "nation's" historians; he belongs to the nation. And for the epoch of national states, one must say: the more he may have reflected on his hermeneutical conditionedness, the more national he knows himself to be. J. F. Droysen, for instance, who saw through the "eunuch-like objectivity" of the historian in all its methodological naïvete, was himself tremendously influential for the national consciousness of bourgeois nineteenth-century culture. He was, in any case, more effective than the epical consciousness of Ranke, which was inclined to foster the nonpoliticality appropriate to an authoritarian state. To understand, we may say, is itself a kind of happening. Only a naïve and unreflective historicism in hermeneutics would see the historical-hermeneutical sciences as something absolutely new that would do away with the power of "tradition." On the contrary, I have tried to present in *Truth and Method,* through the aspect of linguisticality that operates in all understanding, an unambiguous demonstration of the continual process of mediation by which that which is societally transmitted (the tradition) lives on. For language is not only an object in our hands, it is the reservoir of tradition and the medium in and through which we exist and perceive our world.

To this formulation Habermas objects that the medium of science itself is changed through reflection, and that precisely this experience is the priceless heritage bequeathed us by German idealism out of the spirit of the eighteenth century. Habermas asserts that although the Hegelian procedure of reflection is not presented in my analysis as fulfilled in an absolute consciousness, nevertheless my "idealism of linguisticality" (as he calls it)[11] exhausts itself in mere hermeneutical appropriation, development, and "cultural transmission," and thus displays a sorry powerlessness in view of the concrete whole of societal relationships. This larger whole, says Habermas, is obviously animated not only by language but by work and action; therefore, hermeneutical reflection must pass into a criticism of ideology.

In taking such a position, Habermas is tying directly into the central motif in sociological interest in gaining knowledge. Rhetoric (theory) stepped forward against the bewitching of consciousness achieved through the power of speech, by differentiating between the truth and that which appears to be the truth (and which it teaches one to produce). Hermeneutics, being confronted with a disrupted intersubjective understanding, seeks to place communication on a new basis and in particular to replace the false objectivism of alienated knowing with new hermeneutical foundations. Just as in rhetoric and hermeneutics so also in *sociological reflection* an emancipatory interest is at work that undertakes to free us of outer and inner social forces and compulsions simply by making us aware of them. Insofar as these forces and compulsions tend to legitimate themselves linguistically, Habermas sees the critique of ideology as the means of unmasking the "deceptions of language."[12] But this critique, of course, is in itself a linguistic act of reflection.

In the field of psychoanalytical therapy, too, says Habermas, we find the claims for the emancipatory power of reflection corroborated. For the repression that is seen through robs the false compulsions of their power. Just as in psychotherapy it is the goal to identify through a process of reflective development all our motives of action with the real meaning to which the patient is oriented (this goal is of course limited by the therapeutic task in the psychoanalytic situation, which therefore itself represents a limiting concept) so in social reality also (as Habermas would have it) hermeneutics would be at its best when such a fictitious goal situation is operative. For Habermas, and for psychoanalysis, the life of society and the life of the individual consists of the interaction of intelligible motives and concrete compulsions, which social and psychological investigation in a progressive process of clarification appropriates in order to set man, the actor and agent, free.

One cannot dispute the fact that this sociotheoretical conception has its logic. The question we must ask ourselves, however, is whether such a conception does justice to the actual reach of hermeneutical reflection: does hermeneutics really take its bearings from a limiting concept of perfect interaction between understood motives and consciously performed action (a concept that is itself, I believe, fictitious)? I maintain that the hermeneutical problem is universal and basic for all interhuman experience, both of history and of the present moment, precisely because meaning can be experienced even where it is not actually intended. The universality of the hermeneutical dimension is narrowed down, I think, when one area of understood meaning (for instance, the "cultural tradition") is held in separation from other recognizable determinants of social reality that are taken as the "real" factors. But is it not true that we can understand precisely *every* ideology as a form of false linguistic consciousness, one that might show itself not only to us as a conscious, manifest, and intelligible meaning but also might be understood in its "true" meaning? Take for example the interest in political or economic domination. In the individual life, the same thing applies to unconscious motives, which the psychoanalyst brings to conscious awareness.

Who says that these concrete, so-called real factors are outside the realm of hermeneutics? From the hermeneutical standpoint, rightly understood, it is absolutely absurd to regard the concrete factors of work and politics as outside the scope of hermeneutics. What about the vital issue of prejudices with which hermeneutical reflection deals? Where do they come from? Merely out of "cultural tradition"? Surely they do, in part, but what is tradition formed from? It would be true when Habermas asserts that "hermeneutics bangs helplessly, so to speak, from within against the walls of tradition,"[13] if we understand this "within" as opposite to an "outside" that *does not enter* our world — our to-be-understood, understandable, or nonunderstandable world — but remains the mere observation of external alterations (instead of human actions). With this area of what lies outside the realm of human understanding and human understandings (our world) hermeneutics is not concerned. Certainly I affirm the hermeneutical fact that the world is the medium of human understanding or not understanding, but it does not lead to the conclusion that cultural tradition should be absolutized and fixed. To suppose that it does have this implication seems to me erroneous. The principle of hermeneutics simply means that we should try to understand everything that can be understood. This is what I meant by the sentence: "Being that can be understood is language."*

This does not mean that there is a world of meanings that is narrowed down to the status of secondary objects of knowledge and mere supplements to the economic and political realities that fundamentally determine the life of society.

*WM, p. 450.

Rather, it means that the mirror of language is reflecting everything that is. In language, and only in it, can we meet what we never "encounter" in the world, because we are ourselves it (and not merely what we mean or what we know of ourselves). But the metaphor of a mirror is not fully adequate to the phenomenon of language, for in the last analysis language is not simply a mirror. What we perceive in it is not merely a "reflection" of our own and all being; it is the living out of what it is with us — not only in the concrete interrelationships of work and politics but in all the other relationships and dependencies that comprise our world.

Language, then, is not the finally found anonymous subject of all social-historical processes and action, which presents the whole of its activities as objectivations to our observing gaze; rather, it is by itself the game of interpretation that we all are engaged in every day. In this game nobody is above and before all the others; everybody is at the center, is "it" in this game. Thus it is always his turn to be interpreting. This process of interpretation takes place whenever we "understand," especially when we see through prejudices or tear away the pretenses that hide reality. There, indeed, understanding comes into its own. This idea recalls what we said about the *atopon,* the strange, for in it we have "seen through" something that appeared odd and unintelligible: we have brought it into our linguistic world. To use the analogy of chess, everything is "solved," resembling a difficult chess problem where only the definitive solution makes understandable (and then right down to the last piece) the necessity of a previous absurd position.

But does this mean that we "understand" only when we see through pretexts or unmask false pretentions? Habermas's Marxist critique of ideology appears to presuppose this meaning. At least it seems that the true "power" of reflection is evident only when it has this effect, and its powerlessness when one would remain occupied with the supposed phantom of language and spin out its implication. The presupposition is that reflection, as employed in the hermeneutical sciences, should "shake the dogmatism of life-*praxis*." Here indeed is operating a prejudice that we can see is pure dogmatism, for reflection is not always and unavoidably a step towards dissolving prior convictions. Authority is not *always* wrong. Yet Habermas regards it as an untenable assertion, and treason to the heritage of the Enlightenment, that the act of rendering transparent the structure of prejudgments in understanding should possibly lead to an acknowledgment of authority. Authority is by his definition a dogmatic power. I cannot accept the assertion that reason and authority are abstract antitheses, as the emancipatory Enlightenment did. Rather, I assert that they stand in a basically ambivalent relation, a relation I think should be explored rather than casually accepting the antithesis as a "fundamental conviction."[14]

For in my opinion this abstract antithesis embraced by the Enlightenment is a mistake fraught with ominous consequences. In it, reflection is granted a false power, and the true dependencies involved are misjudged on the basis of a fallacious idealism. Certainly I would grant that authority exercises an essential dogmatic power in innumerable forms of domination: from the ordering of education and the mandatory commands of the army and government all the way to the hierarchy of power created by political forces or fanatics. Now the mere outer appearance of obedience rendered to authority can never show why or whether the authority is legitimate, that is, whether the context is true order or the veiled disorder that is created by the arbitrary exercise of power. It seems evident to me that *acceptance* or *acknowledgment* is the decisive thing for relationships to authority. So the question is: on what is this acknowledgment based? Certainly such acceptance can often express more a yielding of the powerless to the one holding power than true acceptance, but really it is not true obedience and it is not based on authority but on force. (And when anyone in an argument appeals to authority, he only pretends.) One need only study the processes of forfeiture and decline of authority (or its rise) to see what authority is and that out of which it lives and grows. It lives not from dogmatic power but from dogmatic acceptance. What is this dogmatic acceptance, however, if not that one concedes superiority in knowledge and insight to the authority, and for this reason one believes that authority is right? Only on this crucial concession, this belief, is acceptance founded. Authority can rule only because it is freely recognized and accepted. The obedience that belongs to true authority is neither blind nor slavish.

It is an inadmissable imputation to hold that I somehow meant there is no decline of authority or no emancipating criticism of authority. Of course, whether one can really say that decline of authority comes about *through* reflection's emancipatory criticism or that decline of authority is *expressed* in criticism and emancipation is a matter we shall leave aside (although we may say that it is perhaps a misstatement of the genuine alternatives). But what is really in dispute, I think, is simply whether reflection always dissolves substantial relationships or is capable of taking them up into consciousness.

In this regard, my presentation in *Truth and Method* of the teaching and learning process (referring principally to Aristotle's *Ethics*) is taken by Habermas in a peculiarly one-sided way. For the idea that tradition, as such, should be and should remain the only ground for acceptance of presuppositions (a view that Habermas ascribes to me) flies in the face of my basic thesis that authority is rooted in insight as a hermeneutical process. A person who comes of age need not — but he also from insight can — take possession of what he has obediently followed. Tradition is no proof and validation of something, in any case not where validation is demanded by reflection. But the point is this: where does reflection demand it? Everywhere? I would object to such an answer on the grounds of the finitude of human existence and the essential particularity of reflection. The real question is whether one sees the function of reflection as bringing something to awareness in order to confront what is in fact accepted with other possibilities — so that one can either throw it out or reject the other possibilities and accept what the tradition *de facto* is presenting — or whether bringing something to awareness *always dissolves what one has previously accepted.*

The concept of reflection and bringing to awareness that Habermas employs (admittedly from his sociological interest) appears to me, then, to be itself encumbered with dogmatism, and indeed, to be a misinterpretation of reflection. For, from Husserl (in his doctrine of anonymous intentionalities) and from Heidegger (in demonstration of the ontological abridgment evident in the subject-object concept in idealism), we have learned to see through the false objectification inherent in the idealist conception of reflection. I would hold that there is most certainly an inner reversal of intentionality in reflection, which in no way raises the thing meant to a thematic object. Brentano, using Aristotelian insights, was aware of this fact. I would not know, otherwise, how the enigmatic form of the being of language could be grasped at all. Then one must distinguish "effective reflection" (*die "effektive" Reflexion*), which is that in which the unfolding of language takes place, from expressive and thematic reflection, which is the type out of which Occidental linguistic history has been formed.[15] Making everything an object and creating the conditions for science in the modern sense, this latter type of reflection establishes the grounds for the planetary civilization of tomorrow.

Habermas defends with extraordinary emotion the sciences of experience against the charge of being a random game of words. But who, from the vantage point of the technical power to place nature at our disposal, would dispute their necessity? The researcher might disclaim the technical motivation of his work and defend his relationship to pure theoretical interests — with full subjective justification. But nobody would deny that the practical application of modern science has fundamentally altered our world, and therewith also our language. But precisely so — "*also* our language." This by no means suggests, however, what Habermas imputes to me: that the linguistically articulated consciousness claims to determine all the material being of life-practice. It only suggests that there is no societal reality, with all its concrete forces, that does not bring itself to representation in a consciousness that is linguistically articulated. Reality does not happen "behind the back" of language;[16] it happens rather behind the backs of those who live in the subjective opinion that they have understood "the world" (or can no longer understand it); that is, reality happens precisely *within* language.

Obviously this fact makes the concept of "natural situation" discussed by Habermas[17] highly questionable. Marx already persuasively held that this concept was the counteridea to the working world of modern class society, but Habermas willingly uses it, not only in his reference to the "natural substance of tradition" but also to "the causality of natural patterns." I believe it is pure romanticism, and such romanticism creates an artificial abyss between tradition and the reflection that is grounded in historical consciousness. However, the "idealism of linguisticality" at least has the advantage that it does not fall into this sort of romanticism.

Habermas's critique culminates in questioning the immanentism of transcendental philosophy with respect to its historical conditions, conditions upon which he himself is dependent. Now this is indeed a central problem. Anyone who takes seriously the finitude of human existence and constructs no "consciousness as such," or "intellectus archetypus," or "transcendental ego," to which everything can be traced back, will not be able to escape the question of how his own thinking as transcendental is empirically possible. But within the hermeneutical dimension that I have developed I do not see this difficulty arising.

The well-known young theologian Wolfhart Pannenberg has presented a highly useful discussion of my book in his article "Hermeneutics and Universal History,"[18] which relates to the question of immanentism but more particularly to the question of whether my philosophical hermeneutics necessarily but unconsciously rehabilitates the Hegelian concept of universal history (such as in the concept of fusion of horizons, where the ultimate horizon is, says Pannenberg, implied or presupposed in the direction of every individual event of fusion). In particular his discussion brought home to me the vast difference between Hegel's claim to demonstrate the presence of reason in history and the conceptions of world history, those constantly outstripped conceptions, in which one unconsciously always behaves like the latest historian.

Hegel's claim to a philosophy of world history can certainly be disputed. Hegel himself knew how finite it was and remarked that the feet of his pallbearers could already be heard outside the door,* and one finds that behind all the disavowals of world history the goal, the end-thought, of *freedom* possessed a compelling evidentness. One can as little get beyond this as one can get beyond consciousness itself.

But the claim that every historian must make and operate within, namely to tie the meaning of all events to today (and of course to the future of this today), is really a fundamentally more modest one than asserting a universal history or a philosophy of world history. Nobody can dispute that history presupposes futurity, and a universal-historical conception is unavoidably one of the dimensions of today's historical consciousness from a practical point of view, or for practical purposes ("In praktischer Absicht"). But does it do justice to Hegel to want to reduce him to the limitations implied by this pragmatic interpretive requirement that the present demands? "In praktischer Absicht" — nobody today goes beyond this claim, for consciousness has become aware of its finitude and mistrusts the dictatorship of ideas or concepts. Even so, who would be so foolish as to try to reduce Hegel to the level of practical purposes? I certainly would not, even while criticizing his claims to a philosophy of universal history. So on this point I think there is really no dispute between Pannenberg and myself, so far as I understand him. For Pannenberg does not propose to renew Hegel's claim either. There is only the difference that for the Christian theologian the "practical purpose" of all universal historical conceptions has its fixed point in the absolute historicity of the Incarnation.

All the same, the question [of universality] remains. If the hermeneutical problematic wishes to maintain itself in the face of the ubiquity and universality of rhetoric, as well as the obvious topicality of critiques of ideology, it must establish its own universality. And it must do so especially over against the claims of modern science to universality, and thus to its tendency to absorb hermeneutical reflection into itself and render it serviceable to science (as in the concept, for instance, of the "methodical development of intelligence" Habermas has in mind). Still, it will be able to do so only if it

*Gadamer expresses this more picturesquely with a quote: "Die Füsse derer, die dich hinaustragen, sind schon vor der Türe." [Trans.]

does not become imprisoned in the impregnable immanence of transcendental reflection but rather gives account of what its own kind of reflection achieves. And it must do it not only within the realm of modern science but also over against this realm, in order to show a universality that transcends that of modern science.

On the Universality of Hermeneutical Reflection

Hermeneutical reflection fulfills the function that is accomplished in all bringing of something to a conscious awareness. Because it does, it can and must manifest itself in all our modern fields of knowledge, and especially science. Let us reflect a bit on this hermeneutical reflection. Reflection on a given preunderstanding brings before me something that otherwise happens *behind my back.* Something – but not everything, for what I have called the *wirkungsgeschichtliches Bewusstsein* is inescapably more *being* than consciousness, and being is never fully manifest. Certainly I do not mean that such reflection could escape from ideological ossification if it does not engage in constant self-reflection and attempts at self-awareness. Thus only through hermeneutical reflection am I no longer unfree over against myself but rather can deem freely what in my preunderstanding may be justified and what unjustifiable.

And also only in this manner do I learn to gain a new understanding of what I have seen through eyes conditioned by prejudice. But this implies, too, that the prejudgments that lead my preunderstanding are also constantly at stake, right up to the moment of their surrender – which surrender could also be called a transformation. It is the untiring power of *experience,* that in the process of being instructed, man is ceaselessly forming a new preunderstanding.

In the fields that were the starting points of my hermeneutical studies – the study of art and the philological-historical sciences – it is easy to demonstrate how hermeneutical reflection is at work. For instance, consider how the autonomy of viewing art from the vantage point of the history of style has been shaken up by hermeneutical reflection (1) on the concept of art itself, and (2) on concepts of individual styles and epochs. Consider how iconography has pressed from the periphery to the forefront, and how hermeneutical reflection on the concepts of experience and expression has had literary-critical consequences (even in cases where it becomes only a more conscious carrying forward of tendencies long favored in literary criticism). While it is of course evident how the shake-up of fixed presuppositions promises scientific progress by making new questions possible, it should be equally evident that this applies in the history of artistic and literary styles. And we constantly experience what historical research can accomplish through becoming conscious of the history of ideas. In *Truth and Method* I believe I have been able to show how historical alienation is mediated in the form of what I call the "fusion of horizons."

The overall significance of hermeneutical reflection, however, is not exhausted by what it means for and in the sciences themselves. For all the modern sciences possess a deeply rooted alienation that they impose on the natural consciousness and of which we need to be aware. This alienation has already reached reflective awareness in the very beginning stages of modern science in the concept of *method*. Hermeneutical reflection does not desire to change or eliminate this situation; it can, in fact, indirectly serve the methodological endeavor of science by making transparently clear the guiding preunderstandings in the sciences and thereby open new dimensions of questioning. But it must also bring to awareness, in this regard, the price that methods in science have paid for their own progress: the toning down and abstraction they demand, through which the natural consciousness still always must go along as the consumer of the inventions and information attained by science. One can with Wittgenstein express this insight as follows: The language games of science remain related to the metalanguage presented in the mother tongue. All the knowledge won by science enters the societal consciousness through school and education, using modern informational media, though maybe sometimes after a great — too great — delay. In any case, this is the way that new sociolinguistic realities are articulated.

For the *natural* sciences, of course, this gap and the methodical alienation of research are of less consequence than for social sciences. The true natural scientist does not have to be told how very particular is the realm of knowledge of his science in relation to the whole of reality. He does not share in the deification of his science that the public would press upon him. All the more, however, the public (and the researcher who must go before the public) needs hermeneutical reflection on the presuppositions and limits of science. The so-called "humanities," on the other hand, are still easily mediated to the common consciousness, so that insofar as they are accepted at all, their objects belong immediately to the cultural heritage and the realm of traditional education. But the modern social sciences stand in a particularly strained relationship to their object, the social reality, and this relationship especially requires hermeneutical reflection. For the methodical alienation to which the social sciences owe their progress is related here to the human-societal world as a whole. These sciences increasingly see themselves as marked out for the purpose of scientific ordering and control of society. They have to do with "scientific" and "methodical" planning, direction, organization, development – in short, with an infinity of functions that, so to speak, determine from outside the whole of the life of each individual and each group. Yet this social engineer, this scientist who undertakes to look after the functioning of the machine of society, appears himself to be methodically alienated and split off from the society to which, at the same time, he belongs.

But is man as a political being the mere object of the techniques of making public opinion? I think not: he is a member of society, and only in playing his role with free judgment and politically real effectiveness can he conserve freedom. It is the function of hermeneutical reflection, in this connection, to preserve us from naïve surrender to the experts of social technology.

Of course, a hermeneutically reflective sociologist like Habermas cannot conceive himself in these shallow terms of social engineering. Habermas's lucid analysis of social-scientific logic has resolutely worked out the authentic epistemological interest, which distinguishes true sociologists from technicians of social structure. He calls it an *emancipating interest* (what a contrast to the interest of the social engineers!), which takes reflection alone as its objective. He points in this regard to the example of psychoanalysis. And it is in psychoanalysis, as a matter of fact, that hermeneutical reflection plays a fundamental role. This is because, as we have emphasized earlier, the unconscious motive does not represent a clear and fully articulable boundary for hermeneutical theory: it falls within the larger perimeter of hermeneutics. Psychotherapy could be described as the work of "completing an interrupted process of education into a full history (a story that can be articulated in language)," so in psychotherapy hermeneutics and the circle of language that is closed in dialogue are central. I think I have learned this fact, above all, from Jacques Lacan.[19]

All the same it is clear that even this is not the whole story, for the psychoanalytic approach turns out not to be universalizable even for the psychoanalyst himself. The framework of interpretation worked out by Freud claims to possess the character of genuine natural-scientific hypotheses, that is, to be a knowledge of acknowledged laws. This orientation inevitably shows up in the role that methodical alienation plays in his psychoanalysis. But although the successful analysis wins *its* authentication in its results, the claim to *knowledge* in psychoanalysis must not be reduced to mere pragmatic validation. And this means that psychoanalysis is exposed again to another act of hermeneutical reflection, in which one must ask: How does the psychoanalyst's special knowledge relate to his own position within the societal reality (to which, after all, he does belong)?

The psychoanalyst leads the patient into the emancipatory reflection that goes behind the conscious superficial interpretations, breaks through the masked self-understanding, and sees through the repressive function of social taboos. This activity belongs to the emancipatory reflection to which he leads his patient. But what happens when he uses the same kind of reflection in a situation in which he is not the doctor but a partner in a game? Then he will fall out of his social role! A game partner who is always "seeing through" his game partner, who does not take seriously what they are standing for, is a spoil sport whom one shuns. The emancipatory power of reflection claimed by the psychoanalyst is a special rather than general function of reflection and must be given its boundaries through the societal context and consciousness, within which the analyst and also his patient are on even terms with everybody else. This is something that *hermeneutical reflection* teaches us: that social community, with all its tensions and disruptions, ever and ever again leads back to a common area of social understanding through which it exists.

Here, I think, the analogy Habermas suggests between psychoanalytical and sociological theory breaks down, or at least raises severe problems. For where are the limits of this analogy? Where does the patient-relationship end and the social partnership in its unprofessional right begin? Most fundamentally: Over against what self-interpretation of the social consciousness (and all morality is such) is it in place to inquire *behind* that consciousness — and when is it not? Within the context of the purely practical, or of a universalized emancipatory reflection, these questions appear unanswerable. The unavoidable consequence to which all these observations lead is that the basically emancipatory consciousness must have in mind the dissolution of all authority, all obedience. This means that unconsciously the ultimate guiding image of emancipatory reflection in the social sciences must be an anarchistic utopia. Such an image, however, seems to me to reflect a hermeneutically false consciousness, the antidote for which can only be a more universal hermeneutical reflection.

NOTES

1. Thus what O. Marquard (Heidelberger Philosophiekongress, 1966) calls "das Sein zum Texte" does not at all exhaust the hermeneutical dimension — unless the word Texte is taken not in the narrow sense but as "the text that God has written with his own hand," i.e., the *liber naturae,* which consequently encompasses all knowledge from physics to sociology and anthropology. And even in this case the model of translation is implied, which is not fully adequate to the complexity of the hermeneutical dimension.

2. See Johannes Lohmann, *Philosophie und Sprachwissenschaft* and his review of my book in *Gnomon,* XXXVII (1965), pp. 709-718. Lohmann's treatment may be seen as a greatly expanded application of what I had briefly sketched as the imprint of the concept of *Sprache*

(language in Occidental thought). He traces "the emergence of the concept (*Begriff*) as the intellectual vehicle by which given objects are momentarily subsumed under one cogitated form" (p. 74). He recognizes in the stem-inflecting verbs of Old Indo-Germanic the grammatical expression of this idea, especially in the copula. From this, he says, we can deduce the possibility of theory, which is a creation peculiar to the occident. The significance of this is more than historical; it also extends into the future. Not only does Lohmann take the transition from stem-inflecting to word-inflecting language types to interpret the history of thought in the occident by showing the development of language forms, he shows that this latter-day development to word-inflecting types makes possible science in the modern sense – science as the rendering disposable to us of our world.

3. I have considered some aspects of this in *WM*, but they can be greatly expanded; see, for instance, the extensive supplements and corrections contributed by Klaus Dockhorn to the Göttingen "Gelehrten-Anzeigen," CCXVIII, Heft 3/4 (1966), pp. 169-206.

4. *PhR*, XIV, Beiheft 5 (1967), pp. 149-180. See also his more recent book, *Knowledge and Human Interests*, (Boston: Beacon Press, 1972).

5. Hermann Gundert has done this in his contribution to *Hermeneia*, 1952, a Festschrift for Otto Regenbogen.

6. Klaus Dockhorn has shown, with profound scholarship, in "Gelehrten-Anzeigen," the extent to which the arousing of emotions has been considered the most important means of persuasion from Cicero and Quintilian to the political rhetoric of the eighteenth century in England.

7. I discussed this in my book, and Dockhorn, "Gelehrten-Anzeigen," has carried out the exploration on a much broader basis.

8. Henri Gouhier in particular has shown this in his *La résistance au vrai*, ed. E. Castelli (Rome: 1955).

9. In this regard see the preface to the second edition (1965).

10. Cf. *Ph R*, XIV, Beiheft 5, pp. 172-174.

11. Ibid., p. 179.

12. Ibid., p. 178.

13. Ibid., p. 177.

14. Ibid., p. 174.

15. On this point I am agreeing with J. Lohmann in *Philosophie und Sprachwissenschaft*.

16. *PhR*, XIV, Beiheft 5, p. 179.

17. Ibid., pp. 173-174.

18. Wolfhart Pannenberg, "Hermeneutik und Universalgeschichte," *Zeitschrift für Theologie und Kirche*, 60 (1963): 90-121. ET. Paul J. Achtemeier in *History and Hermeneutic*, ed. Robert W. Funk and Gerhard Ebeling (New York: Harper & Row, 1967), pp. 122-152.

19. See the collection of his writings now published as *Ecrits* (Paris: Editions du Seuil, 1966).

3

On the Problem of Self-Understanding (1962)

When it was first published in 1941, Rudolf Bultmann's programmatic essay on demythologizing the New Testament produced an enormous sensation.* No one who can remember the impact the essay had at that time or who considers the influence it continues to exert today will fail to see the special problems it raises for theology. For those persons who were acquainted with Bultmann's theological work, however, this essay was hardly sensational. Bultmann only provided a clear formulation for what had already long since taken place in the exegetical work of the theologian. But this point is precisely the one at which philosophical reflection may be able to contribute something to the theological discussion, for the problem of demythologizing undoubtedly also has a general hermeneutical dimension. The theological problems do not have to do with the hermeneutical phenomenon of demythologizing as such, but rather with its dogmatic implications, that is, with whether from the standpoint of Protestant theology Bultmann correctly draws the boundaries within which demythologizing is to be applied. In the discussion

*Cf. Rudolf Bultmann, "Neues Testament und Mythologie," *Kerygma und Mythos,* vol. 1, ed. Hans-Werner Bartsch (Hamburg: Evangelischer Verlag, 1941), pp. 15-48. ET: 'New Testament and Mythology," in *Kerygma and Myth,* ed. Hans-Werner Bartsch (New York: Harper & Row, 1961), pp. 1-44.

that follows, I want to focus my attention on the hermeneutical aspect from a point of view that does not seem to have been sufficiently stressed. I want to pose the question of whether our relation to the New Testament can be understood adequately in terms of the central concept of the self-understanding of faith or whether an entirely different factor is operative in it — a factor that goes beyond the individual's self-understanding, indeed, beyond his individual being. To this end, I will take up the question of the relationship between understanding and "playing." Preparatory considerations are in order, however, to help us indicate the hermeneutical aspect of the problem.

First of all, as a hermeneutical task, understanding includes a reflective dimension from the very beginning. Understanding is not a mere reproduction of knowledge, that is, it is not a mere act of repeating the same thing. Rather, understanding is *aware* of the fact that it is indeed an act of repeating. August Boeckh had already expressed this fact by calling understanding a "knowing of the known.* Boeckh's paradoxical formulation epitomizes the clear insight that romantic hermeneutics had into the reflective structure of the hermeneutical phenomenon. The operation of the understanding requires that the unconscious elements involved in the original act of knowledge be brought to consciousness. Thus romantic hermeneutics was based on one of the fundamental concepts of Kantian aesthetics, namely, the concept of the genius who, like nature itself, creates the exemplary work "unconsciously" — without consciously applying rules or merely imitating models.

This observation indicates the special circumstance in which the hermeneutical problem appears. The problem clearly does not arise as long as one is involved directly in taking up and continuing a specific intellectual tradition. It does not arise, for instance, with the Renaissance humanists, who rediscovered classical antiquity and tried to be the successors of the ancient authors, imitating them, indeed, openly competing with them, rather than merely "under-

*Cf. August Boeckh, *Encyklopädie und Methodologie der philologische Wissenschaften,* ed. Ernst Bratuscheck (Leipzig: Teubner, 1877).

standing" them. The hermeneutical problem only emerges
clearly when there is no powerful tradition present to absorb
one's own attitude into itself and when one is aware of
confronting an alien tradition to which he has never belonged
or one he no longer unquestioningly accepts.

The latter case is the aspect of the hermeneutical problem
that we have to deal with here. For us, the understanding of
the Christian tradition and the tradition of classical antiquity
includes an element of historical consciousness. Even if the
forces binding us to the great Greco-Christian tradition are
still ever so vital, our consciousness of its alien character, of
no longer belonging unquestioningly to it, determines us all.
This point is especially clear when we consider the beginnings
of the historical criticism of the tradition, and especially of
biblical criticism as initiated by Spinoza in his *Tractatus-
Theologico-Politicus*. Spinoza's work makes it quite evident
that the way of historical understanding is a kind of unavoidable detour that the person who understands must take when
immediate insight into what is said in the tradition is no
longer possible for him. Genetic inquiry, whose goal consists
in explaining a traditional opinion on the basis of its historical situation, only appears where direct insight into the truth
of what is said cannot be reached because our reason sets
itself in opposition.

To be sure, the modern age of the Enlightenment was not
the first to take this detour into historical explanation. In
dealing with the Old Testament, for example, Christian theology very quickly faced the problem of eliminating exe-
getically those ideas which were not compatible with Christian dogmatics and moral teaching. Along with allegorical and
typological interpretation, historical considerations also
served this end, as Augustine demonstrated, for instance, in
his *De Doctrina Christiana*. But in all such cases, the dogmatic tradition of the Christian Church remained the unshakable basis of all interpretation. Historical considerations
were unusual and secondary aids to the understanding of
Scripture. The emergence of modern natural science and the
critical perspective it brought with it essentially changed this
state of affairs. On the basis of pure reason, only a small
portion of Scripture could be regarded as being in harmony

with modern science, and hence that portion which one could understand only by recourse to historical conditions grew enormously. For Spinoza, there was certainly still an immediate certitude regarding moral truths that reason recognizes in the Bible. Their certitude is in a certain sense the same as the certitude of Euclid's axioms, which contain truths that illuminate reason so immediately that the question of their historical origin is never raised at all. However, the moral truths in biblical tradition that are certain in this way are for Spinoza only a small part of the biblical tradition taken as a whole. On the whole, Scripture remains alien to reason. If we want to understand Scripture, we must rely on historical reflection, as in the case of the criticism of miracles.

Romanticism began with the deep conviction of a total strangeness of the tradition (as the reverse side of the totally different character of the present), and this conviction became the basic methodological presupposition of its hermeneutical procedure. Precisely in this way hermeneutics became a universal, methodical attitude: it presupposed the foreignness of the content that is to be understood and thus made its task the overcoming of this foreignness by gaining understanding. It is characteristic, therefore, that Schleiermacher did not find it at all absurd to understand Euclid's *Elements* historically, that is, by going back to the creative moments in Euclid's life in which these insights occurred. Psychological-historical understanding took the place of immediate insight into the subject matter and became the only genuinely methodical, scientific attitude. With this development, the exegetical side of biblical scholarship or theology was first elevated to the status of a purely historical-critical science. Hermeneutics became the universal organ of the historical method. As is well known, the application of this historical-critical approach in the area of biblical exegesis led to severe tensions between dogmatics and exegesis, tensions that prevade theological work on the New Testament even in our own time.

In conceiving the historian's task, Friedrich Droysen, the most acute methodologist of the Historical School, thoroughly rejected this total, objectivistic alienation of the object of history. He pursued this "eunuch-like objectivity" with biting ridicule and in opposition to it he pointed to a belonging of the knower to the great moral forces that rule history as the precondition of all historical understanding. His famous formula, that the task of the historian is to "understand by means of careful investigation" (*forschend zu verstehen*), has a theological aspect. The plans of Providence are hidden from men, but in its restlessly searching penetration into the structures of world history, the historical mind has a presentiment of the meaning of the whole, which is concealed from us. Here understanding is more than a universal method that is occasionally supported through the affinity or congeniality of the historian with his historical object. What concerns us is not simply the historian's own fortuitous sympathy. Rather, something of the historicity of the historian's own understanding is already at work in his choice of objects and in the rubrics under which he places the object as a historical problem.

It is certainly difficult for the methodical self-consciousness of historical investigation to grasp this side of the matter, for even historical studies are stamped by the scientific ideal of the modern age. To be sure, the romantic criticism of Enlightenment rationalism destroyed the dominance of natural law, but the path of historical investigation was itself understood as a step toward man's total historical self-illumination, which would dispel the final dogmatic vestiges of the Greco-Christian tradition. The historical objectivism corresponding to this ideal draws its strength from the idea of science that has its background in the philosophical subjectivism of the modern age. Droysen struggled to guard himself against this idea, but only the fundamental critique of philosophical subjectivism that began with Heidegger's *Being and Time* was able to establish philosophically Droysen's historico-theological position and to demonstrate its validity in opposition to Wilhelm Dilthey, who had succumbed so much more completely to the modern concept of science than did his genuine adversary, the Lutheran thinker Count Paul Yorck von Wartenburg. Heidegger no longer regarded the historicity of Dasein as a restriction of its cognitive possibilities and as a threat to the ideal of scientific objectivity, but rather took it up in a positive way into his ontological problematic. As a result of Heidegger's work, the concept of understanding that the Historical School had made methodologically respectable was transformed into a universal philosophical concept. According to *Being and Time,* understanding is the way in which the historicity of Dasein is itself carried out. The futurity of Dasein — the basic character of projection that befits its temporality — is limited by its other basic determination, namely, its "thrownness," which not only specifies the limits of sovereign self-possession but also opens up and determines the positive possibilities that we are. In certain ways, the concept of self-understanding is an heirloom of transcendental idealism and has been propagated in our own time as such an idealism by Husserl. It was only through Heidegger's work that this concept acquired its real historicity, and with this change it became capable of supporting the theological concern for formulating the self-understanding of faith. It is not, therefore, as a sovereign self-mediation of self-consciousness but rather as the *experience* of oneself that what happens to one and (from the theological standpoint) what takes place in the challenge of the Christian proclamation, can remove the false claim of gnostic self-certainty from the self-understanding of faith. In his 1926 essay on Barth's *Commentary on Romans,** Gerhard Krüger sought to radicalize dialectical theology in this direction, and Heidegger's own years in Marburg owed much of their unforgettable excitement to Rudolf Bultmann's theological use of Heidegger's critique of the "objectivistic" subjectivism of the modern age.

Heidegger did not stop, however, with the transcendental schema that still motivated the concept of self-understanding in *Being and Time.* Even in *Being and Time* the real question is not in what way being can be understood but in what way understanding *is* being, for the understanding of being represents the existential distinction of Dasein. Already at this point Heidegger does not understand being to be the result of the objectifying operation of consciousness, as Husserl's phenomenology still did. The question of being, as Heidegger

*Cf. Gerhard Krüger in *Zwischen den Zeiten,* 1926.

poses it, breaks into an entirely different dimension by focusing on the being of Dasein that understands itself. And this is the point at which the transcendental schema must finally founder. The infinite contrast between the transcendental ego and its objects is finally taken up into the ontological question. In this sense, *Being and Time* already begins to counteract the forgetfulness of being that Heidegger was later to designate as the essence of metaphysics. What he calls the "turn" is only his recognition that it is impossible to overcome the forgetfulness of being within the framework of transcendental reflection. Hence all his later concepts, such as the "event" of being, the "there" as the clearing of being, and so on, were already entailed as a consequence of the approach taken in *Being and Time.*

The role that the mystery of language plays in Heidegger's later thought is sufficient indication that his concentration on the historicity of self-understanding banished not only the concept of consciousness from its central position, but also the concept of selfhood as such. For what is more unconscious and "selfless" than that mysterious realm of language in which we stand and which allows what is to come to expression, so that being "is temporalized" (*sich zeitigt*)? But if this is valid for the mystery of language it is also valid for the concept of understanding. Understanding too cannot be grasped as a simple activity of the consciousness that understands, but is itself a mode of the event of being. To put it in purely formal terms, the primacy that language and understanding have in Heidegger's thought indicates the priority of the "relation" over against its relational members – the I who understands and that which is understood. Nevertheless, it seems to me that it is possible to bring to expression within the hermeneutical consciousness itself Heidegger's statements concerning "being" and the line of inquiry he developed out of the experience of the "turn." I have carried out this attempt in *Truth and Method.* Just as the relation between the speaker and what is spoken points to a dynamic process that does not have a firm basis in either member of the relation, so the relation between the understanding and what is understood has a priority over its relational terms. Understanding is not self-understanding in the sense of the self-evident certainty idealism asserted it to have, nor is it exhausted in the revolutionay criticism of idealism that thinks of the concept of self-understanding as something that happens to the self, something through which it becomes an authentic self. Rather, I believe that understanding involves a moment of "loss of self" that is relevant to theological hermeneutics and should be investigated in terms of the structure of the game.

In pursuing this matter we are directed back immediately to antiquity and the peculiar relation between myth and *logos* that we find at the beginning of Greek thought. The customary Enlightenment formula, according to which the process of the demagicification of the world leads necessarily from myth to logos, seems to me to be a modern prejudice. If we take this formula as our starting point, we cannot explain, for instance, how Attic philosophy opposed the tendencies of the Greek Enlightenment and was able to establish its secular reconciliation of religious tradition and philosophical thought. We are indebted to Gerhard Krüger for his masterful illumination of the religious presuppositions of Greek, especially Platonic, philosophizing.* The history of myth and logos in ancient Greece has a completely different and more complicated structure than the Enlightenment formula suggests. In light of this fact, we can begin to comprehend the great distrust that the modern study of antiquity has had of myth as a religious source and its decided preference for the more stable forms of cultic tradition. For the ability of myth to change and its openness for ever new interpretations by the poets compels one to regard it as wrong to ask in what sense an ancient myth was "believed" or, assuming it was no longer "believed" even then, where it passed over into poetic play. In truth, myth is obviously and intimately akin to thinking consciousness. Even the philosophical explication of myth in the language of concepts adds nothing essentially new to the constant movement back and forth between discovery and concealment, between reverential awe and spiritual freedom, that accompanied the entire history of Greek myth. It is useful to remember this point if we are to

---

*Gerhard Krüger, *Einsicht und Leidenschaft: Das Wesen des platonischen Denkens.* (Frankfurt: Klostermann, 1963).

understand correctly the concept of myth that is implied in Bultmann's program of demythologizing. The contrast Bultmann makes between the "mythical picture of the world" and the scientific picture of the world that we hold as true hardly has the tone of finality that has been attributed to it in the course of the demythologizing controversy. In the last analysis, the relation of a Christian theologian to the biblical tradition does not appear to be so fundamentally different from the relation of the Greek to his myths. The casual and somewhat incidental formulation of the concept of demythologizing that Bultmann proposed (indeed, the sum of his general exegetical theology) had anything but an Enlightenment meaning. Rather, as a pupil of the liberal, historical study of the Bible, what Bultmann sought in the biblical tradition was the aspect that had persisted despite all historical explanation, which is the real bearer of the proclamation and represents the real challenge of faith.

This positive dogmatic interest, not an interest in a progressive enlightenment, marks Bultmann's concept of myth. Thus his concept of myth is completely descriptive and retains historical and contingent elements. In any case, although the specifically theological problem involved in demythologizing the New Testament may be fundamental, it is still a matter of practical exegesis and does not directly concern the hermeneutical principle of *all* exegesis. The general hermeneutical implication of this theological concept is that we cannot dogmatically establish a definite concept of myth and then determine once and for all which aspects of Scripture are to be unmasked by scientific explanation as "mere myth" for modern man. "Mere myth" must not be defined on the basis of modern science, but positively from the point of view of the acceptance of the kerygma — in terms of the inner claim of faith. The great freedom that the Greek poet possessed and employed in order to interpret the mythical tradition of his people is another example of such demythologizing. Here too we do not deal with "enlightenment," but rather with a religious basis for the poet's exercise of his spiritual power and critical insight. One need only think of Pindar and Aeschylus in this connection. Hence it is necessary for us to consider the relation between faith and understanding in terms of the freedom of the game.

It may appear surprising at first to combine the deadly seriousness of faith with the arbitrariness of the game. In fact, the sense of this contrast would be completely destroyed if one were to understand the game or playing in the customary way, namely, as a subjective attitude rather than as a dynamic whole *sui generis* that embraces even the subjectivity of the one who plays. Now it seems to me that this latter concept of the game is the truly legitimate and original one,* and it is in terms of this concept of the game that we can best focus attention on the relation between faith and understanding.

The back and forth movement that takes place within a given field of play does not derive from the human game and from playing as a subjective attitude. Quite the contrary, even for human subjectivity the real experience of the game consists in the fact that something that obeys its own set of laws gains ascendency in the game. To the movement in a determinate direction corresponds a movement in the opposite direction. The back and forth movement of the game has a peculiar freedom and buoyancy that determines the consciousness of the player. It goes on automatically — a condition of weightless balance, "where the pure too-little incomprehensibly changes — springs round into that empty toomuch."* Even the intensification of the individual's effort that occurs in competitive situations is marked by something like a possession by the buoyancy of the game in which he has a role. Whatever is brought into play or comes into play no longer depends on itself but is dominated by the relation that we call the game. For the individual who, as playing subjectivity, engages in the game, this fact may seem at first to be an accommodation. He conforms to the game or subjects himself to it, that is, he relinquishes the autonomy of his own will. For example, two men who use a saw

---

*Cf. *WM,* pp. 97-105 and 462-465, where I believe I have shown this to be the case.

**Rainer Maria Rilke, *Duino Elegies,* trans. J. B. Leishman and Stepher Spender (New York: W. W. Norton, 1963), Fifth Elegy, lines 84-86.

together allow the free play of the saw to take place, it would seem, by reciprocally adjusting to each other so that one man's impulse to movement takes effect just when that of the other man ends. It appears, therefore, that the primary factor is a kind of agreement between the two, a deliberate attitude of the one as well as the other. But this attitude is still not the game. The game is not so much the subjective attitude of the two men confronting each other as it is the formation of the movement as such, which, as in an unconscious teleology, subordinates the attitude of the individuals to itself. It is the merit of the neurologist Viktor von Weizsäcker to have conducted experiments on phenomena of this kind and to have analyzed them theoretically in his work *Der Gestaltkreis.* * I am indebted to him also for his reference to the fact that the tension-filled situation in which the mongoose and the snake hold each other in check cannot be described as the reaction of one partner to the attempted attack of the other, but represents a reciprocal behavior of absolute contemporaneousness. Here too, neither partner alone constitutes the real determining factor; rather, it is the unified form of movement as a whole that unifies the fluid activity of both. We can formulate this idea as a theoretical generalization by saying that the individual self, including his activity and his understanding of himself, is taken up into a higher determination that is the really decisive factor.

This is the context in which I would like to consider the relation of faith and understanding. From the theological point of view, faith's self-understanding is determined by the fact that faith is not man's possibility, but a gracious act of God that happens *to* the one who has faith. To the extent that one's self-understanding is dominated by modern science and its methodology, however, it is difficult for him to hold fast to this theological insight and religious experience. The concept of knowledge based on scientific procedures tolerates no restriction of its claim to universality. On the basis of this claim, all self-understanding is represented as a kind of self-possession that excludes nothing as much as the idea that something that separates it from itself can befall it. It is at

*Viktor von Weizsäcker, *Der Gestaltkreis: Theorie der Einheit von Wahrnehmen und Bewegen* (Leipzig, 1940).

this point that the concept of the game becomes important, for absorption into the game is an ecstatic self-forgetting that is experienced not as a *loss* of self-possession, but as the free buoyancy of an elevation above oneself. We cannot comprehend this in a unified way under the subjective rubric of self-understanding. The Dutch historian Huizinga recognized this point when he said that the consciousness of the one who is playing finds itself in an inseparable balance between belief and unbelief: the savage himself knows no conceptual difference between being and playing.*

It is not merely the savage, however, who is unacquainted with this conceptual difference. Wherever the claim of self-understanding is asserted — and where do men not assert it? — it remains within well-defined limits. The hermeneutical consciousness does not compete with that self-transparency that Hegel took to constitute absolute knowledge and the highest mode of being. We are not speaking of self-understanding in the realm of faith alone. In the last analysis, *all* understanding is self-understanding, but not in the sense of a preliminary self-possession or of one finally and definitively achieved. For the self-understanding only realizes itself in the understanding of a subject matter and does not have the character of a free self-realization. The self that we are does not possess itself; one could say that it "happens." And this is what the theologian is actually saying when he asserts that faith is an event in which a new man is established. The theologian says also that we must believe and understand the Word, and that it is through the Word that we overcome the abysmal ignorance about ourselves in which we live.

That the concept of self-understanding has an originally theological stamp can be seen clearly in the work of Johann Georg Hamann. What he meant by the concept was that we do not understand ourselves unless it be before God. But God is the Word. From the earliest times, the human word has provided theological reflection with a concrete visualization of the Word of God and the mystery of the Trinity. Augustine in particular sought to describe the suprahuman mystery of the Trinity by means of innumerable variations on the

*Cf. Johann Huizinga, *Homo Ludens: A Study of the Play Element in Culture* (Boston: Beacon Press, 1955).

word and the dialogue as they occur between men. Word and dialogue undoubtedly include within them an aspect of the game.

Many aspects of the dialogue between men point to the common structure of understanding and playing: risking a word or "keeping it to oneself," provoking a word from the other person and receiving an answer from him or giving an answer oneself. Another indication is the way every word "comes into play" within the definite context in which it is spoken and understood. It is in language games, for example, that the child becomes acquainted with the world. Indeed, everything we learn takes place in language games. This is not to say that when we speak we are "only playing" and do not mean it seriously. Rather, the words we find capture our intending, as it were, and dovetail into relations that point out beyond the momentariness of our act of intending. When does the child who listens to and repeats the language of adults understand the words he uses? When is his playing transformed into seriousness? When does seriousness begin and playing cease? Every determination of word meanings grows, as it were, in playful fashion from the value of the word in the concrete situation. Just as writing represents a fixing of the phonetic constancy [*Lautbestand*] of language and thus reacts upon the phonetic form [*Lautgestalt*] of the language itself by articulating it, so too living speaking and the life of the language have their play in a back and forth movement. No one fixes the meaning of a word, nor does the ability to speak merely mean learning the fixed meanings of words and using them correctly. Rather, the life of language consists in the constant playing further of the game that we began when we first learned to speak. A new word usage comes into play and, equally unnoticed and unintended, the old words die. This is the ongoing game in which the being-with-others of men occurs.

The common agreement that takes place in speaking with others is itself a game. Whenever two persons speak with each other they speak the same language. They themselves, however, in no way know that in speaking it they are playing this language further. But each person also speaks his own language. Common agreement takes place by virtue of the fact that speech confronts speech but does not remain immobile. In speaking with each other we constantly pass over into the thought world of the other person; we engage him, and he engages us. So we adapt ourselves to each other in a preliminary way until the game of giving and taking — the real dialogue — begins. It cannot be denied that in an actual dialogue of this kind something of the character of accident, favor, and surprise — and in the end, of buoyancy, indeed, of elevation — that belongs to the nature of the game is present. And surely the elevation of the dialogue will not be experienced as a loss of self-possession, but rather as an *enrichment* of our self, but without us thereby becoming aware of ourselves.

Now it seems to me that these observations also hold for dealing with written texts and thus for understanding the Christian proclamation that is preserved in Scripture. The life of tradition, and even more, the life of proclamation, consist in such a play of understanding. The understanding of a text has not begun at all as long as the text remains mute. But a text can begin to speak. (We are not discussing here the conditions that must be given for this actually to occur.) When it does begin to speak, however, it does not simply speak its word, always the same, in lifeless rigidity, but gives ever new answers to the person who questions it and poses ever new questions to him who answers it. To understand a text is to come to understand oneself in a kind of dialogue. This contention is confirmed by the fact that the concrete dealing with a text yields understanding only when what is said in the text begins to find expression in the interpreter's own language. Interpretation belongs to the essential unity of understanding. One must take up into himself what is said to him in such fashion that it speaks and finds an answer in the words of his own language. This observation holds true in every respect for the text of the Christian proclamation, which one really cannot understand if it does not seem to speak directly to him. It is in the sermon, therefore, that the understanding and interpretation of the text first receives its full reality. It is the sermon rather than the explanatory commetary of the theologian's exegetical work that stands in the immediate service of proclamation, for it not only communicates to the community the understanding of what Scripture says, but also bears witness itself. The actual completion of understanding does not take place in the sermon as such, but rather in its reception as an appeal that is directed to each person who hears it.

If self-understanding comes about in this way, then it is surely a very paradoxical, if not negative, understanding of oneself in which one hears himself called into dialogue. Such self-understanding certainly does not constitute a criterion for the theological interpretation of the New Testament. Moreover, the texts of the New Testament are themselves already interpretations of the Christian message; they do not wish to call attention to themselves, but rather to be mediators of this message. Does this not give them a freedom in speaking that allows them to be selfless witnesses? We are much indebted to modern theological study for our insight into the theological intention of the New Testament writers, but the proclamation of the gospel speaks through all these mediations in a way that is comparable to the repetition of a legend or the continual renewal and transformation of mythical tradition by great poetry. The genuine reality of the hermeneutical process seems to me to encompass the self-understanding of the interpreter as well as what is interpreted. Thus "demythologizing" takes place not only in the action of the theologian, but also in the Bible itself. But neither in the work of the theologian nor in the Bible is "demythologizing" a sure guarantee of correct understanding. The real event of understanding goes beyond what we can bring to the understanding of the other person's words through methodical effort and critical self-control. Indeed, it goes far beyond what we ourselves can become aware of. Through every dialogue something different comes to be. Moreover, the Word of God, which calls us to conversion and promises us a better understanding of ourselves, cannot be understood as a word that merely confronts us and that we must simply leave as it is. It is not really we ourselves who understand: it is always a past that allows us to say, "I have understood."

4
Man and Language (1966)

Aristotle established the classical definition of the nature of
man, according to which man is the living being who has
logos. In the tradition of the West, this definition became
canonical in a form which stated that man is the *animal
rationale*, the rational being, distinguished from all other
animals by his capacity for thought. Thus it rendered the
Greek word *logos* as reason or thought. In truth, however,
the primary meaning of this word is language. Aristotle once
developed the difference between man and animal in the
following way: animals can understand each other by indicating to each other what excites their desire so they can seek
it, and what injures them, so they can flee from it. That is as
far as nature goes in them. To men alone is the *logos* given as
well, so that they can make manifest to each other what is
useful and harmful, and therefore also what is right and
wrong. A profound thesis. What is useful and what is harmful
is something that is not desirable in itself. Rather, it is desired
for the sake of something else not yet given, in whose
acquisition it aids one. The distinguishing feature of man,
therefore, is his superiority over what is actually present, his
sense of the future. And in the same breath Aristotle adds
that with this the sense for right and wrong is given – and all
because man, as an individual, has the *logos*. He can think

59

and he can speak. He can make what is not present manifest through his speaking, so that another person sees it before him. He can communicate everything that he means. Indeed, even more than this, it is by virtue of the fact he can communicate in this way that there exists in man alone common meaning, that is, common concepts, especially those through which the common life of men is possible without murder and manslaughter — in the form of social life, a political constitution, an organized division of labor. All this is involved in the simple assertion that man is a being who possesses language.

One might think that this obvious and convincing observation had long ago guaranteed a privileged place for the phenomenon of language in our thinking about the nature of man. What is more convincing than the fact that the language of animals — if one wants to confer this name on their way of making themselves understood — is entirely different from human language, in which an objective world is conceived and communicated? Indeed, human language takes place in signs that are not rigid, as animals' expressive signs are, but remain variable, not only in the sense that there are different languages, but also in the sense that within the same language the same expression can designate different things and different expressions the same thing.

In fact, however, Western philosophical thought has not placed the nature of language at the center of its considerations. It is indeed significant that in the Old Testament story of creation, God conferred dominion over the world on the first man by permitting him to name all beings at his discretion. The story of the Tower of Babel too indicates the fundamental significance of language for human life. Nevertheless, it was precisely the religious tradition of the Christian West that hindered serious thought about language, so that the question of the origin of language could be posed in a new way only at the time of the Enlightenment. An important advance occurred when the answer to the question of the origin of language was sought in the nature of man instead of in the biblical story of creation. For then a further step was unavoidable: the naturalness of language made it impossible to inquire any longer about an original condition in which man was without language. With this the very question of the origin of language was excluded altogether. Herder and Wilhelm von Humboldt saw that language is essentially human and that man is an essentially linguistic being, and they worked out the fundamental significance of this insight for man's view of the world. The diversity of human linguistic structures was the field of study of Wilhelm von Humboldt, the one-time minister of culture who withdrew from public life — the wise man of Tegel who through the work of his old age became the founder of modern linguistic science.

Nevertheless, Humboldt's founding of the philosophy of language and linguistic science did not lead to a restoration of the original Aristotelian insight. By making the language of peoples the object of his investigation, Humboldt pursued a path of knowledge that was able to clarify in a new and promising way both the diversity of peoples and times as well as the common human nature underlying them all. But this procedure merely equipped man with a capacity and elucidated the structural laws of this capacity — what we call the grammar, syntax, and vocabulary of a language — and it restricted the horizon of the question of man and language. The aim of such an approach was to comprehend the world-views of different peoples, indeed even the details of their cultural development, through the mirror of language. An example of this approach would be the insight into the cultural situation of the Indo-Germanic family of peoples that we owe to Viktor Hehn's superb studies of cultivated plants and house pets.* Far more than other prehistories, linguistic science is the prehistory of the human spirit.

For this approach, however, the phenomenon of language has only the significance of an excellent manifestation in which the nature of man and his development in history can be studied. Yet it was unable to infiltrate the central positions of philosophical thought, for the Cartesian characterization of consciousness as self-consciousness continued to provide the background for all of modern thought. This unshakable foundation of all certainty, the most certain of all

*Cf. Viktor Hehn, *Kulturpflanzen und Haustiere* (Berlin: Gebrüder Borntraeger, 1870).

facts, that I know myself, became the standard for everything that could meet the requirements of scientific knowledge in the thought of the modern period. In the last analysis, the scientific investigation of language rested on this same foundation. The spontaneity of the subject possessed one of its basic forms in language-forming energy. Also, the worldview present in languages could be interpreted so fruitfully in terms of this principle that the enigma language presents to human thought did not come into view at all. For it is part of the nature of language that it has a completely unfathomable unconsciousness of itself. To that extent, it is not an accident that the use of the concept "language" is a recent development. The word *logos* means not only thought and language, but also concept and law. The appearance of the concept "language" presupposes consciousness of language. But that is only the result of the reflective movement in which the one thinking has reflected out of the unconscious operation of speaking and stands at a distance from himself. The real enigma of language, however, is that we can never really do this completely. Rather, all thinking about language is already once again drawn back into language. We can only think in a language, and just this residing of our thinking in a language is the profound enigma that language presents to thought.

Language is not one of the means by which consciousness is mediated with the world. It does not represent a third instrument alongside the sign and the tool, both of which are also certainly distinctively human. Language is by no means simply an instrument, a tool. For it is in the nature of the tool that we master its use, which is to say we take it in hand and lay it aside when it has done its service. That is not the same as when we take the words of a language, lying ready in the mouth, and with their use let them sink back into the general store of words over which we dispose. Such an analogy is false because we never find ourselves as consciousness over against the world and, as it wore, grasp after a tool of understanding in a wordless condition. Rather, in all our knowledge of ourselves and in all knowledge of the world, we are always already encompassed by the language that is our own. We grow up, and we become acquainted with men and in the last analysis with ourselves when we learn to speak. Learning to speak does not mean learning to use a preexistent tool for designating a world already somehow familiar to us; it means acquiring a familiarity and acquaintance with the world itself and how it confronts us.

An enigmatic and profoundly veiled process! What sort of folly is it to say that a child speaks a "first" word. What kind of madness is it to want to discover the original language of humanity by having children grow up in hermetic isolation from human speaking and then, from their first babbling of an articulate sort, recognize an actual human language and accord it the honor of being the "original" language of creation. What is mad about such ideas is that they want to suspend in some artificial way our very enclosedness in the linguistic world in which we live. In truth we are always already at home in language, just as much as we are in the world. It is Aristotle once again who gives us the most extensive description of the process in which one learns to speak. What Aristotle means to describe is not learning to speak, but rather, thinking, that is, acquiring universal concepts. In the flux of appearances, in the constant flood of changing impressions, how does anything like permanence come about? Surely it is first of all the capacity of retention, namely, memory, that allows us to recognize something as the same, and that is the first great achievement of abstraction. Out of the flux of appearances a common factor is spied here and there, and thus, out of accumulating recognitions that we call experience, the unity of experience slowly emerges. Knowledge of the universal originates in this way as a capacity for disposing over what has been experienced. Now Aristotle asks: Exactly how can this knowledge of the universal come about? Certainly not in such a way that one thing after the other goes by and suddenly knowledge of the universal is acquired when a certain particular reappears and is recognized as the same one. This one particular as such is not distinguished from all other particulars by some mysterious power of representing the universal. Rather, it too is like all other particulars. And yet it is true that at some point the knowledge of the universal actually comes about. Where does it begin? Aristotle gives an ideal image for this: How does an army that is in flight come to take a stand again? Certainly not by the fact that the first man stops, or the second or the third. We cannot say that the army stands when a certain number of fleeing soldiers stops its flight, and also certainly not when the last has stopped. For the army does not begin to stand with him; it has long since begun to come to a stand. How it begins, how it spreads, and how the army finally at some point stands again (that is, how it comes once again to obey the unity of the command) is not knowingly prescribed, controlled by planning, or known with precision by anyone. And nonetheless it has undoubtedly happened. It is precisely this way with knowledge of the universal, because this is really the same as its entrance into language.

We are always already biased in our thinking and knowing by our linguistic interpretation of the world. To grow into this linguistic interpretation means to grow up in the world. To this extent, language is the real mark of our finitude. It is always out beyond us. The consciousness of the individual is not the standard by which the being of language can be measured. Indeed, there is no individual consciousness at all in which a spoken language is actually present. How then is language present? Certainly not without the individual consciousness, but also not in a mere summation of the many who are each a particular consciousness for itself.

No individual has a real consciousness of his speaking when he speaks. Only in exceptional situations does one become conscious of the language in which he is speaking. It happens, for instance, when someone starts to say something but hesitates because what he is about to say seems strange or funny. He wonders, "Can one really say that?" Here for a moment the language we speak becomes conscious because it does not do what is peculiar to it. What is peculiar to it? I think we can distinguish three things.

1. The first is the essential self-forgetfulness that belongs to language. The structure, grammar, syntax of a language — all those factors which linguistic science makes thematic — are not at all conscious to living speaking. Hence one of the peculiar perversions of the natural that is necessary for modern education is that we teach grammer and syntax in our own native language instead of in a dead language like Latin.

A really gigantic achievement of abstraction is required of everyone who will bring the grammar of his native language to explicit consciousness. The actual operation of language lets grammar vanish entirely behind what is said in it at any given time. In learning foreign languages there is a very fine experience of this phenomenon which each of us has had, namely, the paradigm sentences used in text books and language courses. Their task is to make one aware in an abstract way of a specific linguistic phenomenon. In earlier times, when the task of acquisition involved in the learning of the grammar and syntax of a language was still acknowledged, these were sentences of an exalted senselessness that declared something or other about Caesar or Uncle Carl. The modern tendency to communicate a great deal of interesting information about the foreign country by means of such paradigm sentences has the unintended side effect of obscuring their exemplary function precisely to the extent that the content of what is said attracts attention. The more language is a living operation, the less we are aware of it. Thus it follows from the self-forgetfulness of language that its real being consists in what is said in it. What is said in it constitutes the common world in which we live and to which belongs also the whole great chain of tradition reaching us from the literature of foreign languages, living as well as dead. The real being of language is that into which we are taken up when we hear it — what is said.

2. A second essential feature of the being of language seems to me to be its I-lessness. Whoever speaks a language that no one else understands does not speak. To speak means to speak *to* someone. The word should be the right word. That, however, does not mean simply that it represents the intended object for me, but rather, that it places it before the eyes of the other person to whom I speak.

To that extent, speaking does not belong in the sphere of the "I" but in the sphere of the "We." Thus Ferdinand Ebner was right in giving his celebrated work *The Word and Spiritual Realities* the subtitle, *Pneumatological Fragments.* * For the spiritual reality of language is that of the *Pneuma,* the

*Ferdinand Ebner, *Das Wort und die geistigen Realitäten: Pneumatologische Fragmente* (Innsbruck: Brenner, 1921).

spirit, which unifies I and Thou. It has long been observed that the actuality of speaking consists in the dialogue. But in every dialogue a spirit rules, a bad one or a good one, a spirit of obdurateness and hesitancy or a spirit of communication and of easy exchange between I and Thou.

As I have shown elsewhere, the form of operation of every dialogue can be described in terms of the concept of the game.* It is certainly necessary that we free ourselves from the customary mode of thinking that considers the nature of the game from the point of view of the consciousness of the player. This definition of the man who plays, which has become popular primarily through Schiller, grasps the true structure of the game only in terms of its subjective appearance. In fact, however, the game is a dynamic process that embraces the persons playing or whatever plays. Hence it is by no means merely a metaphor when we speak of the "play of the waves," or "the playing flies" or of the "free play of the parts." Rather, the very fascination of the game for the playing consciousness roots precisely in its being taken up into a movement that has own its dynamic. The game is underway when the individual player participates in full earnest, that is, when he no longer holds himself back as one who is merely playing, for whom it is not serious. Those who cannot do that we call men who are unable to play. Now I contend that the basic constitution of the game, to be filled with its spirit — the spirit of bouyancy, freedom and the joy of success — and to fulfill him who is playing, is structurally related to the constitution of the dialogue in which language is a reality. When one enters into dialogue with another person and then is carried along further by the dialogue, it is no longer the will of the individual person, holding itself back or exposing itself, that is determinative. Rather, the law of the subject matter is at issue in the dialogue and elicits statement and counterstatement and in the end plays them into each other. Hence, when a dialogue has succeeded, one is subsequently fulfilled by it, as we say. The play of statement and counterstatement is played further in the inner dialogue of the soul with itself, as Plato so beautifully called thought.

*Cf. *WM*, pt. 3.

3. A third feature is what I would call the universality of language. Language is not a delimited realm of the speakable, over against which other realms that are unspeakable might stand. Rather, language is all-encompassing. There is nothing that is fundamentally excluded from being said, to the extent that our act of meaning intends it. Our capacity for saying keeps pace untiringly with the universality of reason. Hence every dialogue also has an inner infinity and no end. One breaks it off, either because it seems that enough has been said or because there is no more to say. But every such break has an intrinsic relation to the resumption of the dialogue.

We have this experience, often in a very painful way, when a statement is required from us. As an extreme example, we can think of an interrogation or a statement before a court. In such a case, the question we have to answer is like a barrier erected against the spirit of speaking, which desires to express itself and enter into dialogue ("I will speak here" or "Answer my question!"). Nothing that is said has its truth simply in itself, but refers instead backward and forward to what is unsaid. Every assertion is motivated, that is, one can sensibly ask of everything that is said, "Why do you say that?" And only when what is not said is understood along with what is said is an assertion understandable. We are familiar with this fact especially in the phenomenon of the question. A question that we do not understand as motivated can also find no answer. For the motivational background of a question first opens up the realm out of which an answer can be brought and given. Hence there is in fact an infinite dialogue in questioning as well as answering, in whose space word and answer stand. Everything that is said stands in such space.

We can illustrate this idea by an experience each of us has had. What I have in mind is translating and reading translations from foreign languages. The translator has a linguistic text before him, that is, something said either verbally or in writing, that he has to translate into his own language. He is bound by what stands there, and yet he cannot simply convert what is said out of the foreign language into his own without himself becoming again the one saying it. But this means he must gain for himself the infinite space of the saying that corresponds to what is said in the foreign language. Everyone knows how difficult it is. Everyone knows how the translation makes what is said in the foreign language sound flat. It is reflected on one level, so that the word sense and sentence form of the translation follow the original, but the translation, as it were, has no space. It lacks that third dimension from which the original (i.e., what is said in the original) is built up in its range of meaning. This is an unavoidable obstruction to all translations. No translation can replace the original. One might argue that the original assertion, which is projected into this flatness, should be more easily understandable in the translation, since much that was suggestive background or "between the lines" in the original would not be carried over. The reduction to a simple sense achieved by the translation could be taken, therefore, to *facilitate* understanding. But this argument is mistaken. No translation is as understandable as the original. Precisely the most inclusive meaning of what is said — and meaning is always a direction of meaning — comes to language only in the original saying and slips away in all subsequent saying and speaking. The task of the translator, therefore, must never be to copy what is said, but to place himself in the direction of what is said (i.e., in its meaning) in order to carry over what is to be said into the direction of his own saying.

This problem becomes clearest in those translations which make possible a verbal dialogue between men of different native languages by the interposition of an interpreter. An interpreter who only reproduces the words and sentences spoken by one person in the language of another alienates the conversation into unintelligibility. What he has to reproduce is not what is said in exact terms, but rather what the other person wanted to say and said in that he left much unsaid. The limited character of his reproduction must also attain the space in which alone dialogue becomes possible, that is, the inner infinity that belongs to all common understanding.

Hence language is the real medium of human being, if we only see it in the realm that it alone fills out, the realm of human being-together, the realm of common understanding, of ever-replenished common agreement — a realm as indispensible to human life as the air we breathe. As Aristotle said, man is truly the being who has language. For we should let everything human be spoken to us.

5
The Nature of Things and the Language of Things (1960)

The object of our study in this essay will be two common expressions that for all intents and purposes mean the same thing. Our intention is to illuminate a convergence of topics that dominates philosophy today despite every difference in starting points and methodological ideals. While these two expressions seem to say the same thing, we will show that a tension exists between them. At the same time, the power of the same impulse appears in both despite this difference. Linguistic usage alone gives us little indication of all this, for it seems to indicate that the two expressions are completely interchangeable. The two expressions are "it is the nature of things" [*Es liegt in der Natur der Sache*] and "things speak for themselves" [*Die Dinge sprechen für sich selber*], or "they speak an unmistakable language" [*sie führen eine unmissverständliche Sprache*]. In both cases we are dealing with stereotyped linguistic formulas that do not really give the reasons for why we hold something to be true, but rather reject the need for further proof. Even the two basic terms that appear in these expressions, *Sache* and *Ding,* seem to say the same thing. They are both expressions for something that eludes more precise definition. Correspondingly, when we speak of the "nature" of things or the "language" of things, these expressions share in common a polemical rejection of violent arbitrariness in our dealing with things, especially the

69

mere stating of opinions, the capriciousness of conjectures or assertions about things, and the arbitrariness of denials or the insistence on private opinions.

However, if we look more closely and probe the more furtive differences of linguistic usage, the appearance of complete interchangeability is dispelled. The concept of the thing [*Sache*] is marked above all by its counterconcept, the person. The meaning of this antithesis of thing and person is found originally in the clear priority of the person over the thing. The person appears as something to be respected in its own being. The thing, on the other hand, is something to be used, something that stands entirely at our disposal. Now when we encounter the expression "the nature of things," the point is clearly that what is available for our use and given to our disposal has in reality a being of its own, which allows it to resist our efforts to use it in unsuitable ways. Or to put it positively: it prescribes a specific comportment that is appropriate to it. But with this statement the priority of the person over the thing is inverted. In contrast to the capacity persons have to adapt to each other as they please, the "nature of things" is the unalterable givenness to which we have to accommodate ourselves. Thus the concept of the thing can maintain its own emphasis by demanding that we abandon all thought of ourselves and thereby even compelling us to suspend any consideration of persons.

This is where the exhortation to objectivity [*Sachlichkeit*] that we also know as the characteristic attitude of philosophy originates. Bacon's famous words, which Kant chose as the motto for his *Critique of Pure Reason,* express it: "De nobis ipsis silemus, de re autem quae agitur." [About ourselves we keep silent, but we will speak of the subject.]

One of the greatest champions of such objectivity among classical philosophical thinkers is Hegel. He actually speaks of the action of the thing and characterizes real philosophical speculation by the fact that the thing itself is active in it and not simply the free play of our own notions. That is, the free play of our reflective procedures with the thing is not operative in real philosophical speculation. The celebrated phenomenological slogan, "To the things themselves," which at the beginning of the century expressed a new orientation within philosophy, also means something similar. Phenomenological analysis sought to uncover the uncontrolled assumption involved in unsuitable, prejudiced, and arbitrary constructions and theories. And in fact it exposed such assumptions in their illegitimacy by the unprejudiced analysis of the phenomena.

But the concept of the thing [*Sache*] reflects more than the Roman legal concept of *res*. The meaning of the German word *Sache* is permeated above all by what is called *causa,* that is, the disputed "matter" under consideration. Originally, it was the thing that was placed in the middle between the disputing parties because a decision still had to be rendered regarding it. The thing was to be protected against the domineering grasp of one party or the other. In this context, objectivity means precisely opposition to partiality, that is, to the misuse of the law for partial purposes. The legal concept of "the nature of things" does not mean an issue disputed between parties, but rather the limits that are set to the arbitrary will of the legislator in the promulgation of the law and to the judicial interpretation of the law. The appeal to the nature of things refers to an order removed from human wishes. And it intends to assure the triumph of the living spirit of justice over the letter of the law. Here too, therefore, "the nature of things" is something that asserts itself, something we have to respect.

If, however, we pursue what is expressed in the phrase "the language of things," we are pointed in a similar direction. The language of things too is something to which we should pay better attention. This expression also has a kind of polemical accent. It expresses the fact that, in general, we are not at all ready to hear things in their own being, that they are subjected to man's calculus and to his domination of nature through the rationality of science. Talk of a respect for things is more and more unintelligible in a world that is becoming ever more technical. They are simply vanishing, and only the poet still remains true to them. But we can still speak of a language of things when we remember what things really are, namely, not a material that is used and consumed, not a tool that is used and set aside, but something instead that has existence in itself and is "not forced to do any-

thing," as Heidegger says. Its own being in itself is dis-
regarded by the imperious human will to manipulate, and it is
like a language it is vital for us to hear.[1] The expression "the
language of things," therefore, is not a mythological, poetic
truth that only a Merlin the Magician or those initiated into
the spirit of the fairy tale could verify. Rather this common
expression rouses the memory (slumbering in us all) of the
being of things that are still able to be what they are.

Thus, in a certain sense, the same truth is actually spoken
by both phrases. Common expressions are not simply the
dead remains of a linguistic usage that has become figurative.
They are at the same time the heritage of a common spirit,
and if we only understand them rightly and penetrate their
covert richness of meaning, they can make this common
spirit perceivable again. Hence our examination of these
expressions has shown us that in a certain sense they say the
same thing — something that must be kept in mind over
against the despotic character of our capriciousness. This is
not all, however. Even though the two expressions — "the
nature of things" and "the language of things" — are sometimes used interchangeably and are stamped by what they
both oppose, this commonality still conceals a difference that
is not accidental. Rather, there is a philosophical task here of
elucidating the tension perceivable in the subtle undertones
of both expressions. I shall try to show that the arbitration of
this tension that is taking place in philosophy today distinguishes the matrix of problems common to us all.

For the Philosophical mind, the concept of "the nature of
things" brings into focus an opposition to philosophical idealism shared by many persons, and especially to the Neo-
Kantian form in which idealism was renewed in the latter half
of the nineteenth century. This continuation of Kant, which
sought to make him a spokesman for the faith in progress and
pride in science of its own time, really no longer knew what
to do with the thing-in-itself. With all their explicit rejection
of metaphysical idealism, Kant's successors no longer considered a return to the Kantian dualism of thing-in-itself and
appearance. Only by means of a reinterpretation did Kant's
words fit their own self-evident convictions. As a result of
this reinterpretation, their idealism meant the total determi-

nation of the object by cognition. Thus they understood the thing-in-itself as the mere ideal goal of an infinite task of progressive determination. Even Husserl, who, in contrast to Neo-Kantianism, started less from the facts of science than from everyday experience, tried to give a phenomenological demonstration of the doctrine of the thing-in-itself by proceeding from the fact that the various shadings of the things of perception formed the continuum of a single experience. The doctrine of the thing-in-itself could mean nothing other than the possibility of this continuous transition from one aspect of a thing to another, by which the unified matrix of our experience is made possible. Thus even Husserl understood the idea of the thing-in-itself in terms of the idea of the progress of our knowledge, which has its ultimate demonstration in scientific investigation.

There is certainly nothing comparable to this in the moral order, for since Rousseau and Kant it has no longer been possible to assume a moral perfectibility of mankind. Yet here too the phenomenological critique of Neo-Kantianism had its point of departure in the formalism of Kantian moral philosophy. Kant's starting point in the phenomenon of duty and his demonstration of the unconditionedness of the categorical imperative seemed to banish from moral philosophy any filling out of the content of what the moral law demands. As weak as it was on its negative side, Max Scheler's critique of the formalism of Kantian ethics proved its own fruitfulness by its outline of a material ethic of values. Scheler's phenomenological critique of the Neo-Kantian concept of production also represented an important stimulus that led Nicolai Hartmann in particular to reject Neo-Kantianism and to develop his metaphysics of knowledge.[2] The fact that knowledge brought about no alteration in the known, let alone that it meant its production, and the fact that, on the contrary, everything that is remains indifferent to whether it is known or not, seemed to Hartmann to speak against any form of transcendental idealism, even against Husserlian constitutional research. On the positive side, Hartmann believed the way to a new ontology to lie in the recognition of the autonomy of beings and their independence of all human subjectivity. Hence he came into proximity with the "critical realism" that triumphed at the same time in England too — and there completely.

But I believe such a dismissal of transcendental philosophical reflection involves a massive misunderstanding of its meaning and is the result of the decline of philosophical knowledge that began with Hegel's death. There are of course reasons for the continual repetition of such a renunciation, even in the philosophy of our own time. When we contrast the superior reality of the divinely ordained order with our domineering will that is shattered on it (Gerhard Krüger), or man and his history with the indifference of the natural world (Karl Löwith), we can understand such polemical renunciation as an appeal to the nature of things. Nevertheless, it seems to me that such an appeal to the nature of things finds its limitation in a common assumption that remains unquestioned and dominates all these attempts at the restoration of the autonomy of things. It is the assumption that human subjectivity is will, an assumption that retains its unquestioned validity even where we posit being-in-itself as a limit to the determination of things by man's will. In the nature of the case, this means that these critics of modern subjectivism are not really free at all from what they criticize, but only articulate the opposition from the other side. In contrast to the one-sidedness of Neo-Kantianism, which takes the progress of scientific culture as its guideline, they pose the one-sidedness of a metaphysic of being-in-itself, which shares with its opponent the predominance of determination by the will.

In light of this situation, we must ask if "the nature of things" is not a dubious battle cry, and if classical metaphysics does not prove to have a real superiority over against all these attempts and to pose a continuing task. The superiority of classical metaphysics seems to me to lie in the fact that from the outset it transcends the dualism of subjectivity and will, on the one hand, and object and being-in-itself, on the other, by conceiving their preexistent correspondence with each other. To be sure, classical metaphysics' concept of truth — the conformity of knowledge with the object — rests on a theological correspondence. For it is in their creatureliness that the soul and the object are united. Just as the soul is created to encounter beings, so the thing is created true, that is, capable of being known. An enigma that is insoluable for the finite mind is thus resolved in the infinite mind of the Creator. The essence and actuality of the creation consists in being such a harmony of soul and thing.

Now philosophy certainly can no longer avail itself of such a theological grounding and will also not want to repeat the secularized versions of it, as represented by speculative idealism with its dialectical mediation of finite and infinite. But for its part, philosophy may also not close its eyes to the truth of this correspondence. In this sense, the task of metaphysics continues, though certainly as a task that cannot again be solved as metaphysics, that is, by going back to an infinite intellect. Hence we must ask: are there finite possibilities of doing justice to this correspondence? Is there a grounding of this correspondence that does not venture to affirm the infinity of the divine mind and yet is able to do justice to the infinite correspondence of soul and being? I contend that there is. There is a way that attests to this correspondence, one toward which philosophy is ever more clearly directed – the way of language.

It is no accident, it seems to me, that in recent decades the phenomenon of language has come to the center of philosophical inquiry. Perhaps one can even say that under this banner even the greatest kind of philosophical gulf that exists today between peoples – the one between Anglo-Saxon nominalism on the one hand and the metaphysical tradition on the Continent on the other – has begun to be bridged. At any rate, the analysis of language that was developed in England and America after the problematic of logical, artificial language broke down approximates the orientation of Edmund Husserl's phenomenological school in striking fashion. Just as the recognition of the finitude and historicity of human Dasein developed by Martin Heidegger has transformed the nature of the task of metaphysics, the antimetaphysical passion of logical positivism has been dissolved with the recognition of the autonomous meaning of spoken language (Wittgenstein). From information to myth and to the saga [Sage] which, for Heidegger, is a "pointing" [Zeige] as well, language constitutes the common theme. In order to think seriously about language, I believe we must ask if in the end language does not have to be called the "language of things" — the language of things in which the primordial correspondence of soul and being is so exhibited that finite consciousness too can know of it.

In itself, the assertion that language is the medium through which consciousness is connected with beings is nothing new. Hegel had already called language the medium through which subjective spirit is mediated with the being of objects. And in our own time, Ernst Cassirer expanded the narrow starting point of Neo-Kantianism, namely, the facts of science, into a philosophy of symbolic forms that encompassed not only the natural sciences and the human studies, but was to provide a transcendental foundation for human cultural activity in its entirety.

Cassirer took as his starting point the idea that language, art, and religion are "forms" of representation, that is, the presentation of something mental in something sensuous. By transcendental reflection on all these forms of embodied spirit, transcendental idealism would be elevated to a new and authentic universality. The symbolic forms are the spirit's processes of formation within the fleeting temporality of sensuous appearance, and they represent a connecting medium in that they are as much an objective appearance as they are a trace of the spirit. We must certainly wonder, however, if an analytic of the basic spiritual forces Cassirer had in mind really accounts for the uniqueness of the phenomenon of language. For language does not really stand alongside art and law and religion, but represents the sustaining medium of all of these manifestations of the spirit. The concept of language should not merely receive a special distinction among the symbolic forms, that is, among the forms in which spirit is expressed. Rather, as long as it is even conceived as a symbolic form, it is not yet recognized at all in its true dimensions. The idealistic philosophy of language from which Herder and Humboldt start already provokes the critical question that touches the philosophy of symbolic forms as well: by directing attention to the "form" of language, does it not isolate language from what is spoken in and mediated through it? It is not as a formal power or capacity that language presents the correspondence we are seeking, but rather as the preliminary medium that encompasses all beings insofar as they can be expressed in words. Is not language more the language of things than the language of man?

The interconnection of word and thing, which was a problem at the beginning of Western thought about language, gains renewed interest in terms of this question. To be sure, the question the Greeks asked about the correctness of names is more a last echo of that word-magic that understood the word as the thing itself, or better, as its representative being. Indeed, Greek philosophy began with the dissolution of such name-magic and took its first steps as a critique of language. Nevertheless, it preserves in itself so much of the naïve self-forgetfulness of the original experience of the world, that for it the essence of things manifested in the *logos* is the self-presentation of beings themselves. In the *Phaedo*, Plato designates the flight into the *logoi* as his second-best way because being is contemplated there only in the reflected image of the *logos* instead of in its direct reality. But a hint of irony is present in his assertion. In the end, the true being of things becomes accessible precisely in their linguistic appearance — in the ideality of what is intended that is concealed in such fashion that its being intended (the linguistic character of the manifestation of things) is not experienced as such. Since metaphysics understands the true being of things as essences that are directly accessible to the "mind," the linguistic character of the experience of being is concealed.

So too, medieval scholasticism, as the Christian heir of Greek metaphysics, conceived the word wholly in terms of the species, as its perfection, without grasping the enigma of its incarnation. The linguistic character of the experience of the world, to which metaphysical thinking had originally oriented itself, became in the last analysis something secondary and contingent that schematizes the thinking gaze at things through linguistic conventions and closes it off from the primordial experience of being. In truth, however, the illusion that things precede their manifestation in language conceals the fundamentally linguistic character of our experience of the world. In particular, the illusion of the possibility of the universal objectification of everything and anything completely obscures this universality itself. Since at least within the Indo-Germanic family of languages, language has the possibility of extending its universal naming function to any element of the sentence and of making everthing the subject of further assertions, it creates the general illusion of reification, which reduces language itself to a mere instrument of common understanding. Even modern linguistic analysis, as much as it tries to uncover the verbalistic seductions of language by means of artificial sign systems, does not bring the basic assumption of such objectification into question. Rather, through its own self-limitation it only teaches us that there is no liberation from the orbit of language by introducing artificial sign systems, since all such systems already presuppose natural language. Just as the classical philosophy of language showed the question of the origin of language to be untenable, so also the examination of the idea of an artificial language leads to the elimination of this idea and thus to the legitimation of natural languages. But what is implicit in all this discussion remains completely unconsidered. Certainly we know that languages have their reality everywhere they are spoken, that is, where people are able to understand each other. But what kind of being is it that language possesses? Is it that of an instrument of understanding? It seems to me that Aristotle had already indicated the true character of the being of language when he freed the concept of *syntheke* from its naïve meaning as "convention."

By excluding every sense of founding or originating from the concept of *syntheke,* he pointed in the direction of that correspondence of soul and world that comes to light in the phenomenon of language as such and is independent of the forceful extrapolation of an infinite mind by which metaphysics provided this correspondence with a theological foundation. The agreement about things that takes place in language means neither a priority of things nor a priority of the human mind that avails itself of the instrument of linguistic understanding. Rather, the correspondence that finds its concretion in the linguistic experience of the world is as such what is absolutely prior.

This fact can be illustrated beautifully by a phenomenon that itself constitutes a structural aspect of everything linguistic, namely, the phenomenon of rhythm. The essence of rhythm lies in a peculiar intermediary realm between being and the soul, as Richard Höningswald has already emphasized in his analysis from the point of view of the psychology of thought. The succession that is rhythmatized by the rhythm does not necessarily represent the rhythm of the phenomena themselves. Rather, rhythm can be imputed by our hearing even to a regular succession, so that it appears as rhythmatically organized. Or better, wherever a regular succession is to be perceived by the mind, such a rhythmatizing not only can but in the end *must* take place. But what do we mean here when we say "it must"? Something opposed to the nature of things? Obviously not. But then what does "the rhythm of the phenomena themselves" mean? Are the phenomena not first precisely what they are in that they are thus apprehended as rhythmatic or rhythmatized? Thus the correspondence that holds between them is more original than the acoustic succession on the one hand and the rhythmatizing apprehension on the other.

The poets know of this phenomenon, especially those who try to account for the process of the poetic mind that holds sway in them — Hölderlin, for instance. When they differentiate the original poetic experience from the pregiven character of language as well as from the pregiven character of the world (i.e., of the order of things) and describe the poetic conception as the harmony of the world and soul in the linguistic concretization that becomes poetry, it is a rhythmic experience they are describing. The structure of the poem, which thus becomes language, guarantees the process of soul and world addressing each other as something finite. It is here that the being of language shows its central position. The subjective starting point, which has become natural to modern thought, leads us wholly into error. Language is not to be conceived as a preliminary projection of the world by subjectivity, either as the subjectivity of individual consciousness or as that of the spirit of a people. These are all mythologies, just as the concept of genius is. The concept of genius plays so dominant a role in aesthetic theory because it understands the origination of the form as an unconscious production and thus teaches us to interpret it in analogy with conscious production. But the work of art is as little to be understood in terms of the planned execution of a sketch — even an infallibly unconscious one — as the course of history may be conceived for our finite consciousness as the execution of a plan. Rather, here as well as there, luck and success tempt us into *oracula ex eventu* that in fact hide the event — the word or deed — by which they are expressed.

The consequence of modern subjectivism, it seems to me, is that in all such realms self-interpretation receives a primacy that is not justified by the facts. In truth, we may attribute a privilege to a poet in the explanation of his verse just as little as we may attribute it to the statesman in the historical explanation of events in which he had an active part. The real concept of self-understanding that is alone applicable to all such cases is not to be conceived in terms of the model of perfected self-consciousness, but rather in terms of religious experience. Inherent in it is the fact that the false paths of human self-understanding only reach their true end through divine grace. That is, only thereby do we reach the insight that all paths lead us to our own salvation. All human self-understanding is determined in itself by its inadequacy. This holds precisely for work and deed alike. According to their own being, therefore, art and history elude interpretation in terms of the subjectivity of consciousness. They belong to that hermeneutical universe that is characterized by the mode of operation and the reality of language that transcends all individual consciousness.[3] The mediation of finite and infinite that is appropriate to us as finite beings lies in language — in the linguistic character of our experience of the world. It exhibits an experience that is always finite but that nowhere encounters a barrier at which something infinite is intended that can barely be surmised and no longer spoken. Its own operation is never limited, and yet is not a progressive approximation of an intended meaning. There is rather a constant representation of this meaning in every one of its steps. The success of the work constitutes its meaning, not what is only meant by it. It is the right word, and not the subjectivity of the act of meaning, that expresses its meaning.

It is tradition that opens and delimits our historical horizon, not an opaque event of history that happens "in itself."

Thus the disavowal of the act of meaning that we perceive as the common feature in speaking about "the nature of things" and "the language of things" gains a positive sense and a concrete fulfillment. But with this the tension that exists between these two common expressions first appears in its true light. What seemed the same is not the same. It makes a difference whether a limit is experienced from out of the subjectivity of the act of meaning and the domineering character of the will or whether it is conceived in terms of the all-embracing harmony of beings within the world disclosed by language. Our finite experience of the correspondence between words and things thus indicates something like what metaphysics once taught as the original harmony of all things created, especially as the commensurateness of the created soul to created things. This fact seems to me to be guaranteed not in "the nature of things," which confronts other opinions and demands attention, but rather in "the language of things," which wants to be heard in the way in which things bring themselves to expression in language.

NOTES

1. In my essay "Heidegger's Later Philosophy" I have emphasized this idea as the systematic starting-point for Heidegger's later work.

2. The earliest documentation of this stimulus to Hartmann's thought is the review of Scheler that Hartmann had already published in the journal Die Geisteswissenschaften, early in 1914. Cf. Hartmann, Kleine Schriften, vol. 3 (Berlin: DeGruyter, 1958), pp. 365 ff., and my own essay, "Metaphysik der Erkenntnis," in Logos, 12 (1924): 340-359.

3. In addition to WM, cf. "The Universality of the Hermeneutical Problem."

6

Semantics and Hermeneutics (1972)

(Translated by P. Christopher Smith)

It seems to me to be no coincidence that among the various directions which contemporary philosophical research has taken, semantics and hermeneutics have assumed particular importance. Both have as their starting point the linguistic form of expression in which our thought is formulated. They no longer pass over the primary form in which our intellectual experience is given. Insofar as both of them deal with the realm of language, it is clear that semantics and hermeneutics alike have a truly universal perspective. For of that which is given in language, what is, on the one hand, not a sign and what, on the other, is not a moment in the process of coming to understand?

Semantics appears to describe the range of linguistic facts externally, as it were, and does so in a way that has made possible the development of a classification of types of behavior with respect to these signs. For this classification we are indebted to the American scholar Charles Morris.* Hermeneutics, in contrast, focuses upon the internal side of our use of this world of signs, or better said, on the internal process of speaking, which if viewed from the outside, ap-

---

*Charles W. Morris, *Signs, Language and Behavior* (New York: George Braziller, 1955); and *Foundations of a Theory of Signs* (Chicago: University of Chicago Press, 1938). [Translator]

pears as our use of the world of signs. Both semantics and hermeneutics thematize at some time along their own ways the totality of our relationship to the world that finds its expression in language, and both do this by directing their investigations behind the plurality of natural languages.

The merit of semantic analysis, it seems to me, is that it has brought the structural totality of language to our attention and thereby has pointed out the limitations of the false ideal of unambiguous signs or symbols and of the potential of language for logical formalization. The great value of semantic analysis rests in no small part in the fact that it breaks through the appearance of self-sameness that an isolated word-sign has about it. As a matter of fact, it does this in different ways: first, by making us aware of its synonyms and second, and considerably more important, by demonstrating that an individual word-expression is in no way translatable into other terms or interchangeable with another expression. I consider the second achievement more important because it is based on something that transcends all synonymity. The majority of expressions for the same thought or of words for the same thing can be distinguished, arranged, and differentiated if one's approach aims solely at designating or naming a thing. However, the less a particular word-sign is isolated by this method, the more strongly individualized is the meaning of the expression. The concept of synonymity becomes more and more attenuated. Ultimately, it seems a semantic ideal emerges, which stipulates that in a given context only one expression and no other is the right one. Above all, the poetic use of words might be mentioned in this regard, and within it individualization becomes more pronounced as one proceeds from the epic use of words to the dramatic, to the lyric, and to the ultimate poetic creation, the poem itself. The point here is made evident by the fact that lyric poetry is for the most part untranslatable.

The example of a poem might illustrate just what is accomplished by starting from the semantic point of view. There is a verse of Immermann's in which it is said, "Die Zähre rinnt," (meaning roughly, the tear runs), but anyone whose native tongue is German and who hears the carefully chosen use of *Zähre* (for tear) instead of the accustomed

Träne, will perhaps be surprised that such an old-fashioned word replaces the ordinary one. And nevertheless in weighing a context of a poetic sort, one will ultimately come to accept the choice of the poet in instances like this one where it is a matter of a real poem. One will see that a different, quietly changed meaning is brought out by the word *Zähre* in contrast to everyday crying. One might have one's doubts. Is there really a difference in meaning? Is it not solely of aesthetic significance, that is, is the difference not merely in emotional or euphonic valence? Certainly, it might be the case that one hears different things when *Zähre* or *Träne* is spoken. But with regard to their meaning, are they not interchangeable?

One must think through the entire weight of this objection; for, indeed, it is difficult to find a better definition for the sense or meaning of an expression than its interchangeability with another expression. If one expression can take the place of another without changing the meaning of the whole, then that expression has the same meaning as the one it replaces. Still, it is doubtful just in what measure such a theory of meaning in speaking that is based on interchangeability can be valid for the actual entirety of the phenomenon of language. And that it is a matter of the whole of speaking and not of the interchangeable single expression as such is not to be denied. The potential of semantic analysis lies precisely in getting beyond a theory of meaning that isolates words from the whole. Within its wider perspective what emerges is that the theory of interchangeability, which was to define the meaning of words, has limited validity. The structure of a linguistic form cannot be described simply on the basis of the correspondence and the possibility of substitution of single expressions. To be sure, there are such things as equivalent ways of speaking, but such relationships of equivalency are not unchanging correspondences, but rather arise and die out just like the spirit of an era as it is reflected from decade to decade in semantic change. For an example, one need only observe the penetration of English expressions into present German social life. By making such observations semantic analysis is able, in a manner of speaking, to read the differences in times and the course of history. In particular, it has a vantage point from which to make the intrusion of one structural totality into another total structure recognizable. Its descriptive precision points up the incoherence that results when a realm of words is carried over into new contexts — and such incongruity often indicates that something truly new has been discovered.

That is also and particularly true of the logic of the metaphor. Indeed, the metaphor maintains the appearance of carrying something over from one realm to another, that is, it brings to mind the original realm of meaning from which it was taken and out of which it has been carried over into new realms of usage, as long as this context as such is kept in mind. Only when the word has taken root, as it were, in its metaphorical use and has lost its character of having been taken up and carried over does its meaning in the new context begin to become its "proper" meaning. Thus it is certainly a mere convention of grammar books when particular expressions that are used in our language, for example, "blossoming" are accepted as having their proper function in the world of *flora* and the application of the word to the wider realm of living things or even to higher units of life like society or culture, is considered to be an improper and metaphorical use. In fact, the accumulation of vocabulary and the rules of its application establishes only the outline for that which in this way actually builds the structure of a language, namely, the continuing growth of expressions into new realms of application.

Accordingly, a certain limitation is placed on semantics. It is true that one can approach all natural languages guided by the idea of a total analysis of the semantic deep structure of language and can view these languages as forms in which language as such appears. But in so doing, one will find a conflict between the continuing tendency toward individualization in language and that tendency which is just as essential to language, namely, to establish meanings by convention. For to be sure, the fact that one can never depart too far from linguistic conventions is clearly basic to the life of language: he who speaks a private language understood by no one else, does not speak at all. But on the other hand, he who only speaks a language in which conventionality has become total in the choice of words, in syntax, and in style forfeits the power of address and evocation that comes solely with the individualization of a language's vocabulary and of its means of communication.

An exemplary occurrence of the tension I refer to is that which has always existed between terminology and living language. It is a phenomenon well known to the scholar, but even more so to the layman desirous of education, that technical expressions present an obstacle. They have a peculiar profile that prevents them from fitting into the actual life of the language. Nevertheless, such precisely defined, unambiguous terms live and communicate only in as far as they are embedded in the life of the language, and hence it is obviously essential that they enrich their power of making things clear — a power previously limited by their univocality — with the communicative power of multivocal, vague ways of speaking. To be sure, science can ward off such muddying of its concepts, but methodological "purity" is always attainable only in particular areas — the context of world-orientation resting upon our linguistic relationship to the world precedes it. For an example, one need only think of the concept of "force" in physics and the connotations that are heard along with "force" and that make the insights of science meaningful to the layman. On different occasions, I have been able to demonstrate how Newton's accomplishments were integrated into public consciousness in this way by Oetinger and Herder: the concept of force was made comprehensible on the basis of the living experience of force. But as this integration occurred, the technical concept grew into the German language and was individualized to the point of becoming untranslatable. Or, put another way, who would dare to render Goethe's "In the beginning was *die Kraft*" in another language without Goethe's reservation, "Already something warns me that I shall not stop with that"?

As a matter of fact, if we consider the tendency toward individualization that is characteristic of living language, we will come to recognize the ultimate form of that tendency in poetic creation. If that is correct, however, it becomes questionable whether the theory of substitution is really adequate for defining the concept of meaning for a given linguistic expression. The fact characterizing the extreme case of the lyric poem — that it it untranslatable to the point that it can no longer be rendered in another language at all without losing its entire poetic expressiveness — plainly demonstrates the failure of the idea of substitution, of replacing one expression with another. But the point seems also to be valid generally, that is, independently of the special phenomenon of a highly individualized poetic language. The thesis that one expression can be substituted for another is, if I view the matter correctly, contradicted by the moment of individualization in the speaking of a language as such. Even in those cases where, out of an overabundance of available expressions or in correcting ourselves we might, while speaking, replace one expression with another or use one after another since we did not find the best expression at first — even in those cases the intended meaning of what is said emerges within the continuum of expressions that supersede each other, not in separation from the particular flow of this event. Such separation occurs, however, if one attempts to put another word with an identical meaning in the place of the one used.

Here we reach the point where semantics transcends itself and becomes something else. Semantics is a doctrine of signs, in particular, of linguistic signs. Signs, however, are a means to an end. They are put to use as one desires and then laid aside just as are all other means to the ends of human activity. "One masters one's tools," it is said, that is, one applies them purposively. And certainly we would say in a similar fashion that one must master a language, if one is to express oneself to another in that language. But actual speaking is more than the choice of means to achieve some purpose in communication. The language one masters is such that one lives within it, that is, "knows" what one wishes to communicate in no way other than in linguistic form. "Choosing" one's words is an appearance or effect created in communication when speaking is inhibited. "Free" speaking flows forward in forgetfulness of oneself and in self-surrender to the subject matter made present in the medium of language. That is even true in the case of understanding written discourse, in understanding texts. For they too, if one is to understand them, must be merged again with the movement of meaning in speaking.

Thus there emerges behind the field of examination that analyzes the linguistic form of a text as a whole and brings its semantic structure into view yet another direction of questioning and research, namely, that of hermeneutics. Hermeneutical inquiry is based on the fact that language always leads behind itself and behind the façade of overt verbal expression that it first presents. Language is not coincident, as it were, with that which is expressed in it, with that in it which is formulated in words. The hermeneutical dimension that opens up here makes clear the limit to objectifying anything that is thought and communicated. Linguistic expressions, when they are what they can be, are not simply inexact and in need of refinement, but rather, of necessity, they always fall short of what they evoke and communicate. For in speaking there is always implied a meaning that is imposed on the vehicle of the expression, that only functions as a meaning behind the meaning and that in fact could be said to lose its meaning when raised to the level of what is actually expressed. In order to make this point clear, I should like to differentiate between two forms in which speaking extends behind itself in this way: first, in that which is unsaid and nevertheless made present by speaking, and second, in that which for all practical purposes is concealed by speaking.

Let us turn first to that which is said in spite of not being said. What emerges here is the vast realm of the occasionality of all speaking that plays an important role in establishing the meaning of what is said. By occasionality I mean dependency on the situation in which an expression is used. Hermeneutical analysis is able to show that such dependency on the situation is not itself situational, like the so-called occasional expressions (for instance, "here" or "this") that obviously possess no fixed content in their semantical character, but rather are applicable like empty forms and in which, as is the case with empty forms, changing content can be inserted. Hermeneutical analysis is able to show, rather, that such relativity to situation and opportunity constitutes the very essence of speaking. For no statement simply has an unam-

biguous meaning based on its linguistic and logical construction as such, but, on the contrary, each is motivated. A
question is behind each statement that first gives it its meaning. Furthermore, the hermeneutical function of the question
affects in turn what the statement states generally – in that
the statement is an answer. This is not the place to discuss
the as yet unclarified matter of the hermeneutics of the
question. As everyone knows, there are many sorts of questions that do not even need a syntactical character of a
special sort in order, nevertheless, to fully indicate their
interrogative sense. I am referring here to the interrogative
emphasis by which a unit of speech that is syntactically
declarative can assume the nature of a question. Another nice
example, though, is the reverse: namely, that something
which orginally had the character of a question assumes a
declarative character. That is what we call a rhetorical question. For the so-called rhetorical question is in fact a question
only in form. In substance it is an assertion. And if we
analyze how the interrogative character here becomes affirmative and assertive, we shall see clearly that the rhetorical
question becomes affirmative in that it implies its answer.
Through its question it robs one, as it were, of the chance to
answer.

The most clear-cut evidence of the unsaid revealing itself in
what is said is thus that of the latter's roots in the question
behind it. But we must ask ourselves whether this form of
implication is the only one or whether there are other forms
besides. Is this, for example, the proper model for the very
large number of statements that *stricto sensu* are no longer
statements at all, because they are not actually and solely
intended to convey information, to communicate some state
of affairs that is meant, but rather have a completely different function and sense? I mean, for instance, not only phenomena of speaking like the curse or the blessing or the holy
message of a religious tradition, but also the command or
complaint. These are all ways of speaking that make their
proper sense known in such a way that they cannot be
reiterated; their so-called *signatio* (i.e., their transformation
into an informative assertion, "I say I curse you" for instance) fully changes the sense of the statement – (e.g., its

curse character) – if it does not destroy it altogether. The question remains: is that which is said here an answer to a motivating question? Is it comprehensible, solely comprehensible, on the basis of such a question? Certainly, the meaning of all such forms of statements reaching from the curse to the blessing cannot be grasped in its full extent without a determination of meaning derived from a context of action. One cannot contest the fact that these forms of statements also have the character of occasionality in so far as the occasion of their being said is brought to full awareness whenever they are understood.

Yet another level of problems opens up when we have before us a "text" in the special sense of "literature." For the "meaning" of such a text is not motivated by an occasion, but, on the contrary, claims to be understandable "anytime," that is, to be an answer always, and that means inevitably also to raise the question to which the text is an answer. Precisely these texts – those of theology, law, and literary criticism – are the preferred objects of hermeneutics. For such texts present the problem of awakening a meaning petrified in letters from the letters themselves.

Another form of hermeneutical reflection, however, which does not only relate to that which is unsaid, but also to that which is concealed by speaking, penetrates even more deeply into the hermeneutical conditions of our language behavior. We all know that in the case of the lie, language, precisely in being spoken, can in fact conceal. The complicated interweaving of interpersonal relationships encountered in lies ranging from Oriental forms of courtesy to a clear breach of trust between people has in itself no primarily semantic character. He who lies like a book does so without stuttering and without showing embarrassment, that is, he even conceals the concealment that his speaking in fact is. Clearly, the language reality itself has the particular character of a lie only in those cases where we see it as our task to call forth reality by means of language alone, that is, in the case of the linguistic work of art. Within the linguistic totality of a whole of poetic expression this sort of concealing, which one calls lying, does possess its own semantic structures. In the case of texts, for instance, a modern linguist would speak of lie-signals by virtue of which what is said in the text can be identified by intending to conceal. Here lying is not just the assertion of something false; it is a matter of speaking that conceals and knows it. For that reason seeing through the lie, or better said, grasping the lie-character of the lie in one of the senses corresponding to the true intention of the speaker, is the objective of a linguistic explication of any poetic creation.

Opposed to the lie is the quite different concealment of error. Here language behavior in the case of a correct assertion is in no way different from that in the case of a mistaken one. Error is not a semantic phenomenon, but neither is it a hermeneutical phenomenon, though both elements are present in it. Mistaken assertions are "correct" expressions of erroneous opinions, but, taken as phenomena of expression and language, they are not specifically opposed to the expression of correct opinions. The lie, however, is very much a phenomenon of language, but for the most part a harmless case of concealment. I say harmless, not only because lies do not get very far, but also because they are embedded in language behavior in the world, which is reaffirmed in them, since they presuppose the truth value of speaking, a truth value that is reestablished when the lie is seen through or uncovered. He who is caught in a lie acknowledges his lie as such. Only when the lie no longer involves a conscious concealment does it take on a new character — one that determines the liar's whole relationship to his world. We are familiar with this phenomenon as the kind of personal deceitfulness in which a feeling for what is true and, indeed, for truth of any kind has been lost. Such falsity denies its own existence and secures itself against exposure through talking per se. It maintains itself by spreading the veil of talk over itself. Here one encounters the fully developed and all-encompassing power of talk, which persists even after it has been laid bare in the judgment of others. This kind of deceitfulness provides the model for the self-estrangement to which our language consciousness is susceptible and that needs to be broken through by the efforts of hermeneutical reflection. Viewed from the standpoint of hermeneutics, the recognition of deceitfulness means to the one who has recognized it in the other that the latter is excluded from communication because he does not stand behind what he says.

For hermeneutics is primarily of use where making clear to others and making clear to oneself has become blocked. The two powerful forms of concealment through language to which hermeneutical reflection must apply itself above all and that I wish to discuss in what follows concern precisely this kind of concealment through language that determines one's whole relationship to the world. One is an unstated reliance upon prejudices. One of the fundamental structures of all speaking is that we are guided by preconceptions and anticipations in our talking in such a way that these continually remain hidden and that it takes a disruption in oneself of the intended meaning of what one is saying to become conscious of these prejudices as such. In general the disruption comes about through some new experience, in which a previous opinion reveals itself to be untenable. But the basic prejudices are not easily dislodged and protect themselves by claiming self-evident certainty for themselves, or even by posing as supposed freedom from all prejudice and thereby securing their acceptance. We are familiar with the form of language that such self-securing of prejudices takes: namely the unyielding repetitiousness characteristic of all dogmatism. We encounter it, too, however, in science, when, for instance, for the sake of presuppositionless knowledge and scientific objectivity the method of a proven science like that of physics is carried over into such other areas as that of social theory without methodological modification. An even more salient case that occurs more and more in our times is the invocation of science as the highest authority in the decision-making processes of society. Here, as only hermeneutical reflection is capable of demonstrating, the interest that is bound together with knowledge is overlooked. We are familiar with this kind of hermeneutical reflection in the form of ideological critique, which makes a position suspect by pointing up the ideology behind it, that is, which debunks supposed objectivity by showing it to be an expression of the stabilized balance of given social powers. With the help of historical and social reflection, ideological critique seeks to make us aware of the prevailing social prejudices and thus to dispel them. Or put another way, it seeks to penetrate the disguise that cloaks the unchecked effect of such prejudices. That is an extremely difficult task, for one who calls the self-evident into doubt will find the resistance of all practical evidence marshaled against him. Exactly herein, however, lies the function of hermeneutical theory. It makes general acceptance possible in those instances where acceptance by particular individuals might be prevented by powerful habits and prejudices. Ideological criticism represents only a particular form of hermeneutical reflection, one that seeks to dispel a certain class of prejudices through critique.

Hermeneutical reflection, however, is universal in its possible application. As opposed to the sciences, it must also fight for recognition in those cases where it is a matter, not of the particular problem of uncovering ideology through social criticism, but of self-enlightenment with regard to the methodology of science as such. Any science is based upon the special nature of that which it has made its object through its methods of objectifying. The method of modern science is characterized from the start by a refusal: namely, to exclude all that which actually eludes its own methodology and procedures. Precisely in this way it would prove to itself that it is without limits and never wanting for self-justification. Thus it gives the appearance of being total in its knowledge and in this way provides a defense behind which social prejudices and interests lie hidden and thus protected. One need only think of the role of experts in contemporary society and of the way economics, politics, war, and the implementation of justice are more strongly influenced by the voice of experts than by the political bodies that represent the will of the society.

Hermeneutics achieves its actual productivity only when it musters sufficient self-reflection to reflect simultaneously about its own critical endeavors, that is, about its own limitations and the relativity of its own position. Hermeneutical reflection that does that seems to me to come closer to the real ideal of knowledge, because it also makes us aware of the illusion of reflection. A critical consciousness that points to all sorts of prejudice and dependency, but one that considers itself absolutely free of prejudice and independent,

necessarily remains ensnared in illusions. For it is itself motivated in the first place by that of which it is critical. Its
dependency on that which it destroys is inescapable. The
claim to be completely free of prejudice is naïve whether that
naïvete be the delusion of an absolute enlightenment or the
delusion of an empiricism free of all previous opinions in the
tradition of metaphysics or the delusion of getting beyond
science through ideological criticism. In any case, the hermeneutically enlightened consciousness seems to me to establish
a higher truth in that it draws itself into its own reflection.
Its truth, namely, is that of translation. It is higher because it
allows the foreign to become one's own, not by destroying it
critically or reproducing it uncritically, but by explicating it
within one's own horizons with one's own concepts and thus
giving it new validity. Translation allows what is foreign and
what is one's own to merge in a new form by defending the
point of the other even if it be opposed to one's own view. In
this manner of practicing hermeneutical reflection, what is
found in a given formulation of language is altered in a
certain sense; that is, it is taken out of its own linguistically
structured world. But it itself — and not our opinion about
it — is drawn into a new linguistic explication of the world.
In this process of finite thought ever moving forward while
allowing the other to have its way in opposition to oneself,
the power of reason is demonstrated. Reason is aware that
human knowledge is limited and will remain limited, even if
it is conscious of its own limit. Hermeneutical reflection thus
exercises a self-criticism of thinking consciousness, a criticism
that translates all its own abstractions and also the knowledge
of the sciences back into the whole of human experience of
the world. Above all, philosophy, which whether expressly or
not always must be a critique of traditional attempts to
think, is the actualization of such hermeneutics, which blends
the total structures worked out in semantic analysis into the
continuum of translating and comprehending within which
we live and pass away.

7
Aesthetics and Hermeneutics (1964)

If we define the task of hermeneutics as the bridging of personal or historical distance between minds, then the experience of art would seem to fall entirely outside its province. For of all the things that confront us in nature and history, it is the work of art that speaks to us most directly. It possesses a mysterious intimacy that grips our entire being, as if there were no distance at all and every encounter with it were an encounter with ourselves. We can refer to Hegel in this connection. He considered art to be one of the forms of Absolute Spirit, that is, he saw in art a form of Spirit's self-knowledge in which nothing alien and unredeemable appeared, a form in which there was no contingency of the actual, no unintelligibility of what is merely given. In fact, an absolute contemporaneousness exists between the work and its present beholder that persists unhampered despite every intensification of the historical consciousness. The reality of the work of art and its expressive power cannot be restricted to its original historical horizon, in which the beholder was actually the contemporary of the creator. It seems instead to belong to the experience of art that the work of art always has its own present. Only in a limited way does it retain its historical origin within itself. The work of art is the expression of a truth that cannot be reduced to what its creator actually thought in it. Whether we call it the unconscious creation of the genius or consider the conceptual inexhaustibility of every artistic expression from the point of view of the beholder, the aesthetic consciousness can appeal to the fact that the work of art communicates itself.

The hermeneutical perspective is so comprehensive, however, that it must even include the experience of beauty in nature and art. If it is the fundamental constitution of the historicity of human Dasein to mediate itself to itself understandingly — which necessarily means to the whole of its own experience of the world — then *all* tradition belongs to it. Tradition encompasses institutions and life-forms as well as texts. Above all, however, the encounter with art belongs within the process of integration that is involved in all human life that stands within traditions. Indeed, it is even a question as to whether the peculiar contemporaneousness of the work of art does not consist precisely in its being open in a limitless way to ever new integrations. The creator of a work of art may intend the public of his own time, but the real being of his work is what it is able to say, and this being reaches fundamentally beyond any historical confinement. In this sense, the work of art occupies a timeless present. But this statement does not mean that it involves no task of understanding, or that we do not find its historical heritage within it. The claim of historical hermeneutics is legitimated precisely by the fact that while the work of art does not intend to be understood historically and offers itself instead in an absolute presence, it nevertheless does not permit just any forms of comprehension. In all the openness and all the richness of its possibilities for comprehension, it permits — indeed even requires — the application of a standard of appropriateness. It may remain undecided whether the claim to appropriateness of comprehension raised at any particular time is correct. Kant was right in asserting that universal validity is required of the judgment of taste, though its recognition cannot be compelled by reasons. This holds true for every interpretation of works of art as well. It holds true for the active interpretation of the reproductive artist or the reader, as well as for that of the scientific interpreter.

One can ask skeptically if a concept of the work of art that

regards it as being open to ever newer comprehension does
not already belong to a secondary world of aesthetic cultivation. In its origins, is not a work of art the bearer of a
meaningful life-function within a cultic or social context?
And is it not within this context alone that it receives its full
determination of meaning? Still it seems to me that this
question can also be reversed: Is it really the case that a work
of art, which comes out of a past or alien life-world and is
transferred into our historically educated world, becomes a
mere object of aesthetic-historical enjoyment and says nothing more of what it originally had to say? "To say something," "to have something to say" — are these simply meta-
phors grounded in an undetermined aesthetic formative
value that is the real truth? Or is the reverse the case? Is the
aesthetic quality of formation only the condition for the fact
that the work bears its meaning within itself and has something to say to us? This question gives us access to the real
problematic dimension of the theme "aesthetics and herma-
neutics."

The inquiry developed here deliberately transforms the
systematic problem of *aesthetics* into the question of the
experience of *art.* In its actual genesis and also in the foundation Kant provided for it in his *Critique of Aesthetic Judgment,* it is certainly true that philosophical aesthetics covered
a much broader area, since it included the beautiful in nature
and art, indeed, even the sublime. It is also incontestable that
in Kant's philosophy natural beauty had a methodical priority for the basic determinations of the judgment of aesthetic
taste, and especially for his concept of "disinterested pleasure." However, we must admit that natural beauty does not
"say" anything in the sense that works of art, created by and
for men, say something to us. One can rightly assert that a
work of art does not satisfy in a "purely aesthetic" way, in
the same sense as a flower or perhaps an ornament does. With
respect to art, Kant speaks of an "intellectualized" pleasure.
But this formulation does not help. The "impure," intellectualized pleasure that the work of art evokes is still what
really interests us as aestheticians. Indeed, the sharper reflection that Hegel brought to the question of the relation of
natural and artistic beauty led him to the valid conclusion

that natural beauty is a reflection of the beauty of art. When something natural is regarded and enjoyed as beautiful, it is not a timeless and wordless givenness of the "purely aesthetic" object that has its exhibitive ground in the harmony of forms and colors and symmetry of design, as it might seem to a Pathagorizing, mathematical mind. How nature pleases us belongs instead to the context that is stamped and determined by the artistic creativity of a particular time. The aesthetic history of a landscape – for instance, the Alpine landscape – or the transitional phenomenon of garden art are irrefutable evidence of this. We are justified, therefore, in proceeding from the work of art rather than from natural beauty if we want to define the relation between aesthetics and hermeneutics. In any case, when we say that the work of art *says* something to us and that it thus belongs to the matrix of things we have to understand, our assertion is not a metaphor, but has a valid and demonstrable meaning. Thus the work of art is an object of hermeneutics.

According to its original definition, hermeneutics is the art of clarifying and mediating by our own effort of interpretation what is said by persons we encounter in tradition. Hermeneutics operates wherever what is said is not immediately intelligible. Yet this philological art and pedantic technique has long since assumed an altered and broadened form. Since the time of this original definition, the growing historical consciousness has made us aware of the misunderstanding and the possible unintelligibility of all tradition. Also, the decay of Christian society in the West – in continuation of a process of individualization that began with the Reformation – has allowed the individual to become an ultimately indissoluble mystery to others. Since the time of the German romantics, therefore, the task of hermeneutics has been defined as avoiding misunderstanding. With this definition, hermeneutics acquires a domain that in principle reaches as far as the expression of meaning as such. Expressions of meaning are first of all linguistic manifestations. As the art of conveying what is said in a foreign language to the understanding of another person, hermeneutics is not without reason named after Hermes, the interpreter of the divine message to mankind. If we recall the origin of the name hermeneutics, it becomes clear that we are dealing here with a language event, with a translation from one language to another, and therefore with the relation of two languages. But insofar as we can only translate from one language to another if we have understood the meaning of what is said and construct it anew in the medium of the other language, such a language event presupposes understanding.

Now these obvious conclusions become decisive for the question that concerns us here — the question of the language of art and the legitimacy of the hermeneutical point of view with respect to the experience of art. Every interpretation of the intelligible that helps others to understanding has the character of language. To that extent, the entire experience of the world is linguistically mediated, and the broadest concept of tradition is thus defined — one that includes what is not itself linguistic, but is capable of linguistic interpretation. It extends from the "use" of tools, techniques, and so on through traditions of craftsmanship in the making of such things as various types of implements and ornamental forms through the cultivation of practices and customs to the establishing of patterns and so on. Does the work of art belong in this category, or does it occupy a special position? Insofar as it is not directly a question of *linguistic* works of art, the work of art does in fact seem to belong to such nonlinguistic tradition. And yet the experience and understanding of a work of art is different from the understanding of the tool or the practices handed on to us from the past.

If we follow an old definition from Droysen's hermeneutics, we can distinguish between sources [*Quellen*] and vestiges [*Überresten*]. Vestiges are fragments of a past world that have survived and assist us in the intellectual reconstruction of the world of which they are a remnant. Sources, on the other hand, constitute a linguistic tradition, and they thus serve our understanding of a linguistically interpreted world. Now where does an archaic image of a god belong, for instance? Is it a vestige, like any tool? Or is it a piece of world-interpretation, like everything that is handed on linguistically?

Sources, says Droysen, are records handed down for the purpose of recollection. Monuments are a hybrid form of sources and vestiges, and to this category he assigns "works of art of every kind," along with documents, coins, and so on. It may seem this way to the historian, but the work of art as such is a historical document neither in its intention nor in the meaning it acquires in the experience of the work of art. To be sure, we talk of artistic monuments, as if the production of a work of art had a documentary intention. There is a certain truth in the assertion that permanence is essential to every work of art – in the transitory arts, of course, only in the form of their repeatability. The successful work "stands." (Even the music hall artist can say this of his act.) But the explicit aim at recollection through the presentation of something, as it is found in the genuine document, is not present in the work of art. We do not want to refer to anything that once was by means of presentation. Just as little could it be a guarantee of its permanence, since it depends for its preservation on the approving taste or sense of quality of later generations. Precisely this dependence on a preserving will means that the work of art is handed on in the same sense as our literary sources are. At any rate, "it speaks" not only as remnants of the past speak to the historical investigator or as do historical documents that render something permanent. What we are calling the language of the work of art, for the sake of which the work is preserved and handed on, is the language the work of art itself speaks, whether it is linguistic in nature or not. The work of art says something to the historian: it says something to each person as if it were said especially to him, as something present and contemporaneous. Thus our task is to understand the meaning of what it says and to make it clear to ourselves and others. Even the nonlinguistic work of art, therefore, falls within the province of the proper task of hermeneutics. It must be integrated into the self-understanding of each person.[1]

In this comprehensive sense, hermeneutics includes aesthetics. Hermeneutics bridges the distance between minds and reveals the foreignness of the other mind. But revealing what is unfamiliar does not mean merely reconstructing historically the "world" in which the work had its original meaning and function. It also means apprehending what is said to us, which is always more than the declared and comprehended meaning. Whatever says something to us is like a person who says something. It is alien in the sense that it transcends us. To this extent, there is a double foreignness in the task of understanding, which in reality is one and the same foreignness. It is this way with all speech. Not only does it say something, but *someone* says something to someone else. Understanding speech is not understanding the wording of what is said in the step-by-step execution of word meanings. Rather, it occurs in the unitary meaning of what is said — and this always transcends what is expressed by what is said. It may be difficult to understand what is said in a foreign or ancient language, but it is still more difficult to let something be said to us even if we understand what is said right away. Both of these things are the task of hermeneutics. We cannot understand without wanting to understand, that is, without wanting to let something be said. It would be an inadmissible abstraction to contend that we must first have achieved a contemporaneousness with the author or the original reader by means of a reconstruction of his historical horizon before we could begin to grasp the meaning of what is said. A kind of anticipation of meaning guides the effort to understand from the very beginning.

But what holds in this fashion for all speaking is valid in an eminent way for the experience of art. It is more than an anticipation of meaning. It is what I would like to call surprise at the meaning of what is said. The experience of art does not only understand a recognizable meaning, as historical hermeneutics does in its handling of texts. The work of art that says something confronts us itself. That is, it expresses something in such a way that what is said is like a discovery, a disclosure of something previously concealed. The element of surprise is based on this. "So true, so filled with being" [*So wahr, so seiend*] is not something one knows in any other way. Everything familiar is eclipsed. To understand what the work of art says to us is therefore a self-encounter. But as an encounter with the authentic, as a familiarity that includes surprise, the experience of art is *experience* in a real sense and must master ever anew the task that experience involves: the task of integrating it into the whole of one's own orientation to a world and one's own self-understanding. The language of art is constituted precisely by the fact that it speaks to the self-understanding of *every* person, and it does this as ever present and by means of its own contemporaneousness. Indeed, precisely the contemporaneousness of the work allows it to come to expression in language. Everything depends on how something is said. But this does not mean we should reflect on the means of saying it. Quite the contrary, the more convincingly something is said, the more self-evident and natural the uniqueness and singularity of its declaration seems to be, that is, it concentrates the attention of the person being addressed entirely upon what is said and prevents him from moving to a distanced aesthetic differentiation. Over against the real intention, which aims at what is said, reflection upon the means of the declaration is indeed always secondary and in general is excluded where men speak to each other face to face. For what is said is not something that presents itself as a kind of content of judgment, in the logical form of a judgment. Rather, it is what we want to say and what we will allow to be said to us. Understanding does not occur when we try to intercept what someone wants to say to us by claiming we already know it.

All these observations hold especially for the language of art. Naturally it is not the artist who is speaking here. The artist's own comments about what is said in one or another of his works may certainly be of possible interest too. But the language of art means the excess of meaning that is present in the work itself. The inexhaustibility that distinguishes the language of art from all translation into concepts rests on this excess of meaning. It follows that in understanding a work of art we cannot be satisfied with the cherished hermeneutical rule that the *mens auctoris* limits the task of understanding posed in a text. Rather, just this expansion of the hermeneutical perspective to include the language of art makes it obvious how little the subjectivity of the act of meaning suffices to denote the object of understanding. But this fact has a general significance, and to that extent aesthetics is an important element of general hermeneutics. That should be conclusively indicated. Everything that in the broadest sense speaks to us as tradition poses the task of understanding, without understanding in general being taken to mean the new actualization in oneself of another person's thoughts. We learn this fact with convincing clarity not only from the experience of art (as explained above), but also from the understanding of history. For the real task of historical study is not to understand the subjective intentions, plans, and experiences of the men who are involved in history. Rather, it is the great matrix of the meaning of history that must be understood and that requires the interpretive effort of the historian. The subjective intentions of men standing within the historical process are seldom or never such that a later historical evaluation of events confirms their assessment by contemporaries. The significance of the events, their connection and their involvements as they are represented in historical retrospect, leave the *mens auctoris* behind them, just as the experience of the work of art leaves the *mens auctoris* behind it.

The universality of the hermeneutical perspective is all-encompassing. I once formulated this idea by saying that being that can be understood is language.[2] This is certainly not a metaphysical assertion. Instead, it describes, from the medium of understanding, the unrestricted scope possessed by the hermeneutical perspective. It would be easy to show that all historical experience satisfies this proposition, as does the experience of nature. In the last analysis, Goethe's statement "Everything is a symbol" is the most comprehensive formulation of the hermeneutical idea. It means that everything points to another thing. This "everything" is not an assertion about each being, indicating what it is, but an assertion as to how it encounters man's understanding. There is nothing that cannot mean something to it. But the statement implies something else as well: nothing comes forth in the one meaning that is simply offered to us. The impossibility of surveying all relations is just as much present in Goethe's concept of the symbolic as is the vicarious function of the particular for the representation of the whole. For only because the universal relatedness of being is concealed from human eyes does it need to be discovered. As universal as the hermeneutical idea is that corresponds to Goethe's words, in an eminent sense it is fulfilled only by the experience of art. For the distinctive mark of the language of art is that the individual art work gathers into itself and expresses the symbolic character that, hermeneutically regarded, belongs to all beings. In comparison with all other linguistic and nonlinguistic tradition, the work of art is the absolute present for each particular present, and at the same time holds its word in readiness for every future. The intimacy with which the work of art touches us is at the same time, in enigmatic fashion, a shattering and a demolition of the familiar. It is not only the "This art thou!" disclosed in a joyous and frightening shock; it also says to us; "Thou must alter thy life!"

NOTES

1. It is in this sense that I criticized Kierkegaard's concept of the aesthetic (as he himself does). Cf. *WM,* pp. 91 ff.

2. Cf. *WM,* p. 450.

Part II:
Phenomenology, Existential
Philosophy, and Philosophical
Hermeneutics

8

The Philosophical Foundations of the Twentieth Century (1962)

At the end of the nineteenth century, Houston Stewart Chamberlain posed the question of the foundations of his century.* Today a similar question forces itself upon us with respect to the foundations of our own century. From a genuinely historical point of view, the twentieth century is certainly not a chronologically defined period — say the period of time from 1900 to 2000. Just as the nineteenth century lasted in fact from the death of Goethe and Hegel until the outbreak of World War I, so the twentieth century began as the age of the world wars. When we raise this retrospective question, however, something like an epochal awareness seems to separate us from the age of the world wars. The sensibilities of the younger generation no longer appear dominated to such an extent by the anxious expectation that catastrophe will inevitably result from the historical complexities of the present day. Today the predominant expectation is that men may learn to adjust even to the great forces that threaten them with mutual destruction, that a sober assessment of realities and a readiness for rational compromises will open the way into the future. In light of

*The title of Gadamer's essay reflects the title of Houston Stewart Chamberlain's famous book, *Die Grundlagen des 19. Juhrhunderts* (Munich: F. Bruckmann, 1899). [Trans.]

this expectation, what are the foundations of this century in which we live and for whose continuation we hope?

The question of the *foundations* of an epoch, century, or age is directed at something that is not immediately obvious, but that nevertheless has stamped the unified physiognomy of what is immediately present round about us. It sounds trivial perhaps to say that the foundations of the twentieth century lie in the nineteenth century. Yet our point of departure must be the fact that the Industrial Revolution — the rapid industrialization of Western Europe — began in the nineteenth century and that the twentieth century simply continues what was established at that time. The splendid development of the natural sciences in the nineteenth century provided the essential foundations for our own technological and economic development, and to that extent we are only exploiting ever more consistently and rationally the practical possibilities that result from the scientific discoveries of the nineteenth century. Nevertheless, with World War I a genuine epochal awareness emerged that welded the nineteenth century into a unit of the past. This is true not only in the sense that a bourgeois age, which had united faith in technical progress with the confident expectation of a secured freedom and a civilizing perfectionism, had come to an end. This end is not merely an awareness of leaving an epoch, but above all the *conscious withdrawal* from it, indeed, the sharpest rejection of it. The term "nineteenth century" acquired a peculiar ring in the cultural consciousness of the first decades of the twentieth century. It was heard as a term of abuse, designating the very embodiment of inauthenticity, stylelessness, and tastelessness — a combination of crass materialism and an empty cultural pathos. The forerunners of the new age closed ranks in rebellion against the spirit of the nineteenth century. One need only think of modern painting, which made its revolutionary breakthrough in the first decade of our century with the cubist destruction of form; or of architecture, which rejected the past century's art of historicizing façades. An entirely new life-feeling appears in this architecture with increasing clarity. It has no more room for the intimate and favors instead the transparency and openness of every space. Or one may think of the novel that no longer narrates action or of the poem that enigmatizes its message. And even in the greatest devotion to the cultural world of the past, we must acknowledge that all these changes in the actual forms of our life — the dwindling inwardness and the functionalization of social existence in the age of anonymous responsibility — are "right." It was symptomatic of this new age that as early as 1930 Karl Jaspers described the spiritual situation of the time with the concept of "anonymous responsibility." The illusionless recognition of the actual is united in this concept with the passion of existential decision. Philosophy accompanied the events of the time by guarding the limits of the scientific orientation of consciousness to the world.

If we are to speak here of the philosophical foundations of the twentieth century, we do not mean in the sense that philosophy represents the true foundations of the century. For there is some question as to whether what was formerly philosophy still has a place within the totality of present-day life. The old tension between science and philosophy in the modern period of history may culminate in our century, but the problem goes back further, for modern science is not an invention of the nineteenth century, but of the seventeenth century. The task of providing a rational foundation for the knowledge of nature was taken up at that time, and the question was raised as to how science, as the new foundation of our human relation to the world, could be united with the traditional forms of that relation — with the tradition of Greek philosophy, as the embodiment of everything men knew about God, the world, and human life, and with the message of the Christian Church. Then began the Enlightenment that gave the whole of more recent centuries the character of its philosophy. For as triumphant as the march of modern science has been, and as obvious as it is to everyone today that their awareness of existence is permeated by the scientific presuppositions of our culture, human thought is nonetheless continually dominated by questions for which science promises no answer.

In this state of affairs philosophy takes up its task, a task that has remained the same to the present day. The answers it has found in the three centuries of the modern period sound different, but they are answers to the same question. Furthermore, the later answers are not possible without the earlier ones and must be tested successfully against them. Hence the question of the foundations of the twentieth century, when it is posed as a question of philosophy, must be related to the answers that were given in preceding centuries. Leibniz first saw the task in the eighteenth century. He appropriated the new scientific thought with his entire genius, and yet he considered the ancient and scholastic doctrine of substantial forms to be indispensible. Thus he became the first thinker to attempt to mediate between traditional metaphysics and modern science. A century later, German idealism tried to accomplish the same task. The scholastic philosophy of the eighteenth century had been destroyed by the Kantian critique of dogmatic metaphysics with a swiftness that approached a genuine revolution. Actually, its coincidence with Rousseau's critique of the moral arrogance of the Enlightenment and with the immense social upheaval of the French Revolution may have secured Kantian philosophy its victory. After that, a new answer to the old question became necessary, and this answer was given its final systematic cogency by Hegel.

At the beginning of the nineteenth century there stands not only the revolutionary achievement of the Kantian critique, but also the comprehensive synthesis of Hegelian philosophy against which the scientific spirit of the nineteenth century had to make its way. Hegel's philosophy represents the last mighty attempt to grasp science and philosophy as a unity. It is easy today to feel the hopelessness of such a task, and in fact it was the last attempt of this kind. But if it is part of the sensibilities of the nineteenth century, at least in the realm of knowledge of nature, to confirm its own empirical frame of mind by ridiculing the natural philosophy of German idealism, we nonetheless have reason, especially in view of that century itself, to ask to what extent the nineteenth century's scientific idea of progress had different presuppositions from those it was itself aware of. Perhaps Hegel knew more about such presuppositions than did the science that was so full of ridicule for him.

This question forces itself upon us, for in retrospect the

nineteenth century appears to have been influenced by scientific progress only in a very limited way. If we compare the role that the dominance of science over life plays in our own century, the difference is obvious. It may be characteristic of the naïvete of the nineteenth century that it considered the expansive enthusiasm of its knowledge and its civilized faith in the future to rest on the firm basis of a socially sanctioned moral order. The traditional form of the Christian Church, the national consciousness of the modern state, and the morality of private conscience lie unquestioned at the foundation of the bourgeois culture of a century whose scientific achievements have been so fruitful, indeed revolutionary. Today, however, the awareness of such constants of social reality have receded completely into the background. We live with the awareness of a world that is changing in unforeseeable ways, and in conflicts and tensions we expect science, out of its own resources, to constitute the decisive factor. When the issue is avoiding sickness or improving the standard of living we invest our hope in it. Society clings with bewildered obedience to scientific expertise, and the ideal of conscious planning and smoothly functioning administration dominates every sphere of life even down to the level of molding public opinion.

Correspondingly, the culture of inwardness, the intensification of personal conflicts in human life, and the pent-up expressive power of its artistic representation is gradually becoming alien to us. The social order develops forms of such power that the individual is hardly conscious at all any longer of living out of his own decisions, even in the intimate sphere of his own personal existence. Thus we must sharpen the question in our own time as to how man can understand himself within the totality of a social reality dominated by science. It is worth while considering Hegel's answer too, in order to prepare adequate answers of our own. For by subjecting the standpoint of subjective consciousness to an explicit critique, Hegel's philosophy opened up a way to understand the human social reality in which we still find ourselves today. Hence in introducing Hegel's critique of subjective spirit we must also ask how the philosophical thought of our own century is to be distinguished from that first great application of the critique of subjective spirit which we inherit from German idealism, and above all from Hegel.

It is well known that Hegel's speculative idealism is characterized by the most caustic criticism of the philosophy of reflection, which he regarded as an illness of the romantic mind and its feeble inwardness. The concept of reflection as we generally employ it (for instance, when we say that someone engages in reflection or that someone is a relfective man, etc.) is what Hegel calls "external reflection." The layman knows no other concept of reflection. For the layman, as Hegel says, reflection is the *raisonnement* that moves hither and yon and, without settling on a particular content, knows how to apply general principles to any content. Hegel holds this procedure of external reflection to be a modern form of sophism because of the abritrariness with which it brings something given under general principles. His critique of the all too agile, all too facile generalizing of the given has its positive counterpart in the demand that thought immerse itself completely in the objective content of the thing and leave all its own fancies behind. This demand acquires its central significance above all in moral philosophy. From his criticism of Kant's moral philosophy and the explicit foundation that Kant had given to the phenomenon of moral reflection in the principle of ethics, Hegel developed his concept of "spirit" and his criticism of subjective, "external" reflection.

Kant's moral philosophy is based on the so-called categorical imperative. It is obvious that the "formula" of the categorical imperative – (e.g., as Kant says, that the maxim of our action at any time should be thought of as a universal law or a law of nature) – does not represent a moral command that could supplant material commands, such as those of the Decalogue. The formula corresponds instead to what Hegel calls "law-testing reason," and it does not mean that the actuality of the moral life consists in following this command. Rather, it is the highest instance of testing for the binding force of every ought, and it is meant to guide moral reflection in its effort to ascertain the purity of the moral will.

It is obvious, however, that situations of moral action are

not generally ones in which we have the inner freedom for reflection of this kind. And Hegel makes this criticism with cogency. Kant argues, for instance, in the *Foundations of the Metaphysics of Morals,* * that a man considering suicide needs to have retained only enough reflective sense to ask himself if it is in accordance with the law of life to turn life against itself. But it is easy to see that even to consider suicide indicates one no longer has that much reflective sense. The situation in which moral reflection can appear is always an exceptional one, a situation of conflict between duty and inclination, a situation of moral seriousness and distanced self-examination. It is impossible for us to treat the totality of moral phenomena in this way. The moral must be something different. Hegel expressed this point in a provokingly simple formula: morality is living in accordance with the customs of one's land.

This formulation contains the concept of objective spirit implicitly. Present in the customs, the legal order, and the political constitution of a land is a definite spirit that has no adequate reflection in the subjective consciousness of the individual. To this extent, it is in fact *objective* spirit – spirit that surrounds us all and over against which no one has a reflective freedom. The implications of this concept are of fundamental significance to Hegel. The spirit of morality, the concept of the spirit of a people, the whole of Hegel's philosophy of law – all rest on the transcendence of the subjective spirit present in the orders of human community.

Hegel's idea of objective spirit has its origin in the concept of spirit that stems from the Christian tradition, that is, in the concept of *pneuma* in the New Testament – the concept of the Holy Spirit. The pneumatic spirit of love, the genius of redemption, in terms of which the young Hegel interpreted Jesus, indicates precisely this common factor that transcends particular individuals. Hegel quotes an Arabian expression: "a son of the stem of Koresh," an Oriental phrase indicating that, for the men who use it, a particular man is not an individual but a member of a tribe.**

*Cf. Kant, Foundations of the Metaphysics of Morals, trans. Lewis White Beck (Indianapolis and New York: Bobbs-Merrill, 1969), p. 45.
**Cf. Hegel, *Early Theological Writings* (Chicago: University of Chicago Press, 1948), p. 260.

This concept of objective spirit, the roots of which reach far back into antiquity, finds its real philosophical justification in Hegel through the fact that it is itself transcended by what Hegel calls absolute spirit. By absolute spirit, Hegel means a form of spirit that contains nothing more in itself that is alien, other, or in opposition, such as customs, which can stand over against us as something limiting us, or the laws of a state, which restrict our will by expressing prohibitions. Even when we generally recognize that the legal order is the representation of our common social being, it stands in our way in the form of a prohibition. Hegel sees the distinctiveness of art, religion, and philosophy in the fact that no such opposition is experienced in them. We have in these forms a final and adequate mode in which spirit knows itself as spirit, in which subjective consciousness and the objective actuality that supports us permeate each other, as it were, so that we encounter nothing more that is alien, because we know and recognize everything we encounter as our own. It is well known that Hegel's own philosophy of world history claims to know and recognize in the intrinsic necessity of the event even what seems to befall the individual as an alien fate. His philosophy of spirit reaches its culmination in this claim.

In itself, however, such a claim evokes once again the critical question of how we are to conceive the complicated, ambiguous relation between the subjective spirit of the individual and objective spirit that manifests itself in world history. This old question has three forms: how the individual is related to world spirit (Hegel), how he is related to the moral powers that are the genuine sustaining reality of historical life (Droysen), or where he finds himself within the relations of labor, the basic structure of human society (Marx). These three questions are united in the question of where the reconciliation of subjective spirit with objective spirit is to occur – in the absolute knowledge of the Hegelian philosophy, in the restless labor of the Protestant-ethical individual in Droysen, or in the changing structure of society in Marx.

Whoever inquires in this fashion has in fact surrendered Hegel's standpoint of the concept in which the reconciliation has already taken place as reason in reality. What remained

alive in Hegel's critique of subjective spirit at the end of the
nineteenth century, therefore, was not his belief in a reconciliation that knows and conceives everything alien and objective, but rather the alien itself — objectivity in the sense of
the opposition and otherness of what confronts subjective
spirit. In the scientific thought of the nineteenth century,
what Hegel called objective spirit is conceived as the Other of
spirit, and a unified consciousness of method is created after
the model of the knowledge of nature. Just as nature already
appears in Hegel as the Other of spirit, so now the totality of
historical and social reality no longer appears to the active
energy of the nineteenth century as spirit, but rather in its
stubborn actuality, or, to use an everyday word, in its incomprehensibility. One thinks of the incomprehensible phenomenon of money, of capital, and of the concept of the self-
alienation of man as it was developed by Marx. Subjective
spirit does not come to know the incomprehensibility, alien-
ness, opaqueness of social and historical life any differently
than it does nature, which is objective to it. Hence nature and
history are both considered objects of scientific investigation
in the same sense. They constitute the "object of knowledge."

Thus began the development that culminated in Marburg
Neo-Kantianism making the object of knowledge into an
infinite task. The issue for the Neo-Kantians was the determination of the indeterminate, its production in thought. The
model of Neo-Kantian transcendental thought was the infinitesimal method of defining the path or course of a movement. Its watchword was: All knowledge culminates in the
scientific "production" of the object. In the eighteenth century, Leibniz sought to overcome the one-sidedness of the
new science by his new system of monadology. At the
beginning of the nineteenth century, Hegel confronted the
philosophy of reflection with the imposing synthesis of his
philosophy of absolute spirit. Our own century too has felt
the one-sidedness of this scientific methodologism. But we
could indeed ask at this point the skeptical question: Was not
the critique of the dominant Neo-Kantian philosophy that
focused on the concepts "life" and "existence" essentially
romantic in character? Does this question not apply to Dil-

they, Bergson, or Simmel, or to Kierkegaard and existential philosophy, or, with the passion of cultural criticism, to Stefan George, to name but a few representative authors whose work involved a critique of the century? Was their effort anything more than a repetition of the romantic criticism of the Enlightenment? Is it not the case that all such critical attempts contain that indissoluable dialectic of cultural criticism, namely, they continue to value so highly what they condemn that we can apply the same critique to them? We could actually embrace this argument if Nietzsche did not stand behind these philosophical movements of our century. He was the great, fateful figure who fundamentally altered the task of the critique of subjective spirit for our century.

I do not want to take up the question of how far philosophy itself is simply an expression of a new social and personal situation or to what extent it is itself able to alter this situation. If we are concerned with Nietzsche's real and epoch-making significance for this whole matrix of questions, we do not have to decide whether philosophy is the expression of an event or the cause of it. For his criticism aims at the final and most radical alienation that comes upon us from out of ourselves — *the alienation of consciousness itself.* Consciousness and self-consciousness do not give unambiguous testimony that what they think they mean is not perhaps a masking or distorting of what is really in them. Nietzsche hammered this home to modern thought in such fashion that we now recognize it everywhere, and not only in the excessive, self-destructive and disillusioning way in which Nietzsche himself tears one mask after another from the I, until finally no more masks remain — and also no more I. We think not only of the plurality of masks, represented mythologically by Dionysus, the god of masks, but also of the critique of ideology that, since Marx, has been applied increasingly to religious, philosophical, and world-orienting convictions that are held with unconditional passion. Above all, we think of the psychology of the unconscious, of Freud, whose interpretation of psychological phenomena is dominated by his insight that there can be powerful contradictions in man's psychic life between conscious intention and unconscious desire and being and that in any case what we believe ourselves to be doing is in no way identical with what is in fact transpiring in our human being.

At this point one word can provide us with the proper orientation for understanding how deep this incursion into the validity of subjective spirit reaches. It is the concept of interpretation, a philosophical and humanistic concept that, at the beginning of the modern period, was still applied in a wholly naïve fashion to the natural sciences as *interpretatio naturae* and that has now acquired a highly refractory meaning. Since Nietzsche, the claim has arisen that it is interpretation, with its legitimate cognitive and interpretive aim, that first grasps the real which extends beyond every subjective meaning. Consider the role the concept of interpretation plays in the psychological and moral realms, according to Nietzsche. He writes: "There are no moral phenomena, but only a moral interpretation of the phenomena."*

The effects of this idea are beginning to be felt only in our own century. If in earlier times interpretation aimed at nothing more than the explication of the author's true meaning (and I have reasons for believeing that this concept was always too narrow), it is now explicitly the case that interpretation is expected to go behind the subjectivity of the act of meaning.** It is a question of learning to get behind the surface of what is meant. The unconscious (Freud), the relations of production and their determinative significance for social reality (Marx), the concept of life and its "thought-constituting work" (Dilthey and historicism), the concept of existence as it was once developed by Kierkegaard against Hegel — all these are interpretive standpoints that our century has developed as ways of going behind what is meant in subjective consciousness.

This shift is particularly obvious in German philosophy in our century. The epistemology that was still the basic discipline in the Neo-Kantian epoch and that anyone wanting to do philosophy had to study first is disappearing. The epistemological inquiry appealed to Kant and asked: With what right do we use concepts we have produced ourselves for the

---

*Nietzsche, *Beyond Good and Evil,* section 108.
**The verb *hintergehen,* "to go behind," can also mean, "to deceive" or "to double cross." These meanings should not be overlooked in the present context.

knowledge of things and for the description of experience? The question of legitimation, the *questio iuris* stemming from the Cartesian tradition, acquired a new face in our century through phenomenology — or better, it lost its face.

In his first sketches of *The Idea of Phenomenology* in 1907 and afterward with increasing awareness, Husserl traced the concept of the phenomenon and of the pure description of the phenomenon back to the concept of correlation. That is, he always asked how what is intended is revealed, for which consciousness it is revealed, and in what form. Hence from the very beginning he did not conceive of the situation in terms of a subject existing for itself and choosing its objects. Instead, he studied the attitudes of consciousness correlated with the phenomenal objects of intentionality — the "intentional acts," as he called them. Now "intentionality" [*Intentionalität*] does not mean "an act of meaning" [*Meinen*] in the sense of a subjective operation. There are also what Husserl calls "horizontal intentionalities." If I direct my attention to a definite object, for instance, to those two squares on the rear wall, everthing present — the entire room — is simultaneously there for me, like a corona of intentionalities. I can even remember subsequently that at the moment I intended nothing other than the two squares, all of this was also present and cointended. This horizon of intentionalities, the constantly cointended, is not itself an object of a subjective act of meaning. Consequently Husserl calls such intentionalities "anonymous."

Similarly, and with his almost demagogic passionateness, Scheler described the ecstatic character of consciousness by showing that consciousness is not a closed box. The grotesqueness of this image clearly caricatures the false substantializing of the movement of self-reflection. We do not know our representations, we know things, Scheler asserted. There are no images of things in our consciousness that we "really" think and relate in some way to the things of the "external world." All this is mythology. We are always with the beings we intend. Heidegger radicalized this criticism of hypostasized "consciousness" by transforming it into an ontological critique of the understanding of being presupposed by "consciousness." His ontological critique of consciousness found its watchword in the assertion that Dasein is "being-in-the-world." Since that time many have come to regard it as absurd and wholly obsolete to ask how the subject arrives at knowledge of the so-called "external world." Heidegger has called the persistence of this question the real "scandal" of philosophy.

And now we must ask how the philosophical situation of our century, which finally goes back to Nietzsche's critique of consciousness, is to be distinguished from Hegel's critique of subjective spirit. This question is not an easy one to answer, but we could attempt the following argument here. No one knew better than did German idealism that consciousness and its object are not two separated worlds. It even found a word for it by coining the term "philosophy of identity." It showed that consciousness and object are in fact only two sides that belong together and that any bifurcation into pure subject and pure objectivity is a dogmatism. The series of dramatic developments that constitute Hegel's *Phenomenology of Spirit* rests directly on an awareness of the fact that every consciousness that knows an object alters itself and hence also necessarily alters its object once again, so that the truth is known only in "absolute" knowledge — in the complete cancellation of the objectivity of what is thought. Is the critique of the concept of the subject that our century has attempted anything more than a repetition of what German idealism achieved? Indeed, must we not confess that this repetition has an incomparably narrower capacity for abstraction and lacks the intuitive power that the concept then had?

I do not believe this argument is valid. The critique of subjective spirit in our century has altogether different traits at several decisive points because it can no longer renounce Nietzsche's question. There are three points, above all, at which contemporary thought has exposed the naïve assumptions of German idealism that can no longer be considered valid: (1) the naïvete of the assertion; (2) the naïvete of reflection; and (3) the naïvete of the concept.

The first point is *the naïvete of the assertion.* Since Aristotle, the totality of logic has rested on the concept of the proposition, the *apophansis,* that is, the assertion of a judgment. In a classical passage, Aristotle emphasizes that he is dealing with the "apophantic *logos*" alone, that is, with the mode of discourse in which the issue is the truth or falsehood of assertions. He leaves aside such phenomena as the petition, the command, or even the question. To be sure, they are modes of discourse, but they are not concerned simply with revealing that which is existent, that is, with being true. Thus Aristotle established the priority of "judgment" in logic. In modern philosophy, the concept of assertion that originated in this way is connected with the concept of the judgment of perception. Pure perception corresponds to pure assertion. But in our century, roused to doubt by Nietzsche, both have turned out to be inadmissible abstractions that cannot withstand a phenomenological critique. There is neither pure perception nor pure assertion.

The concept of "pure perception" was undermined first by the combined impact of many investigations. In Germany it began to take effect above all when Max Scheler, with the force of his phenomenological intuition, used the results of this research. In *Forms of Knowledge and Society,* he showed the idea of a perception adequated to a stimulus to be a purely artificial product of abstraction. What I perceive in no way corresponds to the sensuous or physchological stimulus that has actually taken place. Rather, the relative adequation of perception − that we see what is actually there, no more and no less − is the final product of a powerful refinement, a final reduction of the excess of fantasy that guides all our seeing. Pure perception is an abstraction. The same holds for the pure assertion, as Hans Lipps in particular has shown.* In this connection, I would point to the legal assertion as an especially relevant phenomenon. It makes clear how difficult it is for a witness to know to any extent the full truth of what he means, within the protocol of the court that is the context of his testimony. Torn from the context of the immediacy of question and answer by omissions, summaries, and so on, the reformulated assertion is like an answer one must give without knowing why the question is asked. And this is not accidental. It is precisely the accepted ideal of a testimony and undoubtedly an essential aspect of all evi-

*Cf. *UhL.*

dence, namely, to testify without knowing what one's own declaration "means." A similar situation exists in an examination when a professor asks the candidate concocted questions that no rational person can answer. Heinrich von Kleist, who had himself been through the Prussian state examinations, took up this theme in his beautiful essay "On the Gradual Composition of Thought in Discourse."* The criticism of the abstraction of the assertion and the abstraction of pure perception has been radicalized by Heidegger's transcendental-ontological inquiry. We must remember, first of all, that the concept of the fact, which corresponds to the concept of pure perception and pure assertion, was exposed by Heidegger as an ontological prejudice affecting the concept of value as well. Thus Heidegger showed the distinction between the judgment of fact and the judgment of value to be problematic, as if there could be a pure determination of facts at all. I would like to characterize the dimension revealed here as the hermeneutical dimension.

Here we find the well-known problem that Heidegger analyzed under the title of the hermeneutical circle. The problem concerns the astounding naïvete of the subjective consciousness that, in trying to understand a text, says "But that is what is written here!" Heidegger showed that this reaction is quite natural, and often enough a reaction of the highest self-critical value. But in truth there is nothing that is simply "there." Everything that is said and is there in the text stands under anticipations. This means, positively, that only what stands under anticipations can be understood at all, and not what one simply confronts as something unintelligible. The fact that erroneous interpretations also arise from anticipations and, therefore, that the prejudices which make understanding possible also entail possibilities of misunderstanding could be one of the ways in which the finitude of human nature operates. A necessarily circular movement is involved in the fact that we read or understand what is there, but nonetheless see what is there with our own eyes (and our own thoughts).

It seems to me, moreover, that this observation needs a

*Cf. Heinrich von Kleist, "Über das allmähliche Verfertigung der Gedanken beim Reden," in *Werke* (Leipzig: Bibliographisches Institut, n.d.), vol. 4, pp. 74-80.

further radicalization — one I have formulated in my own
studies in the following thesis: It is certainly correct that we
have to understand what the author intended "in his sense."
But "in his sense" does not mean "as he himself intended it."
It means rather that understanding can also go beyond the
author's subjective act of meaning, and perhaps even necessarily and always goes beyond it. There was always an awareness of this fact in the earlier stages of hermeneutics before
the psychological turn that we call historicism occurred. And
as soon as we consider an appropriate model — for example,
the understanding of historical actions, of historical events —
we find ourselves in agreement. No one will assume that the
subjective consciousness of the agent, or of the participant in
events, is commensurate with the historical significance of his
actions. It is obvious to us that understanding the historical
significance of an action presupposes that we do not restrict
ourselves to the subjective plans, intentions, and dispositions
of the agents. At least since Hegel's time it has been clear that
history by its very nature does not have its primary focus in
the self-knowledge of the individual, and it holds just as well
for the experience of art. I believe that this same insight must
be applied even to the interpretation of texts whose informational sense is not open to an indeterminate explanation like
the art work. Here too, as Husserl's critique of psychologism
has demonstrated, "what is meant" is not a component of
subjective inwardness.

The second point I would like to consider is *the naïvete of
reflection*. Here our century has consciously delineated itself
from the critique of subjective spirit that was made by
German idealism, and the phenomenological movement deserves the major credit for this fact.

What is at stake here is this: It seems at first as if the
reflective spirit is the absolutely free spirit. In coming back to
itself it is completely at home with itself [*bei sich*]. In fact,
German idealism — for example, in Fichte's concept of action
or even Hegel's concept of absolute knowledge — considered
this achievement of the spirit that is at home with itself as
the highest mode of existence or presence. But if the concept
of assertion has succumbed to the phenomenological critique,
as we have seen, then the central position occupied by the

concept of reflection is also undercut. The kind of knowledge in question here implies that not all reflection performs an objectifying function, that is, not all reflection makes what it is directed at into an object. Rather, there is an act of reflecting that, in the fulfillment of an "intention," bends back, as it were, on the process itself. Let us take a well-known example. When I hear a tone, the primary object of my hearing is obviously the tone. But I am also conscious of my hearing of the tone, and by no means only as the object of a subsequent reflection. A concomitant reflection always accompanies hearing. A tone is always a *heard* tone, and my hearing of the tone is always intrinsically involved. We read this in Aristotle, who already described it with perfect correctness: every *aisthésis* is an *aisthésis aisthéseos*. Every perception is perception of the perceiving and of the perceived in one, and in no way contains "reflection" in the modern sense. Aristotle gives the phenomenon as it showed itself to him, namely, as a unity. Aristotle's commentators were the first to systematize and associate the perception of the perceiving with the concept of the κοινὴ αἴοθεις which Aristotle used in a different connection.

Franz Brentano, Husserl's teacher, founded his empirical psychology substantially on the phenomenon described by Aristltle. He asserted that we have a nonobjectifying consciousness of our psychic acts. I can remember what enormous significance it had for my generation when Heidegger acquainted us for the first time with a scholastic distinction that pointed in the same direction, namely, the distinction between the *actus signatus* and the *actus exercitus*. There is a difference between saying "I see something" and "I am saying that I see something." But the signification "I am saying that . . ." is not the first awareness of the act. The act originally taking place is already such an act, which is to say it is already something in which my own operation is vitally present to me. The transformation into a "signification" founds a new intentional object.

By proceeding from these early and forgotten starting points of phenomenological research, perhaps I can call attention to the role this problem still plays in the philosophy of our century. In demonstrating this procedure, I will restrict myself to Jaspers and Heidegger. Jaspers contrasted the concept of certain knowledge, "world-orientation," as he called it, with the illumination of existence, which comes into play in the boundary situations of the scientific as well as every human capacity for knowledge. According to Jaspers, boundary situations are those situations of human existence in which the possibilities of being guided by the anonymous powers of science break down, and where, for that reason, everything depends upon oneself. In such situations something comes out of a man that remains concealed in the purely functionalized application of science for the purpose of dominating the world. There are many such boundary situations. Jaspers already marked out the situation of death, and also the situation of guilt. In the way one behaves when he is guilty or when he is caught in his guilt, something emerges — *existit*. His mode of behavior is such that he himself is completely immersed in it. That is the form in which Jaspers appropriated the Kierkegaardian concept of existence in a systematic way. Existence is the emergence of what is really up to us, where the guiding power of anonymous science breaks down. What is decisive here is that this emergence is not a fuzzy, emotional event, but an illumination. Jaspers calls it an illumination of existence, that is, what was concealed within a person is raised into the light of an existential commitment that makes him responsible for what he decides to do. It is not an objectifying reflection. Situations — even boundary situations — require a kind of knowledge that is doubtless not an objectifying knowledge and thus cannot be diminished by science's anonymous possibilities of knowing.

Then Heidegger took this motif up into his basic consideration of the meaning of being. The "mineness" of Dasein, being guilty, running ahead toward death, and similar notions are the principal phenomena of *Being and Time*. It is unfortunate that Heidegger's reception during the first decades of his work involved the moralizing of these concepts, which was indeed in accord with Jaspers's concept of existence, but was then extended to the concept of authenticity in *Being and Time*. The authenticity of Dasein, which emerges in boundary situations, in running ahead toward death, was distinguished from the inauthenticity of trivial, thoughtless life, from publicness, from the "They," from idle talk, from curiosity, and so on — from all ways of falling prey to society and its power to reduce things to their lowest common denominator. In short, the authenticity of Dasein emerged as human finitude. All these things reflect something of the passion of a successor to Kierkegaard, who had an enormous impact on our generation. But this influence was undoubtedly more a concealment of Heidegger's real aims than an actual apprehension of the intentions of his thought.

Heidegger was no longer concerned with conceiving of the essence of finitude as the limit at which our desire to be infinite founders. He sought instead to understand finitude positively as the real fundamental constitution of Dasein. Finitude means temporality and thus the "essence" of Dasein is its historicity. These well-known theses of Heidegger's were meant to serve him in asking the question of being. The "understanding" that Heidegger described as the basic dynamic of Dasein is not an "act" of subjectivity, but a mode of being. By proceeding from the special case of the understanding of tradition, I have myself shown that understanding is always an event. The issue here is not simply that a nonobjectifying consciousness always accompanies the process of understanding, but rather that understanding is not suitably conceived at all as a consciousness of something, since the whole process of understanding itself enters into an event, is brought about by it, and is permeated by it. The freedom of reflection, this presumed being-with-itself, does not occur at all in understanding, so much is understanding conditioned at every moment by the historicity of existence.

Finally, there is the third factor, which perhaps defines our present-day philosophy most profoundly, the insight into *the naïvete of the concept.* Here too, it seems to me, the current situation is determined on the one side by the development of phenomenology in Germany and, interestingly enough, also by a development in English-speaking countries that had its origins in Germany. When the layman wonders what philosophy really is, he has the idea that philosophizing means defining, and taking responsibility for the need to define, the concepts in which all men think. Since as a rule we do not see this happen, we have helped ourselves by means of a doctrine of implicit definition. In reality, however, such a "doctrine" is a mere verbalism. For to call a definition implicit obviously means one finally comes to notice, on the basis of a number of sentences someone has spoken, that he was thinking something unambiguous by means of using a concept. In this respect, philosophers are no different from other men, for other men too are in the habit of thinking definite things and avoiding contradictions. The lay opinion appealed to here is in fact dominated by the nominalistic tradition of recent centuries, in considering linguistic reproduction as a kind of application of signs. It is obvious that artificial signs need an organization and arrangement that excludes any ambiguity. Thus the demand arises that the illusory problems of "metaphysics" must be unmasked by establishing univocal, artifical languages. This demand, which came from the Vienna Circle, has given rise to extensive scholarship, expecially in England and America. One of the most radical and successful formulations of this program is found in Wittgenstein's *Tractatus Logico-Philosophicus.* In his late work, however, Wittgenstein showed that the ideal of artificial language is self-contradictory, but not merely for the reason so often cited, namely, that the introduction of any artificial language requires that another language already be in use, thus entailing a natural language. Rather, the knowledge decisive for Wittgenstein's later insights is that language is always right, that is, it has its real function in the achievement of mutual understanding, and that the illusory problems of philosophy do not grow out of a defect in language, but out of a false, dogmatizing thought, an hypostasizing of operative words. Language is like a game. Wittgenstein speaks of language games in order to hold fast to the purely functional sense of words. Language is language when it is a pure *actus exercitus,* that is, when it is absorbed into making what is said visible, and has itself disappeared, as it were.

In his development of phenomenology, Heidegger also came to see that language is a mode of interpreting the world that precedes all reflective attitudes, and his insight was shared by those thinkers who, on the basis of his work, began to draw philosophical consequences, especially from historicism. All thinking is confined to language, as a limit as well as a possibility. This experience is present in every interpretation that is itself linguistic in character. When we do not understand a text, the ambiguity of a particular word and the possibilities for interpreting it undoubtedly lead to a disturbance of the linguistic process in which mutual understanding is achieved. And we are confident we have understood the word when the ambiguity that initially appeared is finally overcome by a clarification of how the text as a whole is to be read. All genuine interpretation of linguistic texts, not just grammatical interpretation, seems to me to be designed to disappear in this way. Interpretation must play, that is, it must come into play, in order to negate itself in its own achievement. Unwelcome as this characterization may be, this much at least may have become clear: something like a convergence is occurring between Wittgenstein's critique of Anglo-Saxon semantics on the one hand and the criticism of the ahistorical art of phenomenological description that is made by the self-criticism of language, that is, by hermeneutical consciousness, on the other hand. The way we trace the use of concepts back into their history in order to awaken their real, living, evocative meaning seems to me to converge with Wittgenstein's study of living language games, and indeed with everything moving in the same direction.

These developments also involve a critique of subjective consciousness in our century. Language and concept are obviously so closely bound to each other that to think we can "apply" concepts – as for instance, when we say "I call it so-and-so" – damages the binding force of philosophizing. Individual consciousness has no such freedom when it wishes to philosophize. It is bound to language – not only the language of the speakers, but also the language of the dialogue that things carry on with us. Today science and the human experience of world encounter each othere in the philosophical problem of language.

It seems to me to follow from these considerations that in contemporary philosophy three great partners of the dialogue down through the centuries stand in the foreground of our consciousness. First of all, there is the presence of the Greeks in contemporary thought, above all because for them word and concept still stand in immediate, easy communication. The flight into the *logoi* with which Plato begins the real Western turn of the metaphysics in the *Phaedo* at the same time holds thought in close proximity to the linguistic world-experience as a whole. The Greeks are so exemplary for us today because they resisted the dogmatism of concepts and the "urge for system." Thanks to this resistance they were able to conceive the phenomena that dominate our quarrel with our own tradition, such as the self and self-consciousness, and thus also the entire realm of ethical and political being, without falling into the dilemma of modern subjectivism.

The second partner in this dialogue through the centuries appears to me to be, now as ever, Kant, for he made binding once and for all the distinction between thinking of oneself and knowledge. We may, of course, consider knowledge to encompass more than the kind of cognition found in mathematical natural science and its treatment of experience, which is the mode Kant had in view. But knowledge is still something different from all thinking about the self, for which experience no longer provides a basis of demonstration. It seems to me that Kant showed that to be the case.

And to my mind, Hegel is the third partner, despite his speculative-dialectical transcendence of the Kantian concept of finitude and its assertion of our dependence upon experience. For the concept of spirit, which Hegel appropriated from the Christian spiritualistic tradition and raised to new life, is still the basis of every critique of subjective spirit, as this critique is posed for us as our own task by the experience of the post-Hegelian epoch. This concept of spirit that transcends the subjectivity of the ego has its true counterpart in the phenomenon of language, which is coming increasingly to the center of contemporary philosophy. The reason is that, in contrast to the concept of spirit that Hegel drew from the Christian tradition, the phenomenon of language has the merit of being appropriate to our finitude. It is infinite, as is spirit, and yet finite, as is every event.

It would be an error to assert that we no longer need these

teachers in the age of scientism. The limit they designate over against the total scientific reduction of our world is nothing we must first devise. It is there as something that has always preceded science. What seems to me to be the most hidden and yet the most powerful foundation of our century is its skepticism over against all dogmatism, including the dogmatism of science.

9
The Phenomenological Movement (1963)

The phenomenological movement, which arose in Germany before World War I, occupies a distinguished place in twentieth-century philosophy. Edmund Husserl, the founder of phenomenology, regarded the method he developed as the only way of elevating philosophy to the status of a rigorous science. His passionate devotion to this task led to the founding of a philosophical school. Even when he was driven from public attention after 1933 because of his Jewish background, his influence continued and produced a veritable renaissance after World War II. Husserl died in 1938. His extensive legacy of literary works, which were taken from Freiburg to Louvain in order to save them from destruction, is currently being edited, and the great series of these volumes keeps philosophical interest in Husserl's thought alive.

It is not at all easy to say what it is that brings this phenomenological movement to the awareness of the general public. For as a school of thought within academic philosophy that avoided any great publicity, it was unable to gain public attention to the degree that existential philosophy later attained it. And yet phenomenology too had its hour, which bound it closely in spirit to other movements. Consider, for example, how nineteenth-century biographical research changed its appearance precisely at this time. Books

130

like Friedrich Gundolf's *Goethe* or Ernst Kantorowicz's *Frederick the Second* had little in common with the nineteenth-century works on the same subject. The biographical study of the individual (the tracing of sources and influences) that had characterized literary work at the end of the nineteenth century is basically overcome here. The object of these new works is not the incidental biographical, historical conditions under which a man and his work took shape, but rather the essential character of these great spiritual figures that reveals itself to us only when our attention is directed to their creative powers and their spiritual life-forces.

Phenomenology was no less critical of the habits of thought of contemporary philosophy. It wanted to bring the phenomena to expression, that is, it sought to avoid every unwarranted construction and to subject the unquestioned domination of philosophical theories to critical examination. Hence it considered it a prejudiced construction, for example, when the effort was made to derive all the phenomena of human social life from a single principle — for example, from the principle of the greatest utility or from the pleasure principle. In opposition to such theories, it asserted that phenomena such as the idea of justice and punishment, or of friendship and love, bear their meaning within themselves and are not to be comprehended in terms of utility or pleasure. But above all, it aimed its attacks at the construction that dominated epistemology, the basic discipline of the philosophy of the time. When epistemological inquiry sought to answer the question of how the subject, filled with his own representations, knows the external world and can be certain of its reality, the phenomenological critique showed how pointless such a question is. It saw that consciousness is by no means a self-enclosed sphere with its representations locked up in their own inner world. On the contrary, consciousness is, according to its own essential structure, already with objects. Epistemology asserts a false priority of self-consciousness. There are no representative images of objects in consciousness, whose correspondence to things themselves it is the real problem of epistemology to guarantee. The image we have of things is rather in general the mode in which we are conscious of things themselves. Only an exceptional case of disturbed certainty, of doubt regarding the correctness of an opinion, requires that I differentiate the mere image I have of an object from the object itself.

A phenomenology of knowledge must account for this fact. The model instance is perception. Here our perceptions grasp the things themselves "in direct givenness." There is no inference here from sense stimuli that are certain to the causes of the stimuli, no subsequent synthesis of various stimulus-effects into the unity of a cause, which we call the thing. These are all constructions that have no warrant in the phenomena. Knowledge is intuition, and in the case of direct perception, that means the direct giveness of what is known in perception. It has its own certainty in itself. Wherever real insight is attained outside of the sphere of what is perceivable, it can mean nothing other than that there too what is intended presents itself in intuitive givenness. There is "categorical" intuition. Husserl said it occurs as a fulfillment of the intention of the act of meaning. That is the plain, descriptive sense of the celebrated "Wesensschau," which has been combatted with a great deal of blind ingenuity. It is no patented procedure, no secret method of a school. Rather, it reestablishes against all constructive theories the simple fact that knowing is a direct intuition. In 1913, when Husserl published his *Ideas* and began the long series of phenomenological yearbooks, in conjunction with Max Scheler, Alexander Pfänder, and later, Martin Heidegger, he wrote regarding the theory of investigation that the editors shared: It is "the common conviction that we can make full use of the great tradition of philosophy in our concepts and problems only by returning to the original sources of intuition and the insights into essences to be derived from them, and that in this way alone can concepts be clarified intuitively, problems be posed anew on an intuitive basis and then solved in principle."*

These words have a faint missionary ring about them. And Husserl was in fact filled with a genuine missionary consciousness. He regarded himself as a master and teacher of patient, descriptive, detailed work, and all rash combinations

JPPF, vol. 1, p.v.

and clever constructions were an abomination to him. In his teaching, whenever he encountered the grand assertions and arguments that are typical of beginning philosophers, he used to say, "Not always the big bills, gentlemen; small change, small change!" This kind of work produced a peculiar fascination. It had the effect of a purgation, a return to honesty, a liberation from the opaqueness of the opinions, slogans, and battle cries that circulated.

Moreover, the content or field upon which this modest sort of work was exercised was itself very modest. One of Husserl's classic themes was the phenomenology of the things of perception. Here, for example, he developed with a really masterful precision the fact that we always see only the side of each thing that is turned toward us and that the change of perspective which results from walking around a thing can do nothing to alter this essential relation, namely, that what we see is always the front and never the reverse side. Many phenomenological analyses were equally trivial. One of Husserl's most gifted pupils, Adolf Reinach, the Göttingen Privatdozent who was killed in World War I, is even said to have spent a whole semester dealing solely with the question of what a mail box is.

Actually Husserl never discussed the great classical themes of philosophy in a manner that could have satisfied the need of the young scholars who listened to him for a worldview. And yet the fascination was there. 1919 was a time of confusion and new organization of German awareness, a time in which debating clubs, both large and small, fairly swarmed. I remember a discussion within a young academic circle that I attended as a wide-eyed, curious student. Every possible means of salvation was offered for the sickness and crisis of the time. One person spoke out for a socialist society; another saw the poet Stefan George as the founder of new human community; a third wanted to build anew on the basis of antiquity and humanism; a fourth saw in Gierke's *Genossenschaftsrecht* the ideas for the construction of a new state. And then a fifth student came forward and said fervently that the only salvation from our difficulties was phenomenology. In retrospect, I think I can say a little more exactly what I did not understand at the time. The shattering of the cultural consciousness that accompanied the collapse of Wilhelminian Germany had spread a general perplexity, and in this confusing situation the wildest talk occurred and the most absurd proposals were made. Some persons who had undergone the rigorous discipline of the art of phenomenological description may have been tempted to say that only rigorous, detailed work that patiently and conscientiously lays new foundations can show the way to a new order, and not this wild thrashing about in the dark.

Husserl's own primary question, which he asked with penetrating conscientiousness, was: How can I become a worthy philosopher? By this he meant: how can I execute each step of my thinking in such fashion that each further step can have a secure ground? How can I avoid every unjustified assumption and thus finally realize the ideal of rigorous science in philosophy too? The shock of World War I, in which he lost one of his sons, brought him back again and again from the progressive realization of his phenomenological investigation to the foundations, which he sought to inspect and justify with ever-new scrupulousness. On the whole, he published little himself, and almost always his publications were only programmatic sketches. The patient, detailed work that he knew how to teach like no other man no longer appeared in his literary work because of his methodological reflections. More than anything else, his *Lectures on the Phenomenology of Internal Time Consciousness,* which date from the time before World War I, give an idea of what phenomenological work was. He experienced a second shock to his philosophical endeavor in the rise of National Socialism, which robbed him of his public influence and which he regarded, along with the philosophical development of the 1920s associated with the names of Jaspers and Heidegger, as the inundation of irrational tendencies that threatened the rationality of human culture and the rigor of scientific philosophical thought.

In truth, this idea of the knowledge of essences that was to renew the morality of philosophizing, this descriptive analysis of the boundless field of "consciousness" that was to precede all scientific knowledge and contain its *a priori* presuppositions, might have a limit beyond which phenomenology itself could not reach. Even a perfected phenomenological knowledge of all essences — including those in the realm of morality and also the realm of "values" — might not be able to reach the actuality of what is actual, the actuality of thinking consciousness as well as the experience of actuality. Even if the distinction between fact and essence might be rightly delimited over against the particular sciences as phenomenology's great field of investigation and the ground cleared for methodically self-conscious work, the factuality of the factual — facticity, existence — is not only a final, last, and contingent factor that is materially determined and grasped exhaustively in its determinateness. It is also a primary and basic factor, one not to be ignored, which on its side supports every insight into essences. The dilemma was that factical human Dasein could be illuminated by phenomenological research only as an *eidos*, an essence. In its uniqueness, finitude, and historicity, however, human Dasein would preferably be recognized not as an instance of an *eidos* but rather as itself the most real factor of all. In this aporia, Husserl and phenomenological investigation in general was to encounter its own limit, finitude, and historicity.

Within the circle of phenomenologists, Max Scheler knew it to be the case. He was at home with every reality and every science. His powerful temperment penetrated the life-problems of modern man with passionateness — problems of the individual, society, the state, and religion. He was an entirely independent and brilliant figure alongside Husserl, even though it was the ethos of the craftsmanship of phenomenological work that Husserl embodied that first disciplined his truly versatile mind. His ethic of material value established a direction of phenomenological research that fused the tradition of Catholic moral philosophy for the first time with the most advanced positions of modern philosophy, and it has this function to the present day. Husserl's doctrine of the "intuition of essences" suited Scheler perfectly, insofar as he had a penetrating intuitive power that gave him access to the broadest fields of science — physiology as well as psychology, anthropology as well as sociology and the historical sciences — and made possible his brilliant insights into the essential lawfulness of human life. He raised philosophical anthropology to the level of a central philosophical science whose influence carried all the way into the doctrine of God, and in the end his restless speculative spirit broke the bonds of the Catholic Church.

In the exciting years after World War I, the intellectual adventure of this distinguished and demonically driven man had no less influence than the quiet continuity of research within the Freiburg phenomenological school. He strove to build a comprehensive synthesis out of the latest scientific knowledge by supplementing phenomenology with a metaphysical science of actuality, and the world of spirit and its deactualizing vision of essences with the actuality of impulse as the elemental ground of all being. Scheler's writings, especially those on the sociology of knowledge and philosophical anthropology, were able to work out the connection between essence and actuality with thematic explicitness. But in the end, the mere supplementing of phenomenology by a philosophical science of actuality was not able to satisfy philosophical consciousness. The dualism of truth and actuality, of spirit and impulse, of the impotence of the spirit the recalcitrant power of the actual, posed a problem rather than solved it. Hence the time was ripe for a more radical approach to philosophizing, which was introduced by Heidegger and by Jaspers's "philosophy of existence."

II

If in the quiet and seclusion of the academic lecture hall the phenomenological movement established a new relation to things and a new interest in the prescientific "life-world," its slogan, "philosophy as a rigorous science," was unable to satisfy the public's need for a worldview. Thus it was the so-called philosophy of existence that gave the strongest philosophical stamp to the period between the two wars.

Its point of departure was the dissatisfaction with the orientation to the facts of the sciences that was the basis of contemporary Neo-Kantian philosophy. The scholastic form of transcendental idealism no longer satisfied a generation shaken by the slaughter of World War I. The limits of liberal cultural consciousness became evident in many areas, for example, in theology, psychiatry, and sociology. Above all else, it was reflection on the Danish philosopher Kierkegaard, the religious author and critic of speculative idealism in the post-Hegelian epoch, that prompted the philosophical critique of Neo-Kantian idealism. With bitter sarcasm, Kierkegaard had asserted that Hegel, the absolute professor, had forgotten existence. "Mediation," that is, the dialectical reconciliation of even the most sharply opposed ideas, takes from human existence the stringency of absolute decision, the unconditioned and irrevocable character of the choice that alone is appropriate to its finitude and temporality. The philosophical reflection that assimilated Kierkegaard's dialectic of existence made its appearance alongside the theological critique of nineteenth-century liberal theology initiated by Karl Barth's *Commentary on Romans* and by Friedrich Gogarten, a critique that turned above all on the immediacy of the Thou and its human claim on the I in contrast to the world of liberal culture and its self-confidence.

Karl Jaspers, in his *Psychology of Worldviews,* was the first to give a new accent to the concept of existence in contrast to all cultural forms of philosophizing. For Jaspers, the scientific idea of the liberal age was embodied in the remarkable scholarly personality of Max Weber. The rigor with which Weber sought to eliminate every aspect of a worldview and all value judgments from the concept of science, but at the same time recognized the limits of science in the necessity for science itself to choose its god, prescribed Jaspers's own philosophical task. That task was to mediate the self-limitation of science that was presented here in so exemplary and almost quixotic a fashion in the life of one man with the claim of philosophy, and to perform this mediation on the basis not of irrational decisions but out of the power of thought to make a choice as to which gods one would follow. That is, the task was to choose in the clear light of reason and at the same time with existential commitment the possibilities that are available at any time to existing man.

This requirement was fulfilled especially by the concept of the boundary situation, which Jaspers created in order to advocate a new commitment for philosophy. Boundary situations are those situations in human life in which the individual must choose and decide without being guided by the certain knowledge provided by science. One has to undergo such extreme situations of decision and choice in his own existence, and precisely how one faces up to them, how one acts, for instance, when death is near, brings out — *existere* — what he himself really is. Many things dwindle into indifference in light of such existentially binding thought. But much that is attained by Dasein that is thus thrown back on itself — especially from philosophy, art, and religion — acquires the seriousness of existentially binding truth. Hence Jaspers's philosophy was constructed in three books, which are the three levels of the soul: world orientation, as supplied by science; illumination of existence, as it occurs for the individual in boundary situations; and metaphysics, in which the cyphers of transcendence become legible for the individual in an existentially binding way.

In Heidelberg, alongside Southwest German Neo-Kantianism, Jaspers had a growing influence on the students. But even before Jaspers's philosophy appeared in print, Martin Heidegger changed the philosophical consciousness of the time with one stroke. He unleashed a critique of cultural idealism that reached a wide public — a destruction of the dominant philosophical tradition — and a swirl of radical questions. Heidegger was a pupil of Edmund Husserl and the heir of his master's great phenomenological art. At the same time he had an intensely revolutionary temperment. His first great masterpiece, the first volume of *Being and Time* (a second volume never appeared), preserved the external form of an affiliation with the transcendental phenomenology of his master. But in truth the force with which the entire academic philosophy of the time was attacked here for the first time in generations was not the professorial pathos that faded away in the hallways of the lecture buildings. Here the academic boundaries were boundaries no longer. Heidegger was a descendent of the great moralists in the style of Montaigne, Pascal, Kierkegaard, Schopenhauer, and Nietzsche, but was at the same time a well-established and highly successful teacher. The chasm that finally opened in the nineteenth century between the academic and worldly forms of philosophy seemed to close up. And the brilliant scheme of *Being and Time* really meant a total transformation of the intellectual climate, a transformation that had lasting effects on almost all the sciences. It repeated and intensified on academic territory the European occurrence that Nietzsche represented, an occurrence absolutely incommensurable with the concept of "rostrum philosophy," to use Schopenhauer's caustic term.

Whoever witnessed Heidegger's influence in those early years of his teaching in Freiburg and Marburg knows that at that time he had the most powerful effect on every direction of scholarly research. In him too there was an existential passion, an emanation of intellectual concentration, that made everything that preceded it seem feeble. Indeed, it was far more powerfully true of Heidegger because it appeared in a more direct way than it did in Jaspers's literary form. One could actually recall the romantic furioso of Van Gogh, whose letters appeared at that time and made a deep impression on the young Heidegger. And in fact, those letters gave representative expression to the life-feeling of the epoch. Just as might have been the case in fifth-century Athens when the young, under the banners of the new sophistic and Socratic dialectic, vanquished all conventional forms of authority, law, and custom with radical new questions, so too the radicalism of Heidegger's inquiry produced in the German universities an intoxicating effect that left all moderation behind.

Today, with the distance of decades, the philosophical impulse that Heidegger represented no longer has the same infatuating relevance. It has penetrated everywhere and works in the depths, often unrecognized, often barely provoking resistance; but nothing today is thinkable without it. The philosophical standpoint of *Being and Time* could be interpreted very easily in terms of the Kierkegaardian concept of existence, and in fact it has been so interpreted. Hence in the 1920s and in the early 1930s, Heidegger and Jaspers stood out as the two representatives of German existential philosophy. In *Being and Time,* and even more in Heidegger's lectures, something occurred that Jaspers had called thinking that makes an appeal [*das appellierende Denken*] — a summons of existence to itself, to the choice of authenticity and the withdrawal from fallenness into the "They," curiosity, and idle chatter. In the "resolution ready to live in anxiety" in "running ahead toward death," Da-sein is placed before itself and has left behind it all the forms of concealment of social intercourse, the cultural complacency of bourgeois life, the bustle of journalism and party politics.

Despite its connection with the methodical discipline of Husserlian phenomenology, what occurred in Heidegger's philosophizing was not really basically a continuation and detailed extrapolation .of a program of phenomenological research. To a far greater degree, it was the themes of pragmatism, Nietzsche's critique of the assertions of self-consciousness, the religious radicalism of a Dostoevski whose flaming sign was displayed at that time on every desk in the form of the red-bound volumes of the Piper edition, that Heidegger's thought pushed to their philosophical consequences.

The doctrine of judgment and its founding, the classical analysis of perception, the logical distinction between expression and meaning, but above all, the incomparably exact and penetrating description of internal time consciousness, in which every sense of duration or timeless validity had to be constructed — these were all themes of Husserl's phenomenology that sprang from a basic intention that was purely theoretical. An ontological hiatus separated them from the pragmatic experience of life, perception directed by the practical meaning of what is ready-to-hand, and the temporality of Dasein that lays hold of itself as a movement of existence, which characterized Heidegger's approach. The explication of this new approach began with *Being and Time.* If it had been Husserl's special merit to analyze conceptually the truths present in the natural consciousness of the world and not just those formulated in science, then in an entirely different way Heidegger's transcendental analysis of everydayness did justice to the experience of real life and to the inner decissions that are part of the leading of each personal life. Heidegger's shattering of the exclusiveness of academic philosophy had a tremendous effect, not only in Germany but also in the whole world. He had the speculative power to develop those things that commanded the attention of a crisis-ridden time, and he did it conceptually on the level of the classical thinkers of philosophy.

It is not difficult today, on the basis of Heidegger's later work, to recognize that even *Being and Time* did not represent a philosophy of existence, but only used its vocabulary to deal with the question that both bound Heidegger to the great line of classical philosophical thinkers stretching from Plato to Nietzsche and at the same time made it necessary to inquire behind this tradition. Today it is clear that the inner and indissoluable connection of the authenticity and inauthenticity of Dasein, of unconcealedness and concealment, of truth and error, indicated the real dimension of the Heideggerian inquiry. At that time, however, his severe style of lecturing and the pointedness of his invective made it appear simply incredible when Heidegger described the world of the "They" and "idle chatter" with bitter acrimony and then added, "this is intended without any negative meaning." The existential seriousness that characterized Heidegger in his lectures seemed to suggest that the rejection of inauthenticity and embracing of authenticity was the meaning of his doctrine. Against his will, then, he became a kind of philosopher of existence. Later, when the chaotic irrationalism of the National Socialist worldview began to confuse the situation, Jaspers similarly had to give the concept of reason priority over that of existence, and indeed, would have better revoked the word "existence" altogether. The reception of Heideggerian thought by the French moralistic tradition strengthened this effect, even though Husserl and Hegel were fused into Heidegger's influences on French thought. Today the style of those "years of decision" has lost its magic, but the task has remained the same, namely, to preserve within an increasingly technical age and its antihistorical ideal the great heritage of Western thought that phenomenology and existential philosophy had appropriated with a new passion.

III

The time seems to have come to write a history of the phenomenological movement. On the one hand, we feel a clear distance from this philosophical current that victoriously dominated the first decades of our century in Germany. On the other hand, the complete edition of Edmund Husserl's works has revealed materials that have determined the present discussion to a very great extent. In particular, the great edition of his works in progress in the Louvain archives is a constant stimulus to discuss the contemporary significance of Husserl's philosophy, especially its relation to the dominant figures in current philosophy. When one leaves the Anglo-Saxon critique of metaphysics out of consideration, this discussion involves, above all others, Heidegger — and Hegel. The discussion is currently in full swing, not only in Germany, but also in France and Italy.

Meanwhile, a series of colloquia have received documentation. Hence one cannot say that phenomenology is of merely historical interest. Nevertheless, it is also the occasion for historical recollection and estimation. For the factor that was felt to be common at that time and that brought the most diverse scholars together, namely, the cultivation of the powers of intuitive description and intuitive exhibition of all the steps of thought, can hardly be found today, even in the works of those who appeal to phenomenology, for example, the distinguished writers of France.[1] There was, to be sure, no phenomenological school, but only various groups of scholars who stood in rather loose relation to each other.[2]

Yet this connection was a strong reality, and became ever stronger, so that out of the common research-orientation of these men the characteristic watchword, "To the things themselves" grew, and it found its literary expression in the phenomenological "yearbook."* It was the aim of many — both before and after World War II — to learn the phenomenological approach and to meet its standards. Even among those scholars who at that time stood outside the phenomenological groups, the best minds tried to work phenomenologically. One thinks, for instance, of Nicolai Hartmann. What one tried to learn was almost like a craft-secret of philosophy. A man could say, for instance, that he had "worked with Husserl" or "with Pfänder," just as a practitioner has special credentials because he served his appren-

*The reference is to *JPPF*, eleven volumes of which were published by Husserl and his associates between 1913 and 1930.

ticeship under a great experimental scientist or a great doctor. Yet the question, "What is phenomenology?" was posed by almost every scholar whom we can assign to this movement, and the question was answered differently by each one.

One's own philosophical standpoint always shines through his description of the basic meaning of phenomenology. It is simply not possible in philosophy to isolate a methodological technique that one can learn independently of its applications and their philosophical consequences. Every phenomenologist had his own opinion about what phenomenology really was. Only one thing was certain: that one could not learn the phenomenological approach from books. The *vox viva* acquired new significance here. Thus the literary production of phenomenology is basically rather slim: eleven yearbooks in two decades and almost nothing at all in any of the other journals, which fairly stagnated at that time, not least of all because of the influence of the new research attitude of a thriving intellectual craft that was not concerned for the needs of the day, but rather for the consummation of the epochal goal of a genuinely scientific philosophy.

The only person who could claim authenticity, because of his unique position, was the founder of phenomenology, Edmund Husserl. And he claimed it. Spiegelberg recounts that at the beginning of the 1920s Husserl used to say, "Phenomenology: that is I and Heidegger, and no one else." As illusory as this assertion was, inasmuch as Husserl misjudged the original intentions of his follower of that time, nevertheless such an assertion was not as completely fantastic as it might seem. Rather, it indicates the fact that the majority of phenomenologists had reservations regarding Husserl's development of transcendental phenomenology and its sphere of operation, which Husserl called constitutional research. To many, this development seemed to be nothing more than an inexplicable relapse into Neo-Kantian idealism.

Reaction to this further development of Husserl's was very negative, even within the narrowest Göttingen circle, so that in reality Husserl had to start again completely anew in Freiburg.[3] Moreover, Max Scheler and Moritz Geiger, whom Nicolai Hartmann followed to a great extent, saw basically a

dangerous one-sidedness in Husserl's preference for the subjective theme. Hence in 1914, Moritz Geiger demanded an
"object phenomenology" as a supplement to Husserl's so-
called act phenomenology. It really was the case that hardly a
single person from the *older* circle of phenomenologists pursued Husserl's way. Husserl was not mistaken when he spoke
in this fashion.

In addition, the other pupils of Franz Brentano who were
active at that time as teachers of philosophy, for example, A.
von Meinong of Graz, the creator of the "theory of objects,"
Oskar Kraus of Prague,[4] and others engaged at least part of
the time in bitter feuding with Husserl. How obvious it was,
from Brentano's point of view, to affirm the Husserl of the
Logical Investigations, but to explain his advance from a
descriptive psychology to "eidetic" phenomenology – and,
even more, its further development to transcendental phenomenology – as a wrong track, is taught by Paul Ferdinand
Linke's *Symptoms of Decline in Contemporary Philosophy.* *
Taken by itself, the slogan "To the things themselves," which
Heidegger still repeats in *Being and Time,* may be regarded as
the common battle cry of all phenomenological researchers.
But even this slogan could be interpreted in the sense of a
phenomenological "realism." This interpretation cannot do
justice to Husserl. It is absurd to interpret this slogan as a
turn to the object and to pose Husserl's later development
over against it as a turn to the subject. How could one
understand the *Logical Investigations* from that point of
view? These investigations did indeed refute psychologism
and thus – in the sense of Frege's critique of Husserl's
Philosophy of Arithmetic – they exhibited the mode of
being of logical objects as a kind of ideal being-in-itself.[5] This
exhibition takes place, however, in a return to the subject
through an analysis of the intentional acts of conscious life.
Only in this way did the *Logical Investigations* succeed in
exposing the error of confusing what is intended with real
psychic experiences. To that extent, Husserl's central assertion, that phenomenological research transcends in principle
the opposition between object and subject and discloses the

*Paul Ferdinand Linke, *Niedergangserscheinungen in der Philosophie der Gen-
genwart* (Munich and Basel, 1961).

correlation of act and object as its own great field of study, already holds good for the *Logical Investigations,* even if this mode of investigation was not yet perfected there by an adequate methodological self-consciousness. Max Scheler and Alexander Pfänder also come into false relief when the motto "To the things themselves" is interpreted from the point of view of the opposition of object and subject. For them too, this motto was not a "realistic" departure from idealism. It was defined instead primarily and simply by their opposition to all theoretical constructions that serve a desire for philosophical explanation not satisfied by the phenomena. Typical examples of such construction are the mechanics of the elements of sensuous representation, or the so-called copy theory of knowledge, which, in order to explain the enigma of knowledge, spoke of copies of perceived things "in" consciousness. Or the reduction of all higher psychic acts, such as sympathy and love, to an original utilitarianism or hedonism. Under the motto "To the things themselves," all this found a devastating critique in Pfänder and Scheler, just as it did in Husserl.

It was clear to all of them too that only the return to intentional acts could produce that "self-givenness" in intuitive self-evidence that constitutes the essence of phenomenology. Without the act of intending there is no such "fulfillment" of what is intended. The "things themselves" are not "objective entities" [*objektive Gegenstände*] posited as transcendent, but rather the intended entities as such, which are experienced in the filling out of intentional acts. The things intended are "immediately perceived" there, not represented by signs or symbols. It is certainly correct that Scheler and Pfänder, as well as Geiger, Reinach, and so on, considered Husserl's "idealistic" modeling of phenomenology on Neo-Kantiansim to be devious. Nevertheless, the priority of self-givenness over against everything merely inferred or postulated was common to them all.

Closely connected with this frontal position of phenomenology as it began is the fact that to Stumph and Husserl, the pupils of Brentano, William James seemed to be almost an ally. His critique of the fundamental concepts of the psychology of that time had in part the same opponents as phenomenology. For example, he also opposed the copy theory of knowledge — despite all the brain mythology he maintained. It is obvious that the phenomenological point of departure is polemically oriented in the first place against contemporary positivism, which appealed to Hume, and only secondarily against dogmatic positions within Neo-Kantianism. Over against the dogmatic physicalism of Avenarius and Mach, Husserl's idea of phenomenology claims to be true positivism.[6] This is also where the concept of "reduction" has its origin. He means the return to the phenomenally given as such, which renounces all theory and metaphysical construction. To this extent, the phenomenological reduction is most closely connected with the *epoche,* the suspension of all positing of being, for the purpose of studying the "pure" phenomena. But we must exclude the associations with the concept of reduction that come from Anglo-Saxon usage and should not think of the oversimplifying reduction of phenomena to a single principle, perhaps in the style of a one-sided naturalism or psychologism, or of Occam's razor, that is, the axiom *entia non sunt multiplicanda.*

The phenomenological reduction is something else entirely. Its goal is not really to reduce to the unity of a principle, but rather to disclose the whole wealth of the self-given phenomena in an unbiased way. The concept of "equiprimordiality" [*Gleichursprünglichkeit*] that becomes important in Heidegger has a good, old phenomenological heritage. The fact that the investigation of the intentionality of consciousness goes back finally to transcendental subjectivity as the ultimate source of all bestowal of meaning and thus brings about Husserl's approximation of Neo-Kantianism in terms of the idea of constitutional research has nothing to do with reduction to a single principle. We do not have to make Husserl's question "How can I become a more honest philosopher?" our own, but we must recognize that Husserl's doctrine of the transcendental reduction is not any sort of borrowing from contemporary theories. It was compelled instead by the attempt to construct a hierarchy of self-evidence with systematic consistency. We need not materially accept the systematic consistency that leads Husserl to the transcendental ego, but we must recognize it nonetheless in its immanent necessity.

Husserl's transcendental turn is not at all, therefore, a kind of one-sidedness that at best one must legitimately concede because it is softened by "realistic" features. It is not without humor when the "passive" constitution of the hyletic data is treated under this rubric. If one is already seeking realistic features, how can they be present in the constitutional analysis of "hyletic data"? This makes sense only if we are operating with a totally obsolete "metaphysical" concept of idealism, which Kant reduced to absurdity and which has *nothing* to do with Husserl. It is just as strange when Husserl's constantly smoldering discussion of the problem of intersubjectivity is quite seriously considered in terms of the question of how far Husserl "succeeded" in avoiding the solipsism that was present in the idealistic approach, for instance, in the sense of Leibnizian monadology. We also cannot find correct access to the concept of the life-world, the most powerful conceptual creation of the later Husserl, if we do not understand it in terms of its connection with the idea of the transcendental reduction. Futhermore, we must not fail to recognize that Husserl did not intend the "new phenomenology" of the life-world to be anything other than transcendental phenomenology itself, carried through faultlessly, that is, free of prejudices, without any "naïve" anticipation. This intention is made perfectly clear by Husserl's persistent appeal to Kant and by his claim really to bring transcendental philosophy to perfection for the first time. With an emphatic radicalness and universality, Husserl even goes beyond the Kantian dissolution of the opposition between realism and idealism, so that it simply does not make sense any longer to speak, as has been done time and time again, of realistic elements within his idealism.

It seems to me to be significant that even the penetrating critique that Adorno directs at Husserl from the point of view of the sociology of knowledge deals with its adversary in this manner.[7] The "static Platonism" of the *Logical Investigations* is certainly easily dissolved by the dialectic of immediacy — except that, after 1907, Husserl himself had already attended to it in the most thorough fashion. Only because of that is there a phenomenological philosophy at all. If Adorno had seen this, he would hardly be so surprised at how close Husserl comes later to abolishing reification.

Philip Merlan is surely correct in finding that Husserl's phenomenology does not so much stand beyond the opposition of realism and idealism as on this side of it.[8] His phenomenology does not intend to contribute anything to the clarification of the problem of this traditional opposition, nor can it. But does that not hold true in the end for speculative idealism as well? Hence I cannot follow Merlan when he sets phenomenology in opposition to idealism and sees its limits, to which we cannot allow ourselves to be confined, in the fact that phenomenology, in contrast to idealism, does not contribute anything to the question of idealism and realism. In my judgment, Merlan's observation might apply to speculative idealism as well. It is of course correct that idealism derives its entire content from the analysis of consciousness, without needing the external in any way. But does that not hold true as well for the plan of Husserlian phenomenology? Husserl certainly does not acknowledge the ideal of derivation. He called it "constitution." But did he not dissociate himself with just as much decisiveness from the epistemological inquiry-standpoint that lies at the foundation of the opposition between idealism and realism? Does he not explicitly emphasize the fact that the turn to transcendental reflection already presupposes the possession of the world by the consciousness that is reflecting, so that seeking its epistemological justification would involve abandoning the transcendental position? It seems to me that at this point the speculative philosophy of identity has no advantage over Husserl.

Heidegger's critique of Husserl too has nothing to do with "realistic" softenings. Rather, it presupposes the consistent carrying out of the transcendental thought in Husserl's phenomenology — admittedly, in order to make it the object of an ontological reflection and critique that takes an entirely different direction. Heidegger's ontological reflection and his doctrine of the ontological difference between Being and beings does not mean the distinction made by metaphysics between *ens qua ens* and *ens qua accidens*. This must be stressed again and again. Rather, it means the completely different dimension of origin of the process of Being's manifestation that precedes and lies at the basis even of metaphysics. Heidegger is thus just as far beyond the opposition between realism and idealism as is Husserl's investigation of the correlation of noesis and noema. If Dasein is Being-in-the-world, human Dasein is not thereby to be defined anthropologically. Rather, it soon becomes apparent that the issue is the completely different one of defining "Dasein in man" ontologically. Heidegger's complete reversal of reflection and his redirection of it toward "Being" — the so-called "turn" — is not so much an alteration of his point of view as it is the indirect result of his critique of Husserl's concept of transcendental reflection, which had not yet become fully effective in *Being and Time.*

It seems as if the opponents of Husserl's transcendental turn do not sufficiently appreciate the fact that Husserl also definitely recognized in principle the ideal of an eidetic ontology "alongside" transcendental constitutional research, for example, an eidetic psychology or an eidetic ontology of the life-world.[9] In his eyes, this "alongside" certainly had no absolutely strict validity. If such an eidetic ontology is also a legitimate task of research, it nevertheless acquires its ultimate philosophical justification for him only in the completion of the transcendental reduction, and thus remains subordinated to transcendental phenomenology. But that changes nothing in the possibility, constantly stressed by Husserl, of turning transcendental phenomenology into an essence-oriented mundane science. We should not sharpen into an antithesis what does not lie on the same level at all.

We can see in the distinguished work of Roman Ingarden *The Literary Work of Art* how one may imagine an "ontological" perspective "alongside" the transcendental-phenomenological one.[10] We will not consider here the special significance of this work, which in a certain sense must be called a classic in literary aesthetics. Instead, we will consider its position with respect to the systematic questions given with Husserl's transcendental self-interpretation. Our approach corresponds after all to the deeper, systematic interests that Ingarden had already expressed in the preface of the first edition of *The Literary Work of Art.* His perspective is initially documented in the German language in his contribution to the Husserl *Festschrift* of 1929. In the meantime it has been supplemented by his contribution to the Krefeld colloquium in 1956. For him, the literary work of art has the philosophical value that "pure intentional objects" are undeniably found in it, that is, objects that claim no immediate correspondence to reality at all. Their mode of being can be thought of neither as real physical being nor as ideal being in itself. Rather, their propositional character stands in a peculiar balance between the identity and intersubjectivity of the work and a mere quasi-reality, which Ingarden calls heteronomy of being. His investigation, therefore, is intended as an ontology of the literary work of art.

He follows Husserl in a far-reaching way when he analyzes the multileveled character of the literary work in its construction (sound, meaning, schematic perspective, presented objectivity). Nevertheless, his systematic intention is clearly to call Husserl's transcendental idealism into question, especially in its later form. Logical structures are autonomous in their being just as the real external world is (despite all the phenomenological aspects they offer as intentional objects). The literary work of art alone, however, is not only phenomenologically but also ontologically structured in such a way that "purely intentional objectivities" appear in it. Hence, over against Husserl, whose *Formal and Transcendental Logic* had appeared at the same time as the first edition of *The Literary Work of Art,* Ingarden wants in fact to advance the task of a real ontology [*Real-Ontologie*] through his investigation of the quasi-reality of art, just as this task is also posed by Hedwig Conrad-Martius. In itself, this task is certainly not incompatible with the consistent execution of the transcendental reduction as it was conceived by the later Husserl. [11] (A later and larger work of Ingarden in Polish, dealing with the "dispute about the existence of the world" is dedicated to this task.)[12] But Ingarden's talk of a "purely intentional object," to which a still more real object corresponds, betrays his position outside of "phenomenological immanence," since for Husserl only a "conversion" of the transcendental-phenomenological into an ontological standpoint would be legitimate. Hence even the questions that Ingarden exposes in his contribution to the Krefeld colloquium are directed against the Husserlian "solution" to the problem of idealism.

When Husserl writes "The real ... in the absolute sense is nothing at all ... , it possesses the whatness of something that in principle is only intentional,"[13] Ingarden understands this in the sense of that heteronomy of being which he regards, for his part justifiably, as the special mode of being of what is presented in literature. He does not understand Husserl's idealism, therefore, as a transcendental idealism but rather (all protestations notwithstanding) as a metaphysical idealism[14] — and, in my opinion, he is incorrect.

IV

The real discussion of Husserl today concerns another level of problems namely, the late elaboration of Husserl's phenomenology and especially *The Crisis of European Sciences and Transcendental Phenomenology*. Ludwig Landgrebe (following the precedent of A. Gurwitch) has emphasized the doctrine of the "life-world" (under the provocative title, "Husserl's Departure from Cartesianism"[15]), which for its part provokes a renewed discussion of the problem.[16]

The word "life-world" has found an astounding resonance in the contemporary mind. A word is always an answer. What does this new word, "life-world," answer? What is the question to which this word presents an answer that has been accepted by the general consciousness of language?

If the question is put in this manner, then it is clear that the issue is not the obvious question of how far Heidegger's analytic of Dasein published in *Being and Time* influenced Husserl's thought, or conversely, grew out of questions pursued in Husserl's thought. It is indeed indubitable that Husserl's late essay — the work of a man in his sixties — had the same constant reference to Heidegger's work as it did to the events of the time that had forced Husserl into his inner emigration. Nevertheless, wherever a new word emerges, it always involves more than what is present consciously, on the surface. An objective concern, persistently pursued and shared by many persons, which has not yet been expressed but has nevertheless long sought proper expression, is what alone permits an individual person's arbitrary conceptual coinage to become a word. Hence what had been sought and inquired after for a long time, especially in Husserl's own thought, was in fact gathered together in the word "life-world."

The counterconcept to "life-world," which provoked the first coining of the new concept, is without doubt the "world of science." Indeed, the first characteristic application of Husserl's phenomenological research, through which his inquiry stood out over against the dominant Neo-Kantianism, had been to show that the task of justifying knowledge did not mean scientific knowledge as much as it did the totality of our natural experience of the world. Neo-Kantianism had never really been interested in this natural experience of the world, because for it science was the model of all knowledge. The progressive determination of the indeterminate permitted the object of knowledge to be defined for all cognition in terms of the idea of an infinite task. Thus it was the fact of science and its transcendental justification alone that could interest Neo-Kantianism.

In contrast to this position, Husserl's phenomenological approach meant from the very beginning the posing of a new task. Instead of the constructive mastery of reality, which had its ideal in the mathematical formalism of the natural sciences, the ideal of knowledge for Husserl was intuition, the concrete givenness of what is perceived. Thus he had the "natural attitude" of "immediately living" consciousness in view just as much as the convincing certainty of mathematical deductions. What interested him about the knowledge of the world in the "natural attitude" was certainly neither the fact actually encountered nor even the actual operation in which that fact was perceived. Rather, he was interested exclusively in the "phenomenon" in its essential nature and the corresponding apprehension of that essence by acts of consciousness. He was concerned exclusively with the legitimation of the ontic validity of that which is intended as existing. The transcendental factor in his method is that this legitimation can only be found in the "antinatural" reflection on the constitutive accomplishments of consciousness. The restriction to the pure phenomenon, this *eidetic* reduction, first opens up the dimension of phenomenological questions. For the need for knowledge was certainly not satisfied with the mere differentiation of essence and fact and the appeal to the self-evidence of what is given directly in the intuition of essences. In the last analysis, the appeal to self-evidence, as it might actually be employed in a natural way, had only the legitimation of a belief in oracles, as Husserl himself recognizes.[17] In order to reach more certain knowledge, a further reduction was clearly needed, one that distinguished within what was given in self-evident intuition something whose nonbeing was absolutely absurd and impossible. Only a self-evidence apodictic in this sense could satisfy the need for a more certain knowledge. Only from such apodictic self-evidence could be extracted a hierarchy of evidence that would satisfy the claim of a philosophy to be a rigorous science. In connection with Kant and Neo-Kantianism, Husserl called this further reduction the *transcendental* reduction. It had its ultimate foundation in the *cogito ego* and on that basis was to make possible constitution, that is, the legitimate derivation of the ontic validity of everything in any way.

The fact that with this idea of the transcendental reduction Husserl followed the Cartesian model as well needs no long explanation. Just as Descartes, by means of universal doubt, suspends everything held as valid in order to reach final certainty in the *fundamentum inconcussum* of the *ego cogito,* so the suspension of the general thesis of reality and the movement of transcendental reduction leads in the same way to the transcendental primal-ego as the source of every bestowal of meaning and being.

Thus it was not the idea of universal doubt but merely Descartes's execution of it that found a critique in Husserl. He found a genuine radicalism missing in it to the extent that this transcendental I that resists all doubt is still conceived by Descartes as a "little bit of the world," a *substantia.* And correspondingly, the way from this foundation of all knowledge of the world was not really understood as a transcendental derivation of meaning. Indeed, it is well-known that for Descartes the detour by way of the proof for the existence of God, that is, by way of the labeled store of ideas of the I-consciousness, is to legitimate the certainty of the mathematically mediated knowledge of the world. Husserl found this approach to be dogmatic. In similiar fashion Husserl later criticized Kant's fundamental position of the transcendental synthesis of apperception and reproached the deduction of the transcendental concepts of the understanding as lacking in radicalism.

This perspective permitted Husserl's *Ideas* of 1913 to develop in programmatic fashion the Cartesian way of a transcendental reduction and a universal investigation of the constitutive accomplishments of the transcendental ego by opening up from below the breadth of a foundation for Marburg Neo-Kantianism.

The decisive question in the execution of this phenomenological program was whether the reduction that was undertaken was really radical enough. That is, whether everything that had validity in the construction of the meaning-accomplishments of consciousness out of the transcendental primal-ego really reached its transcendental legitimation, or whether hidden theses of belief still remained undetected even in this procedure and thus made its justification and certainty dubious. Husserl soon perceived that the general suspension of the positing of actual being that he had demanded in the countermove against the positional consciousness of the sciences reached an ultimate, firm ground in the transcendental ego. But this ultimate ego was basically something empty, with which one really did not know what to do. Husserl saw, in particular, that at least two unnoticed presuppositions were contained in this radical beginning. First of all, the transcendental ego contains the "all of us" of human community, and the transcendental view of phenomenology in no way poses the question explicitly as to how the being of the thou and the we, beyond the ego's own world, is really constituted. (This is the problem of intersubjectivity.) Second, he saw that the general suspension of the thesis regarding reality did not suffice, since suspension of the positing only touched the explicit object of the act of intentional meaning, but not what is cointended and the anonymous implications given along with every such act of meaning. But these implications become fatal for the radicalness of the transcendental reduction, since the critique of the objectivism of science presupposes the validity of the life-world without legitimation and constitutive demonstration.[18] Thus

Husserl arrived at the elaboration of his doctrine of the horizons that in the end are all integrated into the one universal world-horizon that embraces our entire intentional life.

Probably at least as early as the beginning of the 1920s Husserl sought to revise in both these directions the standpoint of the Cartesian reduction taken up in the *Ideas* and set out to try new ways for the reduction of the ego that would be free of such deficiencies. Thus in progressive reductions he went through the entire field of the *nos cogitamus*, that is, the way of a transcendental psychology, in order to reach the transcendental ego from that point. But again it turned out that the progressive *epoche* did not suffice and the "psychical I" itself still had to be subjected to a universal *epoche* through which all prejudices of psychological objectivism would be rendered harmless. But above all, he recognized that in all former attempts at reduction on the part of transcendental reflection and in every previous critique aimed at the objectivism of naïve belief in being (even in Hume's skeptical critique and in the critical destruction of dogmatism by Kant as well as in Descartes's doubting meditation), the universal belief in the world as such was not put in question at all. It was always a question of the dubitability of this or that thing asserted to exist, but just such doubting already presupposed the universal experiential basis of belief in the world.

Thus Husserl came to the characterization of the life-world that still functions as valid, that is, as the pregiven world. Its constitution is the task of the transcendental ego that remained unrecognized before this time. Historically considered, he could justify the fact that this presupposition of belief necessarily remained concealed, for as such it is never explicitly thematic but accompanies all intending consciousness in an anonymous way as a universal horizon of consciousness.

An actual history of the phenomenological movement would have to present this complex of problems in its entirety. It would obviously have to begin with Franz Brentano. It was really with him — with his legitimate appeal to Aristotle[19] — that a momentous distinction is developed between

"inner perception" [*innere Wahrnehmung*] and "inner observation" [*innere Beobachtung*]. To put this another way, not
all consciousness is consciousness of an object, or better,
objectifying consciousness. When we hear a tone, for example, this tone is objectively present to consciousness ("primary object"), but our *hearing* of the tone is not observed as
an object and is nevertheless conscious. Husserl substantially
refined this doctrine of the cogivenness of inner consciousness when he overcame the methodologically key position
that memory had in Brentano's doctrine through his demonstration of the horizontal character of consciousness, and
especially his doctrine of the retentional horizon. The concept of the intentionality of consciousness, the constitution
of the stream of consciousness, and even more, the concept
of the life-world, contribute to the unfolding of this horizontal structure of consciousness.

Heidegger's own effort also presupposes this phenomenological overcoming of the rigid opposition between consciousness and object. When Heidegger once referred to the
scholastic distinction between the *actus signatus* and the
actus exercitus — I believe it was in 1924 in Marburg — it
sounded to us like a new watchword. It corresponded to our
own dissatisfaction with Neo-Kantianism that, over against
the objectifying attitude of consciousness and its culmination
in science, there is a much deeper level in human behavior
and the human experience of the world with which philosophy has to do. But only Heidegger's critique of the concept
of presence-at-hand in *Being and Time* brought the fact home
to general philosophical attention that an ontological task of
thinking "Being" that was not "object-being" was being
posed.

The same complex of problems is the basis of the convergence between Husserl's doctrine of the life-world (first so
designated in *Ideas II* in 1920[20]) and the analysis of world in
Being and Time. I mean this statement objectively, not
genetically: who was the initiator and who the follower,
Husserl or Heidegger, remains undecided.[21]

In *Being and Time* too it is pointed out that the world-
hood of the world as such remains unrecognized in all of
Dasein's experience of the world, and it must be designated

as a particular fundamental characteristic of Dasein, an existential structural aspect of it. Viewed from this perspective, Heidegger's transcendental analytic of everydayness appears as the consistent carrying through of the direction of questioning of Husserlian phenomenology. And its result – the demonstration of the authenticity of Dasein, its existential structure of temporality and historicity – can in fact be interpreted as the execution of the program of transcendental phenomenology right down to the concrete horizons given with the finitude of Dasein. Hence Oskar Becker wrote in the Husserl *Festschrift* of 1929:

> The tendency of hermeneutical phenomenology, though not exclusively, is toward the further *concretization* of the transcendental-idealistic position of the *Ideas*, since many horizons that were left still undefined there are more closely secured, above all be means of the fact that the *finitude* not merely of the "psychological" subject but also of that subjectivity which is relevant in the fundamental ontological respect is established with all its far-reaching consequences (death, historicality, being guilty, etc.).[22]

According to Becker, Heidegger himself operated in methodical dependence on the line of problems of Husserlian phenomenology insofar as he applied Husserl's exhibition of the hidden intentionalities requisite for a really adequate transcendental reduction to the concealedness of the "question of Being" to whose exposition *Being and Time* is dedicated.

At the same time, when we study the great writing of Husserl's last years, *The Crisis of European Sciences and Transcendental Phenomenology,* we cannot hide from the fact that Husserl had become convinced that Heidegger's important work was no longer a continuing effort in the direction planned by him. Even more, the great resonance that Heidegger's philosophizing found at that time seemed to Husserl to be a dubious symptom. It made clear to him the dangers that lurked in the mind of the time and how easily his own philosophical task could be misunderstood. The external situation is already very significant. His efforts of years to develop a sound presentation of the foundation of

phenomenology out of the *Cartesian Meditations* – his addresses published only in French – had come to a standstill.
The success of *Being and Time* forced Husserl to a new
reflection, and thus the *Crisis* appeared. As a result of the
circumstances at that time, however, it appeared not in
Germany, but in Belgrade! What had happened? What did the
explicit thematizing of the life-world mean, and the elaborate
attempt to contrast transcendental phenomenology with the
objectivism of former philosophy interpreted as a whole? So
far as I am familiar with the material, I cannot follow at this
point the opinion of those who want to see an "overcoming"
of the foundation in the transcendental ego in this latest
work of Husserl, and to that extent an approximation of
Heidegger's philosophical approach. One generally refers to
the fragment from the summer of 1935 that was printed as
Appendix XXVIII to Paragraph 73 of the *Crisis.*[23] It is
entirely correct that this text represents a kind of autobio-
graphical motivation for the writing of the *Crisis.* But what
does this motivation appear to be? It begins with the proposition: "Philosophy as science, as serious, rigorous, indeed
apodictically rigorous, science – *the dream is over.*" And
further, "Philosophy once thought of itself as the science of
the totality of what is." "But these times are over – such is
the generally reigning opinion of such people. A powerful
and constantly growing current of philosophy that renounces
scientific discipline, like the current of religious disbelief, is
inundating European humanity."

We misunderstand Husserl's words if we take them to be
his own opinion. In fact, they describe a view he did not
share, indeed, one he contested as a fatal corruption. His old
battle for philosophy as a rigorous science, which had led him
earlier to a sharp demarcation against historicism (1911),
appears now, at the end of his life, in a new phase. Once
again the danger that everything will become a question of
"worldviews," and that a scientific truth of the absolute will
be considered impossible, challenges him to a renewed reflection. "Philosophy is in danger, that is, its future is threatened – shouldn't the question of the present task of philosophy
have a distinctive significance in such a time?" Thus historical
reflection is needed – that is the inference Husserl draws

from his knowledge of the danger. But this inference is in no way to be taken in the sense that the great task of philosophy is recognized as really being a mere dream that has ended. Quite the contrary. Certainly under the altered conditions with respect to the breakthrough of historical relativism into general awareness he must ask himself: "What sort of meaning does it have – must it have – for one engaged in philosophical self-reflection? Is his work lost . . . ?" But this question is certainly answered in the negative. It is not the idea of a scientific philosophy that he surrendered, but rather the carefree, untroubled continuation of it that spares itself the trouble of an explicit historical justification. Thus the *Crisis* reflects well a certain change in his former confidence in finding a foundation for philosophy as an apodictically rigorous science in a direct way. And the systematic accentuation of the life-world is certainly connected somehow with his awareness as changed in this way. But does this change really reach its goal? Husserl writes:

> It is the same here as it is generally for men in danger. For the sake of the life-task that has been taken up, in times of danger one must first let these very tasks alone and do what will make a normal life possible again in the future. The effect will generally be such that the total life-situation, and with it the original life-tasks, has been changed or in the end has even become fully without an object.[24]

How is this general proposition to be applied to Husserl's own special situation? Do we have the right to contend that the transformation of his life-situation leads Husserl too to consider his original life-task of founding philosophy as an apodictically rigorous science to be groundless? What does the *Crisis* give as an answer to this question?

When we view the volume as a whole, the principle of its composition is unmistakable. It is concerned with carrying out a really defensible transcendental reduction. The elaborate survey of the history of objectivism serves the purpose primarily of bringing his own phenomenological program into explicit historical relief. A "transformation of the task of knowledge" is achieved through phenomenology. There is no more assumed experiential basis for it. Even that universal belief in the world which, as the natural reflective life of man, supports the ground of experience in every case of doubt regarding the contents of experience must be suspended and must find its constitution in the transcendental ego. To that extent, the method of phenomenology, in contrast to all scientific methods, is a method dealing with that which has no foundation, the way of a "transcendental experience," not an empirical induction. For it must first create its ground for itself.

The historical reflection that Husserl employs teaches him how it was that the approaches to such a radical transcendental reflection had always been diverted from their proper path by the dominant objectivism. This is true of Descartes, Hume, Kant, and of the leading thinkers of German idealism (Fichte!) In Husserl's eyes it clearly holds also for the surging tide of the philosophy of worldviews in Heidegger's work. The principle of composition in the *Crisis* indicates this fact most clearly. In the effort toward a radical foundation of the transcendental ego, "serious paradoxes" whose solution is indispensable appear ever again. "Further considerations will show how great the temptation is, here, to misunderstand oneself and how much — indeed, ultimately, the actual success of a transcendental philosophy — depends upon self-reflective clarity carried to its limits," Husserl writes at the end of Paragraph 42. And in fact the appearance of paradoxical unintelligibilities in the course of further reflection consists in the difficulty of holding to the purely transcendental sense of the reduction to the ego. Husserl's answer, therefore, is: In the last analysis it is only an apparent problem that the ego that is to function as the source of the validity of all being and meaning is itself a part of the world that is first constituted in it. At work here is the power of what is taken for granted in the natural objective attitude that allows the transcendental attitude to be "constantly threatened by misunderstandings."[25] The transcendental ego is not an I in the world. The enormous difficulty is to recognize this fact and really hold fast to it.

This matter appears once again in the case of the problem of intersubjectivity. Once again it seems in order to ask: How can the Thou and the We, that are themselves both I's, be constituted in a transcendental ego? As much trouble as this difficulty gives Husserl, at no time does it dissuade him from maintaining the methodical primacy of the transcendental ego. There can be no doubt, it seems to me, that in Husserl's eyes it is a question of the difficulties he had perceived long ago in the self-referential character of phenomenology, namely that the phenomenological basis of all philosophy in apodictic certainty must itself have application on this basis too. And it is his conviction that these difficulties had led to fateful errors in Heidegger's "hermeneutic of facticity." The extensive background of historical self-reflection that the *Crisis* represents intends to uncover the grounds of such midunderstandings. Husserl's entire life-situation and the original tasks of his life had in fact changed to this extent: historical self-reflection has become indispensable. It has its place in the critique of the critique in which alone the transcendental reduction can reach completion. The *Crisis* attempts to give an implicit answer to *Being and Time*.

We must ask what the concept of the life-world and the objective meaning attributed to it here can settle in this matter. If the old problem of the metacritique from *Ideas I* finds expression here, namely, the necessary extension of the *epoche* to the universal horizon of the experience of the pregiven world (and every such transcendental reduction includes the task of a constitution; consequently there must be "a doctrine of pure essences of the life-world"), then there can be no doubt that now for the first time the analysis of this essential structure of the life-world reaches its decisive application: *It makes possible the clarification of the problems of historicism.* The relativity present in the concept of the life-world as such appears also in the multiplicity of historical worlds already given to us by historical knowledge in a fashion similar to the general world horizon of our present experience of the world, that is, *a priori* in contrast to all the particular details of historical knowledge. To begin with the transcendental ego, therefore, embraces the entirety of possible "worldviews" whose typical features are the object of constitutional research.[26]

Now all these relativities, even our captivity in our own life-world, which has become historical, lose their disconcerting meaning when the *eidos* "life-world" as such and the range of its variations is known. The result of the analysis of the life-world is unambiguously explained: "After all this it is clear that there is no conceivable meaningful problem of previous philosophy and no conceivable problem of Being at all that transcendental phenomenology would not necessarily reach along its way."

Now one may certainly ask: Must the permeation of the transcendental reduction with historical self-reflection, which characterizes Husserl's late work, not assert itself also in the foundational analysis of self-temporalizing [*Selbstzeitigung*] with which Husserl had heretofor disclosed the basis of his transcendental phenomenology? At least one would expect that the essential finitude that distinguishes the penetration of Husserl's thought by historical elements from Hegel's dialectic of absolute knowledge would stand out clearly. In fact it follows directly from Husserl's long-held aversion to speculative idealism that the universality of the life-world is conceived merely as a universal horizon, so that the idea of an adequate apodictic certainty is to be repudiated here from the very beginning. The idea of a gathering of all the past into the "absolute" present of an "absolute knowledge" proves itself to be absurd. Just as the future, which fades away into the uncertain distance, is incorporated into the immediate flow of the ego as an infinite horizon, so does the past, which also fades into the distance. Husserl resolutely draws the consequences from such an absolute historicity. He writes: "World history in the sense of the infinite idea means the idea of the world projected, as it were, into infinity and continued as corrected by the infinity of factually valid representations of the world." "This requires the idea of an infinite historical past that would be corrected in all past presents by the present as totally determined . . . , but then what will the infinite future mean? One would really be amazed if the world in itself thus presumed can have a meaning, and what that meaning would be."[27] This passage indicates how in the course of his thoughts Husserl is compelled to negate the idea of a world in itself as the projection of an infinite consciousness, and to emphasize radical finitude for the sake of the infinity of the future.

One has to ask if Husserl's insight and the tendency toward historical self-justification that dominates the *Crisis* does not call the methodological foundation of transcendental phenomenology, namely, the reduction to the transcendental ego, into question. In order to lend weight to this question, one might think of the role that the concept of life plays in the later Husserl. It almost seems as if this concept of "life" is intended to replace the I-ness of the transcendental ego. Nevertheless, the "life of consciousness" — an expression that Husserl may well have gotten from Natorp anyway[28] and in which an old mystical connotation can be heard — is for Husserl not a level independent of the transcendental ego. Neither in his exposition of the problem of the life-world nor in that of intersubjectivity do I see a basis for thinking that Husserl was moving toward the revision of his transcendental, Cartesian starting point. As the *Crisis* confirms through wide-ranging historical demonstration, both problem areas offer only particularly tempting starting points — constantly reviving "paradoxes" or difficulties — that entice one to abandon the point of view which led to transcendental founding.

Schutz's hypothesis, with which Fink agrees, that the confines of the transcendental ego finally fell away in the face of the problematic of intersubjectivity is in my opinion wholly indefensible.[29] It represents just the sort of relapse that Husserl tried with all his might to avert. It also seems to me to be a mere illusion when one thinks he sees a development from the theory of intersubjectivity in the *Cartesian Meditations* to the relevant parts of the *Crisis,* according to which Husserl transcended the doctrine that the alter ego is constituted by transcendental empathy. The only thing that can be said is that Husserl had marked out a *methodical* priority of the alter ego, of the experience of the thou namely, for the primordial experience of the transcendence of beings as such. In comparison with the experience of the thou, all experience of the things of the so-called external world is a secondary experience of transcendence. But this changes nothing with respect to the fact that the building up of a hierarchy of evidences, the stratification of constitutive accomplishments, has its unremovable basis in the transcendental ego. There is indeed a discussion in the *Crisis* of the primordiality of the psychic community, and the path of transcendental psychology that leads to it has its own legitimacy as an unfolding of the *nos cogitamus*. According to Husserl, however, this level of the problematic once again absolutely requires its transcendental grounding in the primal ego, so that the reductional procedure of transcendental psychology still leads in the end to "my own" life-world.

It is simply an illusion to follow Fink in taking the new dimension represented by the transcendental primal ego (which in a certain sense has really left the problem horizon of the *Cartesian Meditations* behind) to be the problem of intersubjectivity insofar as the plurality of ego and alter ego finds its origin in it.[30] In fact, the doctrine of the constitution of intersubjectivity by transcendental empathy that is expressed in the *Cartesian Meditations* is in complete agreement with this new dimension. It is explicitly designated as the first step preceding that of the constitution of the objective world and the community of monads.[31] Hence it does not seem to me to be entirely fair to the consistency of Husserl's intellectual achievement when one says — as Jean Wahl does, for instance, in his summary of the results of the colloquium at Royaumont[32] — that two tendencies were at work in Husserl that stood in a fruitful tension with each other, the one directed at the transcendental ego and the other directed at the life-world. In truth, no such tension existed.

The really open questions issuing from Husserl's phenomenology do not lie, therefore, as the *Crisis* teaches us, in "difficulties" that result from his adherence to the process of the transcendental reduction. Husserl believed himself the master of these problems. *In contrast to this, the doctrine of the life-world is intended to make the transcendental reduction flawless.* The point where problems that form the real object of controversy lie is the level of the fundamental question of constitution, that of the primal ego itself, that is, of the self-constitution of temporality.

How can we explain the fact that there is still so much controversy over the meaning of "constitution"? We cannot assume that either Fink or Landgrebe — both of whom had such an active part in Husserl's late philosophy — allowed himself to become entangled in the perversity of an inquiry-standpoint presupposing the old precritical and pretranscendental opposition of realism and idealism. Yet if we inquire after the realistic side of Husserl's phenomenology and perhaps refer to the recognition of the hyletic data in Husserl, we obviously stab at thin air. For who thinks that Husserl was an idealist in the sense that Berkeley was?

In my opinion, this observation holds especially for the concept of constitution. Who will contest the fact that the concept of production with respect to the thing perceived can mean nothing else than the production of its valid sense? But when we take Husserl's transcendental intention seriously, the same holds too for the constitution of the life-world and of the other ego. Constitution is nothing but the movement of reconstruction that follows the accomplished reduction. Just as the latter is transcendental, that is, intends no real negation but only the suspension of ontic validity, so too the process of building up out of the accomplishments of subjectivity is not the real engendering of anything, but rather the way of understanding everything that is to have meaning.[33]

In a very interesting address on Husserl in Royaumont, Fink contended that the concept of constitution is one of a number of Husserl's operative concepts characterized by the fact that they themselves never become thematic. His contention is quite correct. But at Royaumont I had already moved on toward recognizing this fact as being at the same time a problem of transcendental language. To be operative does indeed mean to function in an unthematic way, and this is precisely the mode in which what is linguistic functions. In any case, ambiguity by no means comes into the conceptual meaning of a word when it is of "worldly" origin. Like many another of Husserl's concepts, no matter how much the concept of constitution may have been taken from a commonly known context ("production") and applied in the transcendental realm, production is precisely what he does not mean.

What is to be debated here? In his notes on the *Cartesian Meditations,* Roman Ingarden watches especially carefully, almost jealously, to ensure that the problematic of the tran-

scendental reduction itself does not slip off into the metaphysical. He resists the idea that one can completley deny the
old Göttingen circle an understanding of Husserl's transcendental turn,[34] but he himself still raises noteworthy objections to Husserl's concept of production in logical structures.
The core of the problem lies exclusively in the self-constitution of temporality in its primal source of the present. Hence
it lies in that deepest level of the problematic of constitution
for which even the transcendental ego and the stream of
consciousness (the ultimate source of all accomplishments of
constitution) is transcended in the sense that the immediate
flow of the living present, as the real primal phenomenon, lies
at the basis even of the constitution of the stream of consciousness. Only here, in fact, where the issue is "self-constitution," can one ask if constitution does not also mean
creation.

V

The editing of Husserl's manuscripts in the Louvain Archives is clearly a long term task. Not only their dating but
also the ordering of their contents may at present only be
possible in a provisional way. With things in this state, I could
hardly venture to say anything about the disputed problems
of the self-constitution of the "primal-phenomenal present"
if I did not have before me a copy of the important manuscript C21 from the Husserl Archives in Cologne (for which
Landgrebe and Volkmann-Schluck are to be thanked). In
orienting ourselves to this manuscript, we can consider the
direction and limit of a speculative-dialectical interpretation
that pushes out beyond Husserl's transcendental phenomenology. Such an interpretation is given most impressively by
Fink.

It appears to be the special feature of the primal level that
in no sense can one speak any longer of an activity through
which its ontic meaning comes about as a valid unity. What
exists is instead the transcendental stream of consciousness
itself, which is "I" in all such activities, in every accomplish-
ing act. But it too is constituted — and, indeed, in a passive
way. This talk of the flux and of the I clearly contains

thoroughly illegitimate anticipations. Hence it follows methodically that this being of the transcendental ego too must itself be bracketed and brought to constitution. Only with this do we come upon the "primal" present. How is this primal-phenomenality experienced? Obviously through reflection that knows itself to be the same as that upon which it reflects, and knows it in constant iteration. Thus it is not itself time, but in it the continuing stream of consciousness that has the form of being of time constitutes itself.

Here is where the problem lies. By that primal-phenomenality of the ego do we really mean a mere end result of transcendental reflection? Does not the latter only come to be at all by virtue of that primal-phenomenality (so that in this sense a "creation" [*Kreation*] presents itself)? In fact, Husserl asks: Is primal-phenomenality, the primal ground of temporalizing, the primal I, in the form of time at all? Husserl calls it the present, but in an original sense, and consequently, in contrast to the transcendental ego, an adequate self-givenness is to be attributed to it. He asks himself whether this attribution of self-givenness is not absurd. Is not everything that is given given *to* someone, so that the latter is the recipient and not the giver? But clearly on this deepest level of the self-constitution of temporality, where it is a question of the primal source of the flow of the immediate present, a self-relational character that contains no distinction between what is giving and what is given (or better, what is received) must be assumed. Instead, it is a kind of mutual encompassing, as it is structurally appropriate to life – to Plato's αὐτοκινοῦν. But the classical doctrine of the νόησις νοήσεως and the doctrine of the *intellectus agens* are also confirmed here. This constantly flowing primal-present is at the same time a *nunc stans* that contributes to the constitution of its time horizons in such fashion that it functions as a form for everything that flows through it. What is is a primal change. But the primal transformation is not in time, since time arises first of all within it, in that it builds itself up within the capacity of limitless iteration of reflection as a continuity of form. There seems to me to be no doubt that Husserl saw no breakdown of the phenomenological mode of research in this structure of iteration.[35] On the contrary:

The givenness of the primal change in iterating reflection is, for Husserl, an actual result of the "transcendental reduction." I do not see how the methodological foundations of transcendental phenomenology become ambiguous as a result. The primal life remains a primal ego. In answer to the very pointed question which Hyppolite posed in Royaumont as to whether in Husserl there is a basic level that is egoless, van Breda correctly answered: "For Husserl this solution is unthinkable."[36]

The current discussion of Husserl seems to be determined substantially by the fact that the qualitative difference between the naïve-realistic and the "fundamental ontological" objections to this development does not stand out sharply enough.[37] Landgrebe in particular appears to have given reinforcement to the highly confusing talk of a "fundamental ontological realism,"[38] inasmuch as in his own critique he follows Heidegger's critique of the ontological underdeterminateness of the transcendental consciousness. At any rate, we must keep in mind that a "realistic critique" that intends to proceed to a being that is independent of consciousness in principle[39] completely misses the state of the problem. Husserl's *Crisis* should have made it completely clear that absolutely nothing can escape the universality of transcendental reflection — *nisi intellectus ipse.*

We can do justice to this state of affairs only when we do not fall short of the rigor of Husserl's transcendental philosophical consistency. We do fall short of it, however, when we emphasize "realistic" motives in the problem of the *Hyle,* intersubjectivity or in any other problem. With this the grandeur of Husserl's life work would be unappreciated.

Hence it is incomparably more consistent to follow Fink in carrying Husserl's untiring effort finally to achieve the transcendental reduction out beyond itself, and to start from the insight into the essential impossibility of completing the reduction. Fink makes the doctrine of the self-constitution of the transcendental ego in the "primal present" the starting point for a fundamental critique of Husserl's general transcendental path of reflection. For this purpose, he enlists Hegel and his critique of external reflection, thus supplementing phenomenology, as it were, with its hostile brother, the dialectic. In the wake of Heidegger, however, the "absolute intelligibility of Being," which is involved in the concept of absolute knowledge, remains unacceptable to Fink. Hence at the same time he follows Heidegger by applying to Husserl the inner tension and ambiguity (*Gegenwendigkeit*) of truth and untruth, disclosure and concealment. The essential "shading" that is bound up with every thematization, makes the Husserlian attempt at a "constitutional phenomenology" ultimately impossible. The complete lack of clarity of the concept of constitution in Husserl is itself an example of such a shading.

But was it really Husserl's "shipwreck" on the limiting problems of a transcendental foundation that first provided the new stimulus? Is Heidegger's "hermeneutic of facticity" (which is an answer to this stimulus) really only an answer to such a transcendental limiting problematic, so that, as another answer, one could also introduce Hegel's philosophy of identity, his critique of external reflection and his dialectical negation of "Being"?

In truth, fundamental differences *in content* make their appearance very early and testify to Heidegger's own approach. First of all, there is the persistent dispute concerning the nature of perception. Heidegger's doctrine of the priority of being-ready-to-hand (and also what is similarly expressed in Scheler's reception of pragmatic motives) contradicts the entire order of the building up and founding of intentionalities that Husserl erected in his phenomenology. The return to prepredicative experience that Husserl undertook does not seem to be free from the structure of predication.[40] Is Heidegger not right when he sees an *ontological* prejudice operative in Husserl's foundational structure, a prejudice that finally affects the whole idea of a constitutive phenomenology? To be sure, Husserl can get around this criticism by saying that every sense of being must itself be capable of exhibition in constitutional analysis. Even when "Dasein" comes into the discussion it can only be a matter of the *eidos* "Dasein." All problems of constitution originate precisely in the self-constitution of temporality, in that final limiting stratum of the "primal phenomenal present" which alone, according to Husserl, is not "being" in the same sense as everything that is constituted as being. But Heidegger means more: "The 'essence' of Dasein lies in its existence."[41] This Heideggerian proposition emphasizes not only the ecstatic nature of existence but also the transformation in the meaning of "essence" that is given with the question of Dasein's mode of being. The appeal to the *eidos*-character of Dasein is not sufficient.

Furthermore, the total self-presence involved in the concept of the primal-phenomenal present already fixes every meaning of Being, even the meaning intended in "historicity." The essence of historicity is indeed "the history of the cutting-off of finite mankind's development as it becomes mankind with infinite tasks."[42] But it is self-evident for the Husserlian concept of phenomenology that this history has a *telos,* the knowledge of which constitutes the meaning of phenomenological self-reflection. Teleology remains determinative even when Husserl recognizes the "infinity" of this task, thus repudiating Hegel's absolute knowledge.[43] That is a result which is well known from the history of metaphysics. It indicates that the concept of being that dominates the entire standpoint of Husserl's inquiry is that of metaphysics. Even the final level, the level of the self-constitution of temporality, remains within this horizon as the αὐτοκινοῦν or the νόησις νοήσεως.

I see no possibility here for appealing to Heidegger's doctrine of the interinvolvement of disclosure and concealment. For the Heideggerian doctrine of the "inner tension and ambiguity of truth" does not lie at all in the direction of transcendental philosophical reflection. Thus it does not have its warrant in any way in the paradox of the self-constitution of the primal present as the foundation of the transcendental ego. Rather, it is the essence of metaphysics (i.e., thinking of truth as disclosedness and of Being as the presence of what is present) that still determines Husserl's transcendental question. In contrast, Heidegger recognized the concealment that is necessarily connected with the experience that thinks Being as beings, namely, the concealment of that which first makes possible every disclosure of beings as beings — what he called the ontological difference. Hence he came to see the interinvolvement of disclosure and concealment as the primordial meaning of truth. Just as Being is not mere presence, but rather the "clearing" itself, so in the primordial dimension of the "question of Being," truth turns out to be an event. In metaphysics, the "question of Being" is already construed in such a fashion that it cannot be posed any longer.

I do not believe it advances us at all when we try to combine the direction of Heidegger's inquiry in dialectical fashion, as it were, with the Husserlian problematic of the self-constitution of temporality. This is what we do, however, when (with Fink) we take "finitude" to mean only the limit of total objectification, which for its part presupposes (with the philosophy of identity) the nonobjective whole. Ontologically considered, such an interpretation would mean maintaining precisely the aim of objectification. The nature of the dialectic is the capacity to make fluid only what is secure, to break only what is fixed. It is an Eleatic invention. The interinvolvement of concealment and disclosure, presence and absence, which Heidegger tries to think, is not "dialectical" in this sense and is not conceived as a limiting experience of a "primal present" and an "absolute" truth. Rather, it is itself experienced as Being and truth. Forgetfulness of Being is not forgetfulness of the world.

If this interpretation is right, then the task of philosophy in the face of Husserl's transcendental phenomenology is not a dialectical overcoming of "phenomenological immanence," but a constant confrontation with the attitude of phenomenological research. But then just as little does the direction of Heidegger's inquiry permit a dialectical development. Instead, it requires the constant reference back to the ideal of phenomenological exhibition, even if the ideal of an "ultimate grounding," and thus of a systematic constitutional research, founders on its own ontological prejudices. The concept of fundamental ontology, which has become a common term in our linguistic usage, poorly characterizes Heidegger's path and the consequence of that path. It makes us think at once of another form of grounding for philosophy that would be in competition with the "transcendental reduction" attempted by Husserl. As if it were not the "proposition of reason" [*Satz vom Grunde*] and the idea of grounding itself that are called into question, and Heidegger's transcendental account of *Being and Time* had not proved itself insufficient precisely in the task of grounding Being in time.[44]

It seems to me that it is essential for taking finitude seriously as the basis of every experience of Being that such experience renounce all dialectical supplementation. To be sure, it is "obvious" that finitude is a privative determination of thought and as such presupposes its opposite, transcendence, or history or (in another way) nature. Who will deny that? I contend, however, that we have learned once and for all from Kant that such "obvious" ways of thought can mediate no possible knowledge to us finite beings. Dependence on possible experience and demonstration by means of it remains the alpha and omega of all responsible thought.

But the basis of such demonstration is genuinely universal and, if one can so express it, infinite in a finite way. All our ways of thinking are dependent upon the universality of language.

Hence the problem of *language* finally comes to the center of attention. For Husserl (as for Greek ontology and English empiricism), language was a seduction of thought. Bergson regarded it as the "ice of words" that covered over the living stream. Even for Hegel it was more a preformation of the *Logos* than its perfection. It is astounding how little the problem of language is attended to at all in phenomenology — by Husserl or by Scheler.

It is not as if Husserl did not recognize a field of problems here. We cannot avoid the compelling fact that linguistic formation is a schematization of the experience of the world. And in the minute, descriptive work of phenomenology the investigation of ordinary modes of speech rightly play a great practical role — a point of convergence, moreover, with current Anglo-Saxon analytical philosophy, which will occupy our attention later. Naturally Husserl's constructive order of intentional accomplishments includes language — especially after the discovery of the anonymous intentionalities that build up the "life-world." For him, it is an "upper-level" achievement. But the πρότερον πρὸς ἡμᾶς, which it is, is only eccentrically described.[45] This too, it seems to me, indicates a limit to the projection of the task of phenomenological research. To recognize it means already to have advanced beyond it.

Hence from out of the phenomenological tradition, first Heidegger (though at first not with full force) and, after him, Hans Lipps, gave language the central place that it holds in the current situation of philosophy — not only among the successors of phenomenology, or in Heidegger, but in the ancestral realm of Anglo-Saxon pragmatism and positivism as well.

Hence we must still give some attention to the noteworthy convergence of traditions as opposed to each other as transcendental phenomenology and Anglo-Saxon positivism. [46] The connection between intending and speaking (the "hiatus of the word") acquired a positive side in William James, as Linschoten shows so well.[47] But only in the life work of Ludwig Wittgenstein does it have its full effect — an impact that was felt first of all in England. In Wittgenstein, the problem of language is central from the very beginning, but even there it gains its full philosophical universality only as his thought matures.

Wittgenstein's first endeavor was an attempt to construct a logical critique of language that would banish the problems of philosophy as linguistic bewitchments. Wittgenstein made this attempt in the *Tractatus* of 1921 by seeking to develop the neopositivistic doctrine of elementary propositions into an "all-embracing logic, which mirrors the world"[48] by means of a consistent, logical symbolic.[49] A language that "prevents any logical error"[50] seems possible as a conventionally founded sign language. But in all this Wittgenstein was certainly not a positivist in the sense that he intended to solve "our problems of life" in this way. "There are, indeed, things that cannot be put into words. They *make themselves manifest*. They are what is mystical."[51] But that was only the mystical reverse side of his extreme nominalism. Today it seems to us that the dispute between Husserl and the Vienna Circle regarding the true positivism would have gone against both sides. Wittgenstein's self-criticism within the Vienna Circle's critique of language moves in a direction similar to Heidegger's ontological critique within phenomenology. Wittgenstein's unusually casuistic mode of presentation, which very rarely mentions names — in the *Tractatus,* only Frege and Russell, and in the *Investigations,* occasionally W. James[52] — makes difficult a direct application to the situation in phenomenology. But that Husserl's critique of psychologism was also dispelled by Wittgenstein's critique of language[53] is just as clear as it is that Wittgenstein is not interested in Husserl's transcendental reduction and explicitly criticizes his doctrine of the "ideal unity" of meaning, even if he does not mention his name. But the really astounding thing is that Wittgenstein's self-critique moves in a direction similar to the one we have seen in the evolution of phenomenology.

In the *Tractatus* (and in the surviving diaries, which are published for the first time in the German edition) the *thinking* subject is exposed as a superstition, but only to the advantage of the *acting* subject. "The subject does not belong to the world: rather, it is a limit of the world,"[54] or better, its presupposition. This is all very unclear and sounds like Schopenhauer. It is no less unclear how Wittgenstein intends to go from idealism via solipsism to realism (see the entry in the *Notebooks* for October 15, 1916).

We do not find such obsolete-sounding statements in his later work. There language in its essential finitude occupies the central position. Heidegger had noted earlier that "truth is not propositional truth," and he had put the "existential" of understanding (and its objects) on a completely different basis than that of logic and objective science. Wittgenstein's *Philosophical Investigations,* which he had prepared for publication shortly before his death in 1956, also fundamentally criticized the ideal of a "logical language" in its own way and thus shattered the whole nominalistic presupposition of the critique of language. Even yet, however, the critique of language seeks to free us from the bewitchments of thought by means of language. But in the meantime, Wittgenstein had come to recognize that the logical idealization of language, which the *Tractatus* had sought to establish, contradicted the nature of language itself. He sees now that every proposition of our language "is in order, as it is. That is to say, we are not *striving after* an ideal . . ."[55] Vagueness and indeterminateness of concepts injures its employment so little that we can ask, conversely, if language would succeed at all by means of univocality and if it could even consist of univocal concepts.

The "essence" of language does not lie on the surface, in such fashion that a "propositional logic" can seek to pick it up cartographically, as it were. Wittgenstein asks: What is it?[56] That is, what is it actually, in its actual life? His guiding concept now is the *language game*. Everything is in order in the playing of games or the use of words as it takes place in everyday activities. The reduction of all propositions to a "proposition in itself" or to the form of judgment would bring a false hypostasizing into the actual language game that is played, for instance, in ordering or obeying or in the exclamation and the understanding of it,[57] in short, in linguistic life-forms. The question is to accept what is said intelligibly. Even children's games are of such a nature that we cannot go behind their established rules with any kind of superior knowing. Language games, like those of children, have inexact or changing rules.[58] The particular "aspect" in which something is manifested in seeing or saying, the way we "hear" a word with a particular meaning,[59] is as immediately present as is a thing's contrived play-function in children's games.

Thus it is a question of constantly projecting ourselves into the living usage of language and avoiding hexed "problems" brought about by language. To that extent, the old tendency of the critique of language persists. But this critique no longer aims at language as such, as it actually plays, but rather at linguistic idling, that is, at the false transference that is made from one language game into another, for example, from physics into psychology.[60] The false hyposticizing of "inner processes," encountered especially in the customary thinking of psychology, is pursued in innumerable variations in the *Philosophical Investigations*. We may see a certain agreement here with the phenomenological critique and will recall that Franz Brentano's legacy in Vienna may have influenced Wittgenstein too. We have found in Brentano, as we emphasized earlier, the critique of objectifying observation.

Meanwhile, the range of Wittgenstein's new approach goes far beyond the dedogmatizing of empirical psychology. At the conclusion of the *Philosophical Investigations,* Wittgenstein himself points in this direction: "An investigation is possible in connection with mathematics that is entirely analogous to our investigation of psychology"[61] – an investigation that would not be logical![62] It would obviously "treat" the problems of the foundation of mathematics "like a sickness."[63] It would include, for instance, the problems of the "objectivity and reality of mathematical facts" as philosophizing mathematicians consider them. The same thing could also be said from the phenomenological standpoint – though certainly not with so therapeutic and cathartic a tone.[64] And what would be nearer to the later Husserl and his interest in the life-world or to Heidegger's analytic of everyday Dasein than this sentence: "The aspects of things that are most important for us are hidden because of their simplicity and familiarity. (One is unable to notice something because it is always before one's eyes.) The real foundations of his inquiry do not strike a man at all."[65]

These are, to be sure, all convergences in the object of criticism, not in their own positive intention. For Wittgenstein, a "positive intention" would itself be a highly suspicious concept. In the later Wittgenstein too, the issue is always the demythologizing of grammar – one thinks of Nietzsche at this point. A logical ideal language, therefore, is no longer his aim only because such an ideal language itself proves to be dominated by a mythological assumption. As if there were first objects that we consider subsequently how to name – an "occult process."[66] "Nominalists make the mistake of interpreting all words as *names* and thus do not really describe their application." While it was still his positive task in the *Tractatus* simply to designate the primary elements, he now cites a characteristic passage of Plato's *Theatetus,* according to which the letters and sounds – the real atoms of speech – are undefinable. Now, however, Wittgenstein continues with a large "But," and Augustine's nominalistic theory of language serves him as a point of departure for his self-critique. The question that forces itself upon us is whether he could have learned something from the Platonic *critique* of the theory that was quoted from the *Theatetus,* that is, from Plato's *dialectic.*

But instead, Wittgenstein wants to reach such a complete clarity regarding the use of language by means of his language games that "philosophical problems should *completely* disappear."[67] Hence the goal has remained the same: to eliminate "meaningless" words or signs.[68] Now, however, Wittgenstein pursues this goal without nominalistic prejudices when he demands that we accept the "use" of language and only clarify its aberrations, which arise when language *does not work,* when it "idles,"[69] "takes a holiday."[70] An example: "I can know what someone else is thinking, not what I am thinking. It is correct to say, 'I know what you are thinking,' and wrong to say 'I know what I am thinking.' " [71]

Philosophy, therefore, as a critique of language, a "doctrine of language," is a self-critique of philosophy — we could even say it is the self-healing of self-inflicted wounds, similar to the way the *Tractatus* had already proclaimed its self-negation.[72] Should it not be necessary, however, to define the business of philosophy, and the doctrine of language too, less negatively? In the last analysis, are not the concepts of the "use" or "application" of words, of language as "activity" or as a "life form," for their part in need of "healing," as Wittgenstein says? This insight occasionally emerges in Wittgenstein himself: "If language is to be a means of communication there must be agreement not only in definitions but also (queer as this may sound) in judgments."[73] Perhaps the field of language is not only the place of reduction for all philosophical ignorance, but rather itself an actual whole of interpretation that, from the days of Plato and Aristotle till today, requires not only to be accepted, but to be thought through to the end again and again. At this point, Husserl's transcendental-phenomenological reduction seems to me, despite all its idealism of reflection, to be less prejudiced than Wittgenstein's self-reduction. Over against both of them, we must admit that we are ever and again only "on the way to language."

NOTES

1. Cf. Oskar Becker's description of this phenomenological attitude in *Lebendiger Realismus: Festschrift für Thyssen* (1962).

2. Herbert Spiegelberg has perceived this correctly in his historical introduction to phenomenology, *The Phenomenological Movement* (The Hague: Nijhoff, 1960; Phaenomenologica, Vol. 4 & 5). In general, this two-volume presentation deserves every recognition as a source of reliable information about the past, thanks to its painstaking and conscientious scholarship. The author was close to the Munich circle, especially Alexander Pfänder, and his picture of things is naturally determined in part from that perspective. Hence I have serious objections to many of his emphases. However, in my article in *PhR*, II (1963): 1-45, I inadvertently did him an injustice several times by taking his critical observations to be his own opinion.

3. Cf. Royaumont, pp. 329 f., where Ingarden protests sharply against this all too summary assertion, represented by van Breda.

4. Cf., for instance, Kraus's introduction to Brentano's *Psychologie vom empirischen Standpunkt* (Hamburg: Philosophische Bibliothek (1955) which sounds fatally anachronistic today.

5. Cf. Frege's review of Husserl's *Philosophie der Arithmatik,* which appeared in *Zeitschrift für Philosophie und philosophische Kritik* (1894).

6. On Husserl and Mach, cf. H. Lübbe's essay in *Beiträge zu Wissenschaft und Philosophie: W. Szilasi zum 70. Geburtstag* (1960) pp. 161-184.

7. Cf. Theodor Adorno, *Zur Metakritik der Erkenntnistheorie* (1956).

8. Cf. *Royaumont,* pp. 384 ff.

9. Cf. the interesting contribution of Hedwig Conrad-Martius, published in the Festschrift for Husserl's one-hundredth birthday (Phaenomenologica, Vol. 4, 1959).

10. Cf. Roman Ingarden, *Das literarische Kunstwerk* 2d ed. (Tübingen: Niemeyer, 1960).

11. Cf. n. 34.

12. In the meantime, Ingarden's *Der Streit um die Existenz der Welt* (Tübingen: Niemeyer, 1964) has appeared in German. Here Ingarden delineates his standpoint explicitly as a metaphysical one, as opposed to Husserl's transcendental-constitutive position. This work first appeared in Polish in 1947-1948.

13. Quoted by Ingarden in *Krefeld,* p. 199, from *Ideen,* Vol. 1, p. 94.

14. Cf. *Krefeld,* p. 197.

15. Ludwig Landgrebe, "Husserls Abschied vom Cartesianismus," *PhR,* XI, pp. 133-77.

16. The discussion of the problem of the life-world that follows was presented in November 1960, in Cologne, and in June 1961, in Berlin.

17. Cf. *K,* p. 192 (ET. pp. 188-189).

18. *K,* p. 136.

19. Cf., Aristotle, *De Anima* 425b12 ff., and *Metaphysics* 12. 9.

20. Cf. *Husserliana,* Vol. 4, pp. 372 ff. (Beilage XIII).

21. In the final analysis, this question is posed in an altogether mistaken way. Heidegger's note in *SuZ*, p. 38, testifies to Husserl's "liberal" turning over of manuscripts. Such an action would be unthinkable if Husserl himself at that time had not found the sorting out of his own property and, generally, the spectacle of giving and taking between himself and Heidegger to be inappropriate.

22. Oskar Becker, in *Husserl Festschrift*, (1929), p. 39.

23. So, most recently, Landgrebe, *PhR*, IX (1963), p. 157. However, it should be emphasized that Spiegelberg, *Phen. Movement*, vol. 1, p. 77, n. 2, correctly understands the text in question: "He was speaking in bitter irony about the times, not about himself."

24. *K*, p. 592 (ET, p. 392).

25. *K*, p. 183 (ET. p. 180).

26. Cf. Husserl's letter to Levy-Bruhl, given in Spiegelberg, *Phen. Movement*, vol. 1, pp. 161 ff. But it would be a mistake if, because of this letter, the above doctrine were referred only to the mythical-magical "world" and not to all "alien" worlds, and above all to the historical world.

27. *K*, p. 501.

28. From the first edition of Natorp's *Einleitung in die Psychologie* (1886).

29. Cf. A. Schutz, "Das Problem der transzendentalen Intersubjektivität bei Husserl," *PhR*, V (1957), pp. 105 ff. For Fink's agreement, cf. *Royaumont*, p. 268. Meanwhile, M. Theunissen has investigated the problem in his wide-ranging analysis, *Der Andere* (Berlin, 1965). His analysis leads from the "loneliness" of transcendental phenomenology to the foundering of philosophy on "the other person" in general — a contesting of transcendental phenomenological immanence that deals with principles and that lays no claim to being an immanent interpretation of Husserl.

30. Cf. *Royaumont*, p. 113.

31. Husserl, *Cartesian Meditations* (The Hague: Nijhoff, 1964), paragraph 50.

32. *Royaumont*, p. 429.

33. In Royaumont, I pointed out that the meaning of the word constitution already points in this direction. To constitute does not mean to produce, but rather to bring into a constituted state, to bring about, as in Kant's distinction between constitutive and regulative. Of course such a determination is formulated from a wholly naïve, extra-phenomenological standpoint. As Fink rightly says, the distinction between being and valid sense, taken strictly, has no meaning at all in the sphere of phenomenological immanence. But when on this account one calls the disputed concept ambiguous, because it also contains the sense of pure creation, as Fink continually stresses, then he himself makes such a naïvely realistic concept fundamental. In my opinion. he therefore must be prepared to have his opinion tested against Husserl's text.

34. Cf. n. 11. The considerations against the "production" of logical structures – or, to say this in another way, their subsistence in their "ideal in-itselfness," as distinct from structures characterized by "heteronomy of being" such as the "literary work of art" (cf., p. 165-166 above) – certainly betray the fact that Husserl's transcendental idealism is not shared by Ingarden. Accordingly, he does not consider the "painful questions" Husserl raised in his *Formal and Transcendental Logic* (p. 30) to be settled by Husserl's consistent carrying out of the transcendental reduction. Cf. *Das lit. Kunstwerk,* Ch. 13 (this was also clear at Krefeld; cf., *Krefeld,* pp. 190 ff.)

35. A "speculative" development of this line of thought, as presented, for instance, by Hubert Hohl, *Lebenswelt und Geschichte: Gründzüge der Spätphilosophie E. Husserls* (Freiburg and Munich, 1962), would have been rejected by Husserl as unphenomenological.

36. *Royaumont,* pp. 323, 333.

37. This is even the case to some extent in Thomas Seebohm's otherwise excellent defense of the consistency with which Husserl carries through his idea of transcendental phenomenology. Seebohm, *Die Bedingungen der Möglichkeit der Transzendental-philosophie: Edmund Husserls transzendental-phänomenologischer Ansatz* (Bonn, 1962).

38. Cf. Seebohm, p. 151.

39. Ibid., p. 155.

40. Against Heidegger, Husserl's *Erfahrung und Urteil,* (p. 62 and par. 15) resolutely holds to the foundational structure that has "pure" perception at its basis.

41. *SuZ,* p. 42.

42. *K,* p. 325 (ET, p. 279).

43. On this basis, we can exhibit elements of a philosophical theology in Husserl: God as the Logos who bears the "ontological uniqueness in himself." Cf. Hohl, p. 85.

44. Cf. *HB,* p. 17.

45. The valuable analyses that Roman Ingarden gives in *Das lit. Kunstwerk* do, to be sure, deal thoroughly with the linguistic constitution of the work of art, but from the perspective of the "ideal concepts existing in autonomy of being" as mere (partial) actualization of their sense (*Das lit. Kunstwerk,* chaps. 16, 66). The real interest of the author is focused on the "existence of ideal concepts." Only in this way, he believes, is deliverance from total subjectification possible – in the case of the literary work of art as well as in that of scientific work (chap. 60). Linguistically this remains a secondary phenomenon.

46. Cf. also H. Lübbe, " 'Sprachspiele' und 'Geschichten,' Neopositivismus und Phänomenologie im Spätstadium," *Kantstudien,* 52 (1960-61), pp. 220-243.

47. Cf. J. Linschoten, *Auf dem Wege zu einer phänomenologischen Psychologie* (Berlin, 1961), pp. 92 ff.

48. *T,* 5.511.

49. *T*, 5.475.

50. *T*, 5.4731.

51. *T*, 6.522.

52. *PI*, I, 342, 413, 610; II, xi.

53. For instance, "Intending is no experience," (*PI* II, xi), or "The meaning of a word is not the experience one has in hearing or saying it." (*PI*, II, vi).

54. *T*, 5.632; 641.

55. *PI*, I, 98.

56. *PI*, I, 92.

57. *PI*, I, 27.

58. *PI*, I, 83.

59. *PI*, I, 534.

60. Aristotle had already recognized that many philosophical errors arise from false transferences. Cf. *Topics* 139b 32 ff.

61. *PI*, II, 14.

62. Alexander Israel Wittenberg, *Denken in Begriffen* (1957), represents an effort in this direction.

63. *PI*, I, 255.

64. Cf. Oskar Becker's analysis of "mathematical existence" in *JPPF* 8 (1927), 441-809.

65. *PI*, I, 129.

66. *PI*, I, 38.

67. *PI*, I, 133.

68. *T*, 6.53.

69. *PI*, I, 132.

70. *PI*, I, 38.

71. *PI*, II, xi.

72. *T*, 6.53, 6.54.

73. *PI*, I, 242.

10
The Science of the Life-World (1969)

Although the science of the life-world is the most discussed part of the doctrine of the later Husserl, there seems to be a permanent necessity to examine what is novel in this doctrine. Does it open new paths of investigation or is it only a new and clearer outline of the programmatic intentions phenomenology had from the beginning? It is a peculiar characteristic of Husserl's style of thinking that self-correction and self-repetition are indistinguishable from each other. Therefore the introduction of the concept of the *Lebenswelt* wavers between a mere description of the authentic approach that Husserl chose for his phenomenological investigation (and that distinguished him and his philosophical interest from the dominant Neo-Kantian and positivistic scientism) and a new self-criticism that if it did not attain the great goal for which Husserl longed throughout all his work, namely, to found philosophy as a rigorous science, would at least make this goal appear attainable. We may add that Husserl's self-interpretation is anything but a trustworthy canon for the understanding of his meaning. His self-interpretation also oscillates between continually renewed self-criticism on the one hand and, on the other, a teleological self-interpretation that allows him, for example, to pretend that his *Philosophy of Arithmetic* is a prefiguration of constitutional research.

And even the critical objections that Scheler and Heidegger raised against his foundation of phenomenology encounter nothing but his obstinate insistence that they had not understood the real meaning of his "transcendental reduction." That is the only fixed point in his self-interpretation. It seems to me, therefore, to be methodologically required that we interpret the doctrine of the life-world against the background of this permanent complaint that he raises against his philosophical contemporaries.

One must concede, however, that the new word, life-world – one of the few new words proposed by a philosopher that has had a success of its own in ordinary language – has a very broad meaning that expresses very well the specific character of Husserlian thinking over against the dominant philosophies of Neo-Kantianism and positivism. It does not restrict the task of philosophy to the foundations of science, but extends it to the wide field of everyday experience. It is quite understandable, then, that this wider sense of the concept of the life-world proposed in Husserl's later work should be accepted and acclaimed by many scholars who by no means intended to follow him on his path toward transcendental reduction. Rather, in perfect opposition to it, they have used the popular term "life-world" in the sense of turning away from Cartesianism, or at least they sought to legitimate their own investigations as independent analyses of the social and historical world in the context of a phenomenological anthropology. This use is not unjustified, insofar as Husserl himself acknowledged that it is a genuine though secondary task to work out an ontology of the life-world. To do so does not necessarily require that one follow Husserl's own way of transcendental phenomenology and transcendental reduction.

As a matter of fact, it is not only the intention of Husserl's phenomenology to go back behind the whole of scientific experience to the simple phenomenological data, like sense-perception, or practical experience, and to legitimate claims of validity over against the sciences – it is also quite justified that the life-world claims its own phenomenal legitimacy. This field of themes represents a mode of givenness, or better, a realm of original modes of givenness, and it is clearly unjustified to ignore these modes of givenness by directing our attention to a structure of scientific knowledge of the world that lies "behind" them —to an ontology of the genuinely objective world — and to do it because the objective science of nature encompasses everything that is knowable. One of Husserl's first important insights, present in his *Philosophy of Arithmetic,* was to recognize in the example of the symbolic number that there exist no monolithic and dogmatic concepts of givenness at all. What could the concept of givenness mean, for example, in the case of infinite numbers, which by definition can never actually be produced but nevertheless have a well-defined mathematical meaning? In the same sense, the modes of givenness of the life-world must be made objects of intentional analysis and constitutively founded in their character as phenomena without being reduced to the world of "physics." Such an analysis, which follows the correlation between intentional object and intentional act and determines the meaning of the intended by the intention, necessarily entails that the "life of consciousness," the stream of intentional experiences, offers a way of access and exhibition for what is given in the life-world and by no means only for the objectivity of scientific experience. It is thus important to observe that even the first step of Husserl's investigations went beyond the Neo-Kantian task of conceiving the objects of experience in the sense of the science of facts.

Only the analysis of this correlation between intentional act and intentional object is able to disclose the naïvete of an ontology of the world based on the objectivism of mathematical natural science. Such an ontology of the world misses the decisive question of the idealizations involved in its method and therefore floats in the air, as Husserl says. But on the other side, intentions within the life-world horizon also represent idealizations and therefore contain intentional acts that participate in its building-up. It was already the program of the correlative constitutional analysis in the *Logical Investigations* not only to thematize the constitutive intentionalities correlated with objects but also to work out the basic structure of consciousness as a whole, which by its own streaming temporality builds up validity of objects. In this sense, the thematic of the life-world is not completely new, but is clearly in view when Husserl investigates the deepest level of phenomenological research, the self-constitution of internal time-consciousness, investigations that go back to a time before the first programmatization of the idea of transcendental phenomenology.

But later, when the philosophical project of transcendental reduction integrated all Husserlian investigations into one systematic philosophical framework and when philosophy was programmatized as a rigorous science by starting from ultimate founding in apodictic evidence, it became necessary to test the rigorousness and clarity of the procedure to transcendental reduction. It was at that time that the problem of the life-world emerged and that the term "life-world" was created. It is well known that in the *Ideas* Husserl interpreted the new style of scientific philosophy founded in the analysis of transcendental subjectivity in the sense that in it for the first time an idealism of a really transcendental character would be achieved. To demonstrate it he followed the Cartesian method of gaining the apodictic certainty of the *ego cogito* by means of a universal methodical doubt. This Husserlian Cartesianism was very far from the authentic motives of Descartes, as Husserl was fully aware. In particular, it was clear to him that Descartes's universal doubt of the world could not result in a systematic foundation of all knowledge in a new philosophical certainty, but served rather to legitimate the mathematical natural sciences as the real knowledge of the objective world. Therefore the ego, that *fundamentus inconcussum* that resists the most universal doubt, was by no means the transcendental ego, by which Husserl sought to build up the order of evidences and to found philosophy as pure phenomenology. The Cartesian ego was only a little piece of the world that remained after all doubting and by which in quite different theological ways the cognition of the world could be legitimated. Nevertheless, what Husserl gained from the example of Descartes's doubt was the universality of suspending all validity of belief in the world. Thus he developed his own doctrine of the transcendental *epoche,* which brackets and suspends all positing of reality and also the validity of eidetic sciences such as mathematics undisturbed by the claims of modern science, the phenomena, the modes of givenness as such, must be demonstrated and acknowledged in their ontological status by investigating their phenomenological constitution.

The enormous field of investigations involved in transcendental phenomenology was outlined in its full methodical autonomy in the *Ideas* and claimed to be all-embracing. By means of the methodical rigor of the transcendental reduction, Husserl went back behind all the usual philosophical debates about standpoints and worldviews. He felt misunderstood when people expected from his analysis of transcendental subjectivity a decision regarding the usual philosophical standpoints or even imagined they found realistic elements, for example, in his doctrine of the hyletic data grounding sense-perception. And I think he was correct. With no less resoluteness he combatted the confusion between phenomenology and psychology, for all sciences of facts were excluded from the inner field of transcendental phenomenology. Only on the basis of transcendental phenomenology could they regain their legitimacy in the form of eidetic "sciences in a new style." But it lay well within the claim of transcendental phenomenology to provide the sciences too with a new, clarified basis that no crisis could disturb. That was the claim Husserl made in the *Ideas* and retained and repeated in his last work, the so-called *Crisis.*

Certainly Husserl recognized the enormous difficulty of maintaining the transcendental attitude firmly and unerringly. He not only protested to his adversaries that they were regressing into an uncritical natural attitude or that they did not understand the radicalism of the transcendental reduction, but he also acknowledged that the danger of regressing into the natural attitude is always present for everyone. In many of his phenomenological investigations, therefore, he discussed untiringly the problem of intersubjectivity: how can we grasp the constitution of an alter ego by the transcendental ego, when this alter ego has in itself the same character as the transcendental ego? But in the end he always relies on the same unambiguous solution to this difficulty: only on the basis of transcendental subjectivity, in the radical solitude of the transcendental ego — that is, only from the standpoint of a transcendental solipsism — can one legitimate the concept of "we" that is the experience of other subjects, each of which is in and of itself an "ego." To be sure, the problem of intersubjectivity was considered to be crucial, not only by Husserl but also by his school; and many scholars treating this problem postulated a breakthrough and a rejection of the transcendental attitude as a whole. Some of them even argued that Husserl himself had already done so. But Husserl was right in contending that this argument is an illusion. It is only from the side of the transcendental ego and its constitutive accomplishments that the problem of intersubjectivity can be resolved, that the "like ego," the intentionality of the so-called transcendental empathy, can be understood. It is curious enough that a mere object of perception, a corporeal thing, is only able to become an alter ego by means of a form of idealizing apprehension. Husserl acknowledged explicitly that the problem of intersubjectivity did not receive sufficient consideration within the framework of his appropriation of Cartesian doubt. He therefore dedicated numerous papers to invalidating all the objections to his theory of transcendental reduction that followed from this point. But it seemed to him absolutely certain that there was no real danger here to his foundation of philosophy as a rigorous science.

The same holds for the problem of the life-world. Nevertheless, even more than the problem of intersubjectivity, this problem remains alive and unsettled in Husserl's later works. What exactly was the problem? Husserl recognized it in a double form: in the form of a self-criticism directed against his own description of the transcendental reduction in the *Ideas* and also in another form, one in which the problem of the life-world is entangled in peculiar fashion with the transcendental foundation of philosophy. To be sure, in the end he contends that the entanglement of the problem of the life-world with the transcendental reduction can be resolved and that it appears as irresolvable only as long as the way of reduction is not worked out exactly. But he came increasingly to recognize that the problem of the life-world contained special difficulties and paradoxes for the working out of the reduction.

From this point on, he found a rigorous consideration of the historical world unavoidable. In his famous *Logos* article of 1911, which marked the beginning of his philosophical program, he recognized *Weltanschauungsphilosophie* as a second danger equal to that of a naïve and unreflective naturalism. In it he saw the danger of an impatient demand for hasty philosophical decisions, a confusing relativism, and, as a result, "skepticism and weariness." The terrible convulsions of World War I had a personal impact on him, not only in the loss of one of his şons, but also in the dissolution of the Hapsburg Empire and separation from Moravia, his native land. Soon thereafter, other events claimed his attention: the collapse of popular idealism, the rise of dialectical theology, and the emergence of Scheler, Jaspers, and Heidegger. The deep earnestness of his basically unpretentious and innocent personality was focused from then on upon the single question: How can I become a worthy philosopher? A philosopher for him was a self-thinker, a man who sought to give an ultimate account for all his thoughts and convictions, beginning with the basic problems of science (Husserl was a mathematician) but extending to all the problems of human life, and a man for whom every uncontrolled and unproven conviction must appear as a loss of his own inner self-confidence. It was in the context of this lifelong quest for a final self-justification in this sense that the demons of historicism and the skepticism it involved continued to disquiet him. In the explanation of the life-world he hoped to find the way to a final clarity and the beginning of a new honesty and rationality that would fundamentally transform all future generations of man.

He began by acknowledging a mistake he had made in the construction of philosophy as a rigorous science, that is, in his carrying out of the transcendental reduction — a mistake that had as its consequence the demands of *Weltanschauungsphilosophie* that were threatening to burst the dams of responsible scientific thinking. In his *Ideas* he believed that by the bracketing of all posited reality, of all objects of science, he had reduced what is not objective, the field of pure subjectivity and apodictic evidence. He did not realize that in the bracketing of all objects in the world by the suspension of the general thesis of reality, the belief in the world as such, in the horizon-intentionality of the world antecedent to every positing of entities, was not also suspended — and that meant precisely that uncontrolled prejudices might slip into the constitutional research that claimed to build up every objective validity by starting with transcendental subjectivity. It was not really a pedantic desire for absolute precision and rigorousness that directed the reductional procedure and discovered an incidental mistake. This mistake would be a fatal one. For the horizon of the life-world in which life goes on unquestioningly and that is never an object by itself, represents a cardinal problem for any philosopher. Clearly, he himself, as the one who engages in transcendental reflection, is surrounded by this horizon of the world without ever questioning it. One look at such fields of investigation as ethnology or history informs us that spaces and times produce highly different life-worlds in which highly different things pass as unquestioningly self-evident.

Of course it seems to be the way of science to recognize the objective facts and the objective laws and to make them controllable and at the disposal of everyone. Here alone does truth seem to reside. But the way of scientific investigation follows quite different aims posed by deliberate decisions that go beyond the natural self-givenness of the life-world and involve a specific idealization or mathematical description of the world. In this respect the bracketing of the scientific cognition of facts by the *epoche* presupposes the validity of the life-world dimension of pure self-givenness; but "now we are embarrassed as to what else could be claimed scientifically as established for everyone and for all time," writes Husserl in the *Crisis*. The word "now," of course, means here not "now after the first *epoche*," but "now after we have recognized the manifoldness and the relativity of life-worlds and their priority for all scientific objectivity." In this sense, the thematic insight into the basic validity of the life-world, which as such was not perfectly new, involves nevertheless the emergence of new problems. Certainly the subjective relativity of life-worlds may be analyzed in its universal structure and the *a priori* of a life-world, a universal *a priori,* can be disclosed as one that by no means is the objective *a priori* of the traditional metaphysics or the sciences but that grounds all the sciences because as *Bodengeltung,* as basic validity, it precedes every science, including logic. Is it not a new fundament for all truth and does it not displace the transcendental ego?

When we read the explicit summary of the new role of transcendental reduction that Husserl gives in the *Crisis* (it is the only one we possess), we are astonished to find that the old, well-known problems and insights of the earlier program have returned, though in a somewhat altered form. The analysis of the *a priori* of the life-world and its methodical founding involves a change of attitude that is none other than the familiar transcendental *epoche* of the *Ideas.** What is new in the new description and differs from the older Cartesian way of graded doubting or "graded reduction" is that the turn of attitude is achieved all at once in its totality. Every graded bracketing of validities would only occupy the universal ground in another way but would not suspend its validity.

It is true that the thematizing or bracketing of the basic validity of the life-world is a new aspect of the transcendental investigation of the autonomous realm of "experiences," since what comes into view is precisely the universal structure of the manifold life-worlds with their changing horizons. Or we might also say that the *edios* "life-world" persists in all forms of the life-world. The way through the life world is not only a "new" way of reduction but an important new insight insofar as the transcendental ego to which the reduction also leads proves to be the solution to an otherwise insoluable difficulty. This difficulty consists in the fact that the universal horizon of the life-world also necessarily embraces transcendental subjectivity. As a matter of fact the life-world manifests itself in its subjective and relative structure. The immediate living in "the" world, however, in one world that

---

*It should be noted that the title of paragraph XXXVIII, whoever its author may be, is erroneous. There are not "two fundamental modes of thematizing the life-world," but the unthematic validity of the horizon of the life-world as opposed to the thematization of it by a universal turn of interest — an *Interessenwendung.*

claims to be essentially singular, proves to be ambiguous since it encompasses a variable wealth of modes of givenness. The world is never self-given; it is only the pole of objectivity, that is, it remains functional as a polar direction in the ever-continuing advance and disclosure of life-world experience. In this way, the *epoche*, that is, the deliberate thematization of it, reveals the transcendental subject-object correlation in its purity.

But what is involved here with all its mysterious implications? What is this world-constitutive subjectivity that is itself a part of this world? It is we, the human beings for whom this world is valid. We are many egos among whom I am one ego. It is necessary to clarify this dimension of intersubjective experience of the world by constitutive analysis. One can investigate all these modes of givenness. For example, what is an acquaintance? What common horizon of the life-world is involved and presupposed in the phenomenon of having acquaintances? A whole series of constituent elements: being present to others and having others present to oneself, a circle of acquaintances with the open possibility of its expansion, internal levels of closer and more distant acquaintances, of friends and enemies. Furthermore, there is the anonymous horizon of society with all its patterns and rules with which one is familiar and which is nevertheless quite a different thing from the circle of one's own acquaintances. It is the world itself that is concretized in such intersubjective experiences: it, and not an "objective" world mathematically describable *a priori,* is *the* world.

Even if we realize all these things, and consider that, like myself, every I has the possibility of freely deciding to adopt the change of attitude involved in the *epoche* and to investigate this transcendental *a priori* of correlations — and thus that transcendental subjectivity permits and even demands a transcendental community — we still cannot escape the paradox that the world-constitutive subjectivity, though it may be a manifold of such constitutive subjectivities, is a part of the world constituted by these subjectivities and therefore brings into play all the special subjective, relative characters of the personal horizon that distinguishes the Negroes of the Congo or Chinese farmers, for example, from Professor Husserl. In light of the unsuspendably specific character of the pregiven horizons of the life-world, how is phenomenology as a "rigorous science" possible at all?

When we follow the text of the *Crisis,* the solution of the problem explained there seems neither new nor problematic — it is the old answer that the transcendentally functioning subjectivity of the ego, by which belief in the world is constituted, may not be confused with the ego that is a part of the world and is constituted with all its experiences of the world. That which constitutes all the forms of world, for example, the world of dreams, the world of children, the world of animals, historical worlds, the problems of birth and death, the problem of the sexes, is not one ego beside others and is not in the world as one of its parts, but functions only as the ultimate functioning ego in all its absolute apodicticity but also in its unique philosophical solitude.

But it is not the text of the article alone that is the source here — though this source is unclear enough, since the discussion of newly arising difficulties always interrupts the stream of thinking. Besides this text (which was never completed) there exists a series of articles and notes from the same period that give the correct picture of what it is that concerns Husserl and drives him on. But the composition of the *Crisis* itself confirms it also. Husserl speaks almost apologetically of historical investigations that became unavoidable with his recognition of the great wealth of subjective-relative lifeworlds.

The historical investigation that he undertakes in this respect concerns the origins of scientific objectivism in the physics of Galileo, who was fully aware of the specific problematic and idealization grounding the natural sciences. Husserl's analysis is a genetic ideal-typical construction and treats Descartes, Hume, and Kant under the norm of the ultimate founding of transcendental phenomenology, especially as it pertains to the life-world. Admittedly, the overlooking of the life-world and the lack of radicalness in Kant's transcendentalism and in Neo-Kantianism comes from the narrowness of their concept of scientific experience, but does it follow from this that the new thematic of the life-world cannot be investigated apart from historical clarifications?

This conclusion is by no means the case. When Husserl describes the *eidos* "life-world" in such fashion that "it takes into account all imaginable possibilities that are included in the horizon or into which the horizon can be resolved in its explications," what is implied is "the problem of the idealization of the world of life."* But does this point the way to historical investigations, for which Husserl was poorly equipped? It is certainly the case that penetration into these life-world horizons cannot avoid beginning by uncovering the style of the present life-world and in the end thinking the world "in its concrete and infinite historicity." ** But when we read, "All possible worlds are variants of the world which is valid for us," or that the world is built up only as a "perpetually streaming" constituted something, in the sense of an infinite idea, it means certainly that the life-world, because it is an "idea," is not the world itself that constructs itself in a continually streaming change by a continuous series of corrections, nor can it ever be the object of a science in the traditional sense of objective science. Precisely this un-questioning recognition of the horizon of validity of objective science is the error that is uncovered only in light of the life-world in which it is grounded. The life-world is in princi-ple an intuitively given world, given, of course, only in the flowing and fluctuating of its streaming horizon, while the world of science has rather the symbolic givenness of a logical substruction that can no more be given by itself than the infinite series of numbers.†

Thus the life-world has the universal structure of a finite, subjective-relative world with indeterminately open horizons. By starting from our own finite life-world and our historical recollection of its well-defined variations since classical Greece and by limiting the objective *a priori* of the world of science, we can disclose the life-world in its validity. But can it be doubted that the *a priori* of the life-world too becomes accessible in the old phenomenological fashion by varying and methodically changing our examples?†† The very self-

*K, p. 499.
**K, p. 500.
†K, p. 131 (ET, p. 127).
††Cf. K, p. 383 (ET, p. 375).

interpretation of the historical way that Husserl uses in his analysis of Galileo, written in 1936, treats the starting point in his own life-world merely as his access to the *aeterna veritas*,* and it certainly takes a firm grasp of the transcendental meaning of the ego — as the pure working ego [*Vollzugs-Ich*] — to disentangle the paradoxes that result from the continuing validity of the life-world for every imaginable I. The text of the article makes that sufficiently clear.

Nevertheless, the differentiation of the science of the life-world from the objective science that has determined the way of human civilization from the time of the Greeks is not an arbitrary one. For objective science is a factor in our own life-world. It is a factor that can be understood by historical exploration of its origin and its limits of validity, and the prejudices involved in it can be overcome. Rigorous science in the sense that the young Husserl professed and never revoked may indeed be science, but a new style of science, namely a universal account and self-examination based on a change of attitude and certainly not derived from the idea of objective science but from the situational cognition involved in the direct form of life-interests. This is nothing new. But one must concede that in a certain sense Husserl's own lifelong task changed the moment he entered the way of historical self-clarification, thematizing the personal life-world presuppositions of philosophizing. This way is presented in the *Crisis*. Nevertheless, without any doubt this new way leads to the old goal of transcendental phenomenology, a goal that is firmly based in the transcendental ego (and its self-constitution as ego). This way alone is rigorous science, clearly not in the traditional sense of science or traditional philosophy, but in the sense of a new will to live, "to become acquainted with oneself in one's former and predetermined future being.**But this aim is the old one of an ultimate and absolute self-cognition, and in it one hears the old familiar tones. The life-world in all its flexibility and relativity can be the theme of a universal science, but not, of course, as a general theory in the form of traditional philosophy or traditional science.†

*K, p. 385 (ET, p. 377).
**K, p. 472.
†K, p. 462 (ET, pp. 382-383).

Furthermore, the appendices and the preface planned for the *Crisis* make it clear enough that external, contemporary reasons led Husserl, after the general discovery of the *a priori* of the life-world and its historicity, to attach historical considerations to this "new way of transcendental reduction." Their purpose is to oppose the spirit of the time and the historical skepticism it entailed. The names of Scheler and of Heidegger are mentioned* and many reflections are concerned with the right use of historical studies. But here too the result is no different than what we find in all the other ways of Husserl's thinking: transcendental phenomenology (and the transformation of philosophy into phenomenology), is the final meaning of the history of philosophy.

To summarize all the texts published in the sixth volume of the *Husserliana*, Husserl would agree with Oskar Becker, who formulated it long ago, namely, that the contribution of *Being and Time* to the problematic was restricted to the "fixing of horizons" of historical existence left open by Husserl himself. And the claim of rigorous science remains untouched. Self-reflection culminates in a knowledge for everyone, and, Husserl adds proudly, in a "universal praxis" of humanity that is ready to be led consciously by phenomenology.**

Really? Is this the way to bridge the growing gulf between practical, political judgment and the anonymous validity of science? Can phenomenology prescribe and determine the ways of men in the "life-world" by recommending that they follow the philosopher, who finds his own justification in surveying the complex relations between the "practical knowledge" that underlies and determines human activities in the life-world and the proud and rigorous science — science "in a new style" — that is grounded in transcendental phenomenology? It was the ultimate aim of the lifelong thinking of Husserl to become a worthy philosopher. And perhaps this goal seemed to him to be attainable through his insight into the mutual interweaving of the basic reality of the life-world and the speculative, ultimate grounding in the transcendental ego. Whoever will become a philosopher must give an account

*K, p. 439.
**K, p. 503.

of all his prejudices and all his self-evident assumptions, and his "Sitz im Leben" is determined by this requirement as his own unique act.

What I am alluding to here is the problem of the self-referential character of phenomenology, a problem Husserl himself reflected upon. It became entangled, however, in the dubious question of science and praxis "in a new style" that is described above. Actually it was only in Heidegger's ontological critique of the concepts of subjectivity and objectivity that we acquired the philosophical means for uncovering the illusion that persisted undetected in Neo-Kantianism, and not in it alone. It is the illusion that from science — in whatever style — rational decisions can be derived that would constitute a "universal praxis." Even if Heidegger's own question aimed in an altogether different direction and cripples the relation of philosophy to the sciences in a dangerous way, we are nonetheless indebted to him for rehabilitating the "modes of knowledge" implied in Aristotle's concept of *phronesis* and in his critique of Plato's knowledge of the good, a tradition that, as *philosophia practica,* continued all the way into the eighteenth century before losing its legitimacy. It is a mistake to consider the knowledge that is behind our practical decisions nothing other than the application of science — no matter how much the application of science enters into our practical knowledge. In light of this fact, the notion of the "life-world" has a revolutionary power that explodes the framework of Husserl's transcendental thinking. What confronts us here is not a synthesis of theory and practice nor science in a new style, but rather the prior, practical-political limitation of the monopolistic claims of science and a new critical consciousness with respect to the scientific character of philosophy itself. As early as the prolegomena to his *Logical Investigations* (1900), a certain ambiguity is present in Husserl's notion of the application of science. If the application of science were simply the problem of how, with the help of science, we might do everything we can do, then it is certainly not the application we need as human beings who are responsible for the future. For science as such will never prevent us from doing anything we are able to do. The future of humanity, however, demands that we do not simply do everything we can but that we require rational justification for what we should do. In this sense, I agree with the moral impulse that lies at the basis of Husserl's idea of a new kind of life-world praxis, but I would like to connect it with the old impulse of an authentic practial and political common sense.

11
Martin Heidegger and Marburg Theology (1964)

Let us turn our thoughts back to the 1920s, to that tension-filled time when the theological break with historical and liberal theology took place in Marburg, to the time when the philosophical abandonment of Neo-Kantianism occurred, the Marburg School dissolved, and new stars arose in the philosophical heavens. It was at that time that Eduard Thurneysen delivered an address to the theological community in Marburg. For the younger of us, he was a first herald of dialectical theology in Marburg and after this address he received the more or less hesitant blessing of the Marburg theologians. The young Heidegger also took a part in that discussion. He had just come to Marburg as an assistant professor, and even today I find unforgettable the way he concluded his contribution to the discussion of Thurneysen's address. After evoking the Christian skepticism of Franz Overbeck, he said it is the true task of theology, which must be discovered once again, to seek the word that is able to call one to faith and preserve one in faith. A genuine Heidegger-statement, full of ambiguity. In speaking these words, Heidegger seemed to be posing a task for theology. Yet perhaps he conjured up more than Overbeck's attack on the theology of his time, for his statement reflected a despair at the possibility of theology itself. What a turbulent epoch of philosophical and theologi-

198

cal controversy was beginning at that time! On the one side, there was the dignified reserve of Rudolf Otto; on the other, the sharp and gripping exegesis of Rudolf Bultmann. On the one side, there was Nicolai Hartmann's finely chiselled thought; on the other, the breath-taking radicalism of the Heideggerian questions, which brought theology too under its spell. In its earliest form, *Being and Time* was an address that Heidegger gave before the theological community in Marburg in 1924.

What Heidegger expressed in his discussion of the Thurneysen address can be traced through to the present day as a central motif of his thinking: the problem of language. No ground had been prepared for this theme in Marburg. The Marburg School, which for decades had been distinguished within contemporary Neo-Kantian circles for its methodological rigor, had concentrated on the philosophical foundation of the sciences. It assumed without question that what can be known is really grasped by the sciences alone, and that the objectification of experience by science completely fulfills the meaning of knowledge. The purity of the concept, the exactness of the mathematical formula, the triumph of the infinitesimal method – these were the philosophical concerns of the Marburg School, not the intermediary realm of fluctuating linguistic configurations. Even when Ernst Cassirer brought the phenomenon of language into the program of Marburg Neo-Kantian idealism, he did so under the methodological principle of objectification. To be sure, his *Philosophy of Symbolic Forms* had nothing to do with a methodology of the sciences. It saw myth and language as symbolic forms, as configurations of objective spirit, and yet in such fashion that they should have their methodological basis in a fundamental dimension of transcendental consciousness.[1]

At the same time phenomenology began to attract attention in Marburg. Max Scheler's founding of the ethics of material value, which was connected with a vigorous critique of the formalism of Kantian moral philosophy, had already left a deep impression on Nicolai Hartmann, who represented the avant-garde in the Marburg School of that time.[2] Scheler had shown persuasively – as had Hegel a century earlier – that it is simply not possible to approach the whole range of ethical phenomena by starting with the phenomenon of the "ought" in the imperative form of ethics. In the field of moral philosophy, therefore, a basic limitation of the subjective starting point of transcendental consciousness came to light. The consciousness of the "ought" could not encompass the entire domain of moral value. But the phenomenological school had an even stronger impact by no longer sharing the Marburg School's orientation to the facts of the sciences as self-evident. It went behind scientific experience and the categorical analysis of its methods, and it brought the natural experience of life — that is, what the later Husserl named with his now-famous expression, the "life-world" — into the foreground of its phenomenological investigation. Both the turning away from imperative ethics in moral philosophy and the abandonment of the methodologism of the Marburg School had their theological parallels. When the problem of speaking of God was reawakened, the foundations of systematic and historical theology were shaken. Rudolf Bultmann's critique of myth, his concept of the mythical picture of the world, especially to the extent that it is still dominant in the New Testament, was at the same time a critique of the total claim of objectifying thinking. Bultmann's concept of having something at one's disposal [*Verfügbarkeit*], with which he sought to encompass both the procedure of historical science and mythical thinking, plainly forms the counterconcept to the authentically theological expression.

And now Heidegger appeared in Marburg. No matter what he lectured on — whether Descartes or Aristotle, Plato or Kant formed the starting point — his analysis always penetrated behind the concealments of traditional concepts to the most primordial experience of Dasein. An early manuscript, which Heidegger had sent to Paul Natorp in 1922, and which I read, attests well to this fact. (It was a basic introduction to the interpretation of Aristotle, prepared by Heidegger, and it spoke especially of the young Luther, of Gabriel Biel and of Augustine. Heidegger would surely have called it a working out of the hermeneutical situation: it tried to make the reader aware of the questions and the intellectual resistance with which we confront Aristotle, that master of the tradition.) Today no one would doubt that the basic purpose in

Heidegger's preoccupation with Aristotle was a critical and destructive one. At that time, however, this purpose was not so clear. The remarkable phenomenological power of intuition Heidegger brought to his interpretation liberated the original Aristotelian text so profoundly and strikingly from the sedimentations of the scholastic tradition and from the lamentably distorted image of Aristotle contained in the criticism of the time (Cohen loved to say, "Aristotle was an apothecary") that it began to speak in an unexpected way. Perhaps what happened then, not only to the students, but to Heidegger himself, was that the power of Aristotle, though an adversary, came to dominate him for a time.[3] Indeed, Heidegger's interpretation took this risk, true to the Platonic axiom of making the opponent's position stronger.[4] For what else is interpretation in philosophy but coming to terms with the truth of the text and risking oneself by exposure to it?

I became aware of something of this for the first time when I met Heidegger in 1923. At that time he was still in Freiburg, and I participated in his seminar on Aristotle's *Nichomachean Ethics.* We studied the analysis of *phronesis.* Heidegger pointed out to us in the text of Aristotle that every *techne* poses an intrinsic limit: its knowledge is not a full uncovering of something because the work it knows how to produce is delivered into the uncertainty of a use over which it does not preside. Then he began to discuss the difference that distinguishes all such knowledge, and especially mere *doxa,* from *phronesis:* λήθη τῆς μὲν τοιαύτης ἕξεως ἔστιν, φρονήσεως δὲ οὐκ ἔστιν.[5] We were unsure of this sentence and completely unfamiliar with the Greek concepts; as we groped for an interpretation, he declared brusquely: "That is the conscience!" This is not the place to reduce the pedagogical overstatement involved in this assertion to its proper proportions, and even less, to indicate the logical and ontological force that the analysis of *phronesis* actually had in Aristotle. Today it is clear what Heidegger found in it, and what so fascinated him in Aristotle's critique of Plato's idea of the Good and the Aristotelian concept of practical knowledge. They described a mode of knowledge (an εἶδος γνώσεως)[6] that could no longer be based in any way on a final objectifiability in the sense of science. They described, in other words, a knowledge within the concrete situation of existence. Could Aristotle perhaps even help in overcoming the ontological prejudice in the Greek concept of *Logos,* which Heidegger later interpreted temporally as presence-at-hand and presence [*Anwesenheit*]? The violent rending of the Aristotelian text here recalls Heidegger's own thematic concerns. In *Being and Time,* for instance, it is the call of conscience that first makes "Dasein in man" manifest in its ontological and temporal event-structure. Of course it was only much later that Heidegger defined his concept of Dasein in terms of the "clearing," and thus disengaged it from all transcendental reflection.[7] Could the word of faith also ultimately find a new philosophical legitimation by means of Heidegger's criticism of the *logos* and of the traditional understanding of being as presence-at-hand? In somewhat the same way, later on Heidegger's "remembrance" [*Andenken*] never allows us to forget entirely its old proximity to "devotion" [*Andacht*], which Hegel had already observed. Was that the ultimate meaning of his ambiguous contribution to the Thurneysen discussion?

Later, in Marburg, a similar instance attracted our attention. Heidegger was dealing with a scholastic distinction and spoke of the difference between the *actus signatus* and the *actus exercitus.*[8] These scholastic concepts correspond approximately to the concepts "reflective" and "direct" and mean, for instance, the difference between the act of questioning and the possibility of directing attention explicitly to the questioning as questioning. The one can lead over into the other. One can designate the questioning as questioning, and hence not only question but also say that one questions, and say that such and such is questionable. To nullify this transition from the immediate and direct into the reflective intention seemed to us at that time to be a way to freedom. It promised a liberation from the unbreakable circle of reflection and a recapturing of the evocative power of conceptual thinking and philosophical language, which would secure for philosophical thinking a rank alongside poetic use of language.

Certainly Husserl's phenomenology had, in its analysis of

transcendental constitution, already gone beyond the realm
of explicit objectifications. Husserl spoke of anonymous intentionalities, that is, conceptual intentions in which something is intended and posited as ontically valid, of which no
one is conscious thematically as individually intended and
performed, which nonetheless are binding for everyone. Thus
what we call the stream of consciousness is built up in
internal time consciousness. The horizon of the life-world too
is such a product of anonymous intentionalities. Nevertheless, not only the scholastic distinction that Heidegger cited
but also the Husserlian constitutional analysis of the anonymous "accomplishments" of transcendental consciousness
proceeded from the unrestricted universality of reason, which
can clarify each and every thing intended in constitutional
analysis, that is, can make them into the object of an explicit
act of intending – in other words, objectify them.

In contrast to this objectification, Heidegger himself went
resolutely in quite another direction. He pursued the intrinsic
and indissoluable interinvolvement of authenticity and inauthenticity, of truth and error, and the concealment that is
essential to and accompanies every disclosure and that intrinsically contradicts the idea of total objectifiability. The direction in which this carried him is clearly indicated by the
insight that instructed us and moved us most deeply in those
times, namely, that the most primordial mode in which the
past is present is not remembering, but forgetting.[9] Heidegger's ontological opposition to Husserl's transcendental subjectivity becomes evident at the very center of the phenomenology of internal time consciousness. Indeed, in contrast to
the role that memory played in Brentano's analysis of time,
Husserl's analysis sought the more precise phenomenological
differentiation of explicit recollection (which always implies
a "having-been-perceived") from the actual existence of the
present that is retained in the process of sinking away into
the past, and that Husserl called "retentional consciousness."
All consciousness of time and of entities in time rests on the
function of retentional consciousness.[10] To be sure, these
were "anonymous" functions but precisely functions of a
keeping-present, of a stopping, as it were, of the process of
passing away. The now, which emerges out of the future and

sinks into the past, is still understood in terms of the present-at-hand. In contrast to this, Heidegger had in view the
primordial ontological dimension of time that lies in the
fundamental dynamic of Dasein. From this perspective, light
is cast on the enigmatic irreversibility of time, which never
permits time to arise but always merely to pass away.
Furthermore it also becomes clear that time has its being not
in the "now" or the succession of nows, but rather in the
essentially futural character of Dasein. That is obviously the
actual experience of history, the mode in which historicity
happens to us. The fact that more happens to one here than
one does testifies to forgetting. It is one way in which the
past and passing away demonstrate their reality and power.
Heidegger's thought clearly pushes out beyond the transcendental philosophical direction of reflection that, with the
help of Husserl's anonymous intentionalities, had thematized
these structures of temporality as the consciousness of internal time and its self-construction. In fact, in the end, the
critique of the ontological prejudice involved in the Aristotelian concept of being and substance, and in the modern
concept of the subject, necessarily brought about the dissolution of the idea of transcendental reflection itself.

This *actus exercitus* in which reality is experienced in a
quite unreflective way — for example, the experience of the
tool in the inconspicuousness of its actual use, or of the past
in the inconspicuousness of its receding — is not transformed
into a signified act without a new concealment. The upshot
of Heidegger's analysis of Dasein as being-in-the-world was
rather that the being of beings experienced in this way, and
especially the worldliness of the world, is not encountered
objectively. Rather, it conceals itself in an essential way.
Being and Time had already discussed the holding-in-itself of
the ready-to-hand [*Ansichhalten des Zuhandenen*] upon
which "being-in-itself" [*Ansichsein*] — unexplainable in
terms of being-present-at-hand — ultimately rests.[11] The
being of the ready-to-hand is not simply a concealment and
concealedness whose disclosure and disclosedness is at issue.
Its "truth" — its authentic, undisguised being — obviously lies
precisely in its inconspicuousness, unobtrusiveness, inob-
stinacy. Here already in *Being and Time* were hints of a

radical abandonment of the "clearing" and the "disclosedness" that were oriented toward the self-understanding of
Dasein. For even if this holding-in-itself of the ready-to-hand
is finally founded in Dasein as the ground [*Worumwillen*] of
every involvement, it is nevertheless clear as regards being-in-
the-world itself that its "disclosedness" is not a total transparency of Dasein, but entails instead an essential domination
of indefiniteness.[12] The holding-in-itself of the ready-to-hand
is not so much a withholding and concealment as it is a
being-included and being-saved in the world-relation in which
it has its being. The inner tension in which "disclosure"
stands not only with concealment [*Verbergung*] but also
with saving [*Bergung*] also probes, in the final analysis, the
dimension in which language appears in its versatile being and
can be of use to the theologian in his understanding of the
Word of God.

In the realm of theology too the concept of self-understanding experienced a corresponding transformation. The
self-understanding of faith — the main concern of Protestant
theology — clearly cannot be grasped appropriately through
the transcendental concept of self-understanding. We are acquainted with this concept from transcendental idealism.
Fichte, especially, proclaimed that his *Wissenschaftslehre* had
consistently carried through the transcendental idealism that
understands itself. One recalls his critique of Kant's concept
of the thing-in-itself.[13] In his critique, Fichte declared, with
characteristically scornful coarseness, that if Kant had understood himself, then only such and such could have been
meant by "thing-in-itself." If Kant did not think that, then
he was only a half-wit and no thinker at all.[14] Hence at the
basis of the concept of self-understanding lies the fact that all
dogmatic assumptions are dissolved by the inner self-produc-
tion of reason, so that at the end of this self-construction of
the transcendental subject it is totally transparent to itself. It
is astounding how close Husserl's idea of transcendental phenomenology comes to this requirement set by Fichte and
Hegel.

For theology, however, such a concept could not be retained without transformation. For if anything is inseparable
from the idea of revelation, it is precisely this: man cannot

reach an understanding of himself by his own means. It is an age-old motif of faith, which already pervades Augustine's reflection on his life, that all of man's efforts to understand himself out of himself, and in terms of the world over which he presides as his own, ultimately founder. It would seem, in fact, that the word and concept "self-understanding" owe their first use to a Christian experience. We find both in the correspondence between Hamann and his friend Jakobi. From the standpoint of a pietistic certainty of faith, Hamann tries to convince his friend that he can never reach a genuine self-understanding with his philosophy and the role that faith plays in it.[15] By "genuine self-understanding," Hamann obviously means more than the complete self-transparency possessed by thought in harmony with itself. Rather, self-understanding contains historicity as a determining aspect. Something happens and has happened to one who attains true self-understanding. Thus the meaning of the self-understanding of faith is that the believer is conscious of his dependence upon God. He gains insight into the impossibility of understanding himself in terms of what he has at his disposal.

In his concept of having something at one's disposal and the necessary shattering of any self-understanding founded on it, Bultmann put Heidegger's ontological critique of the philosophical tradition to work for theological purposes. He delineated the position of the Christian faith over against the self-consciousness implicit in Greek philosophy. In keeping with his own scholarly background, however, Greek philosophy, for him, was the philosophy of the Hellenistic age, and his attention focused not on ontological foundations but on existential self-understanding. In particular, Greek philosophy meant the Stoic ideal of self-control, interpreted as the ideal of complete self-sufficiency and criticized as untenable from the point of view of Christianity. From this point of departure, under the influence of Heideggerian thinking, Bultmann explicated his position by means of the concepts of inauthenticity and authenticity. Dasein that has fallen into the world, that understands itself in terms of what is at its disposal, is called to conversion and experiences the turn to authenticity in the shattering of its self-sufficiency. For Bultmann, the transcendental analytic of Dasein seemed to describe a neutral anthropological basic constitution in terms of which the call of faith could be interpreted "existentially," independently of its content, and within the fundamental dynamics of existence. It was therefore precisely the transcendental philosophical conception of *Being and Time* that fit in with his theological thinking. Of course it was no longer the old idealistic concept of self-understanding and its culmination in "absolute knowledge" that could represent the *a priori* of the experience of faith. For what the conceptual interpretation of the event of faith had to make possible was the *a priori* of an event — the *a priori* of the historicity and finitude of human Dasein. And it was just this interpretation of Dasein in terms of temporality that Heidegger achieved.

It is beyond my competence to discuss here the exegetical fruitfulness of the Bultmannian approach. It was certainly a triumph of the new existential exegesis that Paul and John were interpreted, with the rigorous methods of historical philology, in terms of their self-understanding of the faith. Precisely in such an interpretation the kerygmatic meaning of the New Testament proclamation was brought to its highest fulfillment.

Meanwhile, Heidegger's way of thinking went in the opposite direction. Transcendental philosophical self-knowledge proved to be ever more inappropriate to the inner concern of Heidegger's thought — the concern that drove him on from the very beginning. The discussion that arose later on, regarding the turn [*Kehre*] that eliminated every existential sense from the language of Dasein's authenticity, and thus obliterated the concept of authenticity itself, could no longer be combined, it seems to me, with Bultmann's basic theological concern. In this way, however, Heidegger was now really approaching for the first time the dimension in which his early demand (that theology find the word that not only calls one to faith but would also be able to preserve one in faith) could find fulfillment. If the call to faith — the claim that challenges the complacency of the I and compels it to self-examination in faith — could be interpreted as self-understanding, perhaps a language of faith that could preserve one in faith was something else. It was just this language for which a new foundation was sketched out ever more clearly

in Heidegger's thought, namely, truth as an event containing
its own error within itself, a disclosure that is concealment
and thus at the same time saving, and also the celebrated
phrase from the *Letter on Humanism,* that language is the
"house of being." All of this points beyond the horizon of
any self-understanding, be it ever so frail and historical.

Yet one can also advance in the same direction from the
experience of understanding and the historicity of self-understanding, and it is at this point that my own efforts to
develop a philosophical hermeneutic began. First of all, the
experience of art presents indisputable evidence for the fact
that self-understanding does not yield an adequate horizon of
interpretation. This fact is certainly no new piece of wisdom
for the experience of art. Even the concept of genius, upon
which the modern philosophy of art has been founded since
Kant, contained unconsciousness as an essential ingredient.
For Kant, there is an inner parallel between nature's creativity, whose forms favor us with and establish for men the
miracle of beauty, and the genius, who, like a favorite of
nature, creates what is exemplary unconsciously and without
the application of rules. It is a necessary result of this
account that the artist's self-interpretation is deprived of its
legitimation. When such interpretive declarations by the artist
do arise, they are the product of subsequent reflection, in
which the artist has no particular privilege over against anyone else who confronts his work. Such declarations of the
artist are indeed documents, and in certain circumstances
constitute points of departure for subsequent interpretation.
But they do not have a canonical status.

The consequences become even more decisive, however,
when we look beyond the limits of the aesthetics of genius
and *Erlebnis*-art, and consider that the interpreter belongs
intrinsically to the movement of meaning of the work. For
then even the standard of an unconscious canon that is seen
in the "miracle of the creative mind" is given up. The whole
universality of the hermeneutical phenomenon appears behind the experience of art.

In fact, a deeper penetration into the historicity of all
understanding necessarily leads in this direction. An insight
with important implications emerges, especially from the

study of the older hermeneutics of the seventeenth and eighteenth centuries. Can the *mens auctoris*, what the author meant, be acknowledged in an unqualified way as the standard for understanding a text? If we give a broad and sympathetic interpretation to this hermeneutical axiom, it certainly contains something convincing. That is, if by "what the author meant" we understand "what in general he could have meant" – what lay within his own individual historical horizon – and therefore exclude "whatever could not have occurred to him at all," then this axiom seems sound.[16] It protects interpretation from anachronisms, from arbitrary interpolations and illegitimate applications. It seems to formulate the ethic of the historical consciousness, the conscientiousness of the historical mind.

However, if one considers the interpretation of texts together with the understanding and experience of the work of art, then this axiom too still involves something that is fundamentally questionable. There may also be historically appropriate and to that extent authentic modes of experience of the work of art. But the experience of art surely cannot be restricted to them. Precisely because we hold fast to the historical task of integration that is posed for every experience of the work of art as human experience, we may not embrace completely a Pythagorizing aesthetic. Nonetheless, we must acknowledge that the work of art represents a structure of meaning of a unique kind, whose ideality approaches the unhistorical dimension of the mathematical.[17] Our experience and interpretation is obviously in no sense limited by the *mens auctoris*. Now when we add that the inner unity of understanding and interpreting, which the romantics had already exhibited, transports the object of understanding – whether a work of art, a text or whatever kind of tradition – into the present and brings it again to speech in its own language, then I think I see certain theological consequences adumbrated.

The kerygmatic meaning of the New Testament, which gives the form of application of the *pro me* to the gospel, cannot ultimately contradict the legitimate investigation of meaning by historical science. This is, I contend, an unalterable requirement of the scientific consciousness. It is impossible to assume a relation of mutual exclusion between the meaning and the salvation-meaning of a scriptural text. But can it be a question here at all of a mutual exclusion? Does not the intended meaning of the New Testament authors — even what they may concretely have in mind — move in the direction of the meaning of salvation for which one reads the Bible? This is not to say that an adequate and appropriate self-understanding is to be attributed to their statements. They belong completely to the genre which Franz Overbeck characterized as *Urliteratur*. If by the meaning of a text we understand the *mens auctoris*, that is, the "actual" horizon of understanding of the original Christian writers, then we do the New Testament authors a false honor. Their honor should lie precisely in the fact that they proclaim something that surpasses their own horizon of understanding — even if they are named John or Paul.

This assertion in no way entails an uncontrollable theory of inspiration or pneumatic exegesis. Such things would dissipate the gain in knowledge that we derive from New Testament scholarship. In fact, however, it is not a question of a theory of interpretation. That becomes clear if we consider the hermeneutical situation of theology together with that of jurisprudence, with the human studies and with the experience of art, as I have done in my efforts toward a philosophical hermeneutic. Nowhere does understanding mean the mere recovery of what the author "meant," whether he was the creator of a work of art, the doer of a deed, the writer of a law book, or anything else. The *mens auctoris* does not limit the horizon of understanding in which the interpreter has to move, indeed, in which he is necessarily moved, if, instead of merely repeating, he really wants to understand.

The surest testimony to this seems to me to lie in the character of language. Not only does all interpretation occur within the medium of language, but insofar as it has to do with linguistic forms it also carries over the form of what is understood into its own linguistic world when it raises it into its own understanding. That is not a secondary act standing over against "understanding" as such. Since Schleiermacher, the ancient distinction that was always maintained by the Greeks between "thinking" (νοεῖν) and "expressing" (λέγειν)[18] no longer holds a prominent position in hermeneutics. What is at issue here is not even basically a matter of translating, at least not from one language to another. The hopeless inadequacy of all translations can well illustrate the difference we have in mind. When one who understands attempts to explicate his comprehension, he is not in the unfree situation of the translator, who must coordinate his efforts word for word with a given text. He participates in the freedom that belongs to actual speaking, which is to say what the text means. Certainly every understanding is only "underway"; it never comes entirely to an end. And yet a whole of meaning is present in the free achievement of saying what is meant — even in what the interpreter means. Understanding that is linguistically articulated has free space around it which it fills in constant response to the word addressing it, without filling it out completely. "There is much to say" is the basic hermeneutical relation. Interpretation is not a subsequent fixing of fleeting meanings — anymore than speaking is something of that sort. What comes to language, even in literary tradition, is not some sort of meanings as such, but rather by means of it, the very experience of the world, which always entails the whole of our historical tradition. Tradition is always porous for what is handed on [tradiert] in it. Not only the word that theology must seek but every answer to the address of tradition is a word, a word that preserves.

NOTES

1. For Cassirer's discussion of this point, see his *Philosophy of Symbolic Forms*, vol. 1 (New Haven: Yale University Press, 1953), pp. 73-114. (Trans.)

2. Cf. N. Hartmann's review of the *JPPF*, vol. 1, in *Die Geisteswissenschaften*, vol. I (1914), pp. 35, 97 ff. Also cf. Hartmann, *Kleine Schriften*, vol. III (Berlin: De Gruyter, 1958), pp. 365 ff.

3. In this connection, one might consider the reference to Aristotle's *Nichomachean Ethics* VI and *Metaphysics* XII in *SuZ*, p. 225.

4. Plato, *Sophist* 246d.

5. Aristotle, *Nichomachean Ethics*, VI, 9, 1149b 29.

6. Ibid., 1141, 633 ff.

7. That the Aristotelian concept of φύσις was at the same time also

important for Heidegger is clear in his interpretation of Aristotle's Physics BI. Cf. Heidegger in *Il Pensiero* (Milan-Varese, 1958).

8. On the historical background of this distinction, cf. "The Philosophical Foundations of the Twentieth Century."

9. Cf. *SuZ*, p. 339.

10. Cf. Husserl, "Vorlesungen zur Phänomenologie des inneren Zeitbewusstseins," ed. by Martin Heidegger, in *JPPF*, IX (1928), pp. 395 ff. ET by James S. Churchill, *The Phenomenology of Internal Time Consciousness* (Bloomington, Ind.: University of Indiana Press, 1964), pp. 57 ff.

11. Cf. *SuZ*, p. 75.

12. *SuZ*, p. 308.

13. Cf. Johann Gottlieb Fichte, "Zweite Einleitung in die Wissenschaftslehre," in *Sämmtliche Werke*, ed. I. H. Fichte, vol. I, pp. 471 f., 474 ff., 482. ff.

14. Ibid., p. 482.

15. Cf. the Heidelberg dissertation of Renate Knoll, "J. G. Hamann und Fr. H. Jacobi," *Heidelberger Forschungen*, vol. 7 (Heidelberg: Karl Winter Verlag, 1963).

16. Cf. Chladenius, quoted in *WM*, p. 172.

17. When Oskar Becker wishes to play the "Pythagorean" truth off against my attempt to interpret the aesthetic experience hermeneutically too, he touches no really controversial issue. Cf. Becker, "Die Fragwürdigkeit des Transzendierung der ästhetischen Dimension der Kunst," in *PhR* X (1962), pp. 225-238, esp. p. 237.

18. This distinction first appears in Parmenides's didactic poem. Cf. H. Diels, *Fragmente der Vorsokratiker*, 5th ed., 2, 7 f., 8, 35 f.

12
Heidegger's Later Philosophy (1960)

When we look back today on the time between the two
world wars, we can see that this pause within the turbulent
events of our century represents a period of extraordinary
creativity. Omens of what was to come could be seen even
before the catastrophe of World War I, particularly in painting and architecture. But for the most part, the general
awareness of the time was transformed only by the terrible
shock that the slaughters of World War I brought to the
cultural consciousness and to the faith in progress of the
liberal era. In the philosophy of the day, this transformation
of general sensibilities was marked by the fact that with one
blow the dominant philosophy that had grown up in the
second half of the nineteenth century in renewal of Kant's
critical idealism was rendered untenable. "The collapse of
German idealism," as Paul Ernst called it in a popular book
of the time,* was placed in a world-historical context by
Oswald Spengler's *The Decline of the West*. The forces that
carried out the critique of this dominant Neo-Kantian philosophy had two powerful precursors: Friedrich Nietzsche's
critique of Platonism and Christendom, and Søren Kierkegaard's brilliant attack on the *Reflexionsphilosophie* of spec-

*Cf. Paul Ernst, *Der Zusammenbruch des deutschen Idealismus.* (Munich: G.
Müller, 1918).

ulative idealism. Two new philosophical catchwords confronted the Neo-Kantian preoccupation with methodology. One was the *irrationality of life,* and of historical life in particular. In connection with this notion, one could refer to Nietzsche and Bergson, but also to the great historian of philosophy Wilhelm Dilthey. The other catchword was *Existenz,* a term that rang forth from the works of Søren Kierkegaard, the Danish philosopher of the first part of the nineteenth century, whose influence was only beginning to be felt in Germany as a result of the Diedrichs translation. Just as Kierkegaard had criticized Hegel as the philosopher of reflection who had forgotten existence, so now the complacent system-building of Neo-Kantian methodologism, which had placed philosophy entirely in the service of establishing scientific cognition, came under critical attack. And just as Kierkegaard — a Christian thinker — had stepped forward to oppose the philosophy of idealism, so now the radical self-criticism of the so-called dialectical theology opened the new epoch.

Among the forces that gave philosophical expression to the general critique of liberal culture-piety and the prevailing academic philosophy was the revolutionary genius of the young Heidegger. Heidegger's appearance as a young teacher at Freiburg University in the years just after World War I created a profound sensation. The extraordinarily forceful and profound language that resounded from the rostrum in Freiburg already betrayed the emergence of an original philosophical power. Heidegger's *magnum opus, Being and Time,* grew out of his fruitful and intense encounter with contemporary Protestant theology during his appointment at Marburg in 1923. Published in 1927, this book effectively communicated to a wide public something of the new spirit that had engulfed philosophy as a result of the convulsions of World War I. The common theme that captured the imagination of the time was called existential philosophy. The contemporary reader of Heidegger's first systematic work was seized by the vehemence of its passionate protest against the secured cultural world of the older generation and the leveling of all individual forms of life by industrial society, with its ever stronger uniformities and its techniques of communication and public relations that manipulated everything. Heidegger contrasted the concept of the authenticity of Dasein, which is aware of its finitude and resolutely accepts it, with the "They," "idle chatter" and "curiosity," as fallen and inauthentic forms of Dasein. The existential seriousness with which he brought the age-old riddle of death to the center of philosophical concern, and the force with which his challenge to the real "choice" of existence smashed the illusory world of education and culture, disrupted well-preserved academic tranquility. And yet his was not the voice of a reckless stranger to the academic world — not the voice of a bold and lonely thinker in the style of Kierkegaard or Nietzsche — but of a pupil of the most distinguished and conscientious philosophical school that existed in the German universities of the time. Heidegger was a pupil of Edmund Husserl, who pursued tenaciously the goal of establishing philosophy as a rigorous science. Heidegger's new philosophical effort also joined in the battle cry of phenomenology, "To the things themselves." The thing he aimed at, however, was the most concealed question of philosophy, one that for the most part had been forgotten: What is being? In order to learn how to ask this question, Heidegger proceeded to define the being of human Dasein in an ontologically positive way, instead of understanding it as "merely finite," that is, in terms of an infinite and always existing Being, as previous metaphysics had done. The ontological priority that the being of human Dasein acquired for Heidegger defined his philosophy as "fundamental ontology." Heidegger called the ontological determinations of finite human Dasein determinations of existence "existentials." With methodical precision, he contrasted these basic concepts with the categories of the present-at-hand that had dominated previous metaphysics. When Heidegger raised once again the ancient question of the meaning of being, he did not want to lose sight of the fact that human Dasein does not have its real being in determinable presence-at-hand, but rather in the dynamic of the care with which it is concerned about its own future and its own being. Human Dasein is distinguished by the fact that it understands itself in terms of its being. In order not to lose sight of the finitude and temporality of human Dasein, which cannot ignore the question of the meaning of its being, Heidegger defined the question of the meaning of being within the horizon of time. The present-at-hand, which science knows through its observations and calculations, and the eternal, which is beyond everything human, must both be understood in terms of the central ontological certainty of human temporality. This was Heidegger's new approach, but his goal of thinking being as time remained so veiled that *Being and Time* was promptly designated as "hermeneutical phenomenology," primarily because self-understanding still represented the real foundation of the inquiry. Seen in terms of this foundation, the understanding of being that held sway in traditional metaphysics turns out to be a corrupted form of the primordial understanding of being that is manifested in human Dasein. Being is not simply pure presence or actual presence-at-hand. It is finite, historical Dasein that "is" in the real sense. Then the ready-to-hand has its place within Dasein's projection of a world, and only subsequently does the merely present-at-hand receive its place.

But various forms of being that are neither historical nor simply present-at-hand have no proper place within the framework provided by the hermeneutical phenomenon of self-understanding: the timelessness of mathematical facts, which are not simply observable entities present-at-hand; the timelessness of nature, whose ever-repeating patterns hold sway even in us and determine us in the form of the unconscious; and finally the timelessness of the rainbow of art, which spans all historical distances. All of these seem to designate the limits of the possibility of hermeneutical interpretation that Heidegger's new approach opened up. The unconscious, the number, the dream, the sway of nature, the miracle of art — all these seemed to exist only on the periphery of Dasein, which knows itself historically and understands itself in terms of itself. They seem to be comprehensible only as limiting concepts.

It was a surprise, therefore, in 1936, when Heidegger dealt with the origin of the work of art in several addresses. This work had begun to have a profound influence long before it was first published in 1950, when it became accessible to the general public as the first essay in *Holzwege*.* For it had long been the case that Heidegger's lectures and addresses had everywhere aroused intense interest. Copies and reports of them were widely disseminated, and they quickly made him the focus of the very "idle chatter" that he had characterized so acrimoniously in *Being and Time*. In fact, his addresses on the origin of the work of art caused a philosophical sensation.

It was not merely that Heidegger now brought art into the basic hermeneutical approach of the self-understanding of man in his historicity, nor even that these addresses understood art to be the act that founds whole historical worlds (as it is understood in the poetic faith of Hölderlin and George). Rather, the real sensation caused by Heidegger's new experiment had to do with the startling new conceptuality that boldly emerged in connection with this topic. "World" and "earth" were key terms in Heidegger's discussion. From the very beginning, the concept of the world had been one of Heidegger's major hermeneutical concepts. As the referential totality of Dasein's projection, "world" constituted the horizon that was preliminary to all projections of Dasein's concern. Heidegger had himself sketched the history of this concept of the world, and in particular, had called attention to and historically legitimated the difference between the anthropological meaning of this concept in the New Testament (which was the meaning he used himself) and the concept of the totality of the present-at-hand. The new and startling thing was that this concept of the world now found a counterconcept in the "earth." As a whole in which human self-interpretation takes place, the concept of the world could be raised to intuitive clarity out of the self-interpretation of human Dasein, but the concept of the earth sounded a mythical and gnostic note that at best might have its true home in the world of poetry. At that time Heidegger had devoted himself to Hölderlin's poetry with passionate intensity, and it is clearly from this source that he brought the concept of the earth into his own philosophy. But with what justification? How could Dasein, being-in-the-world, which

*Cf. Martin Heidegger, "Über den Ursprung des Kunstwerkes," in *Holzwege* (Frankfurt: Klostermann, 1950), pp. 7-68.

understands itself out of its own being, be related ontologically to a concept like the "earth" - this new and radical starting point for all transcendental inquiry? In order to answer this question we must return briefly to Heidegger's earlier work.

Heidegger's new approach in *Being and Time* was certainly not simply a repetition of the spiritualistic metaphysics of German idealism. Human Dasein's understanding of itself out of its own being is not the self-knowledge of Hegel's absolute spirit. It is not a self-projection. Rather, it knows that it is not master of itself and its own Dasein, but comes upon itself in the midst of beings and has to take itself over as it finds itself. It is a "thrown-projection." In one of the most brilliant phenomenological analyses of *Being and Time,* Heidegger analyzed this limiting experience of Dasein, which comes upon itself in the midst of beings, as "disposition" [*Befindlichkeit*], and he attributed to disposition or mood [*Stimmung*] the real disclosure of being-in-the-world. What is come upon in disposition represents the extreme limit beyond which the historical self-understanding of human Dasein could not advance. There was no way to get from this hermeneutical limiting concept of disposition or moodfulness to a concept such as the earth. What justification is there for this concept? What warrant does it have? The important insight that Heidegger's "The Origin of the Work of Art" opened up is that "earth" is a necessary determination of the being of the work of art.

If we are to see the fundamental significance of the question of the nature of the work of art and how this question is connected with the basic problems of philosophy, we must gain some insight into the prejudices that are present in the concept of a philosophical aesthetics. In the last analysis, we need to overcome the concept of aesthetics itself. It is well known that aesthetics is the youngest of the philosophical disciplines. Only with the explicit restriction of Enlightenment rationalism in the eighteenth century was the autonomous right of sensuous knowledge asserted and with it the relative independence of the judgment of taste from the understanding and its concepts. Like the name of the discipline itself, the systematic autonomy of aesthetics dates from the aesthetics of Alexander Baumgarten. Then in his third Critique — the *Critique of Aesthetic Judgment* — Kant established the problem of aesthetics in its systematic significance. In the subjective universality of the aesthetic judgment of taste, he discovered the powerful and legitimate claim to independence that aesthetic judgment can make over against the claims of the understanding and morality. The taste of the observer can no more be comprehended as the application of concepts, norms, or rules than the genius of the artist can. What sets the beautiful apart cannot be exhibited as a determinate, knowable property of an object, but manifests itself in a subjective factor: the intensification of the *Lebensgefühl* (life-feeling) through the harmonious correspondence of imagination and understanding. What we experience in beauty — in nature as well as in art — is the total animation and free interplay of all our spiritual powers. The judgment of taste is not knowledge, yet it is not arbitrary. It involves a claim to universality that can establish the autonomy of the aesthetic realm. We must acknowledge that this justification of the autonomy of art was a great achievement in the age of the Enlightenment, with its insistence on the sanctity of rules and moral orthodoxy. This is particularly the case at just that point in German history when the classical period of German literature, with its center in Weimar, was seeking to establish itself as an aesthetic state. These efforts found their conceptual justification in Kant's philosophy.

Basing aesthetics on the subjectivity of the mind's powers was, however, the beginning of a dangerous process of subjectification. For Kant himself, to be sure, the determining factor was still the mysterious congruity that obtained between the beauty of nature and the subjectivity of the subject. In the same way, he understood the creative genius who transcends all rules in creating the miracle of the work of art to be a favorite of nature. But this position presupposes the self-evident validity of the natural order that has its ultimate foundation in the theological idea of the creation. With the disappearance of this context, the grounding of aesthetics led inevitably to a radical subjectification in further development of the doctrine of the freedom of the genius from rules. No longer derived from the comprehensive whole of the order of being, art comes to be contrasted with actuality and with the raw prose of life. The illuminating power of poesy succeeds in reconciling idea and actuality only within its own aesthetic realm. This is the idealistic aesthetics to which Schiller first gave expression and that culminated in Hegel's remarkable aesthetics. Even in Hegel, however, the theory of the work of art still stood within a universal ontological horizon. To the extent that the work of art succeeds at all in adjusting and reconciling the finite and the infinite, it is the tangible indication of an ultimate truth that philosophy must finally grasp in conceptual form. Just as nature, for idealism, is not merely the object of the calculating science of the modern age, but rather the reign of a great, creative world power that raises itself to its perfection in self-conscious spirit, so the work of art too, in the view of these speculative thinkers, is an objectification of spirit. Art is not the perfected concept of spirit, but rather its manifestation on the level of the sense intuition of the world. In the literal sense of the word, art is an intuition of the world [*Welt-Anschauung*].

If we wish to determine the point of departure for Heidegger's meditation on the nature of the work of art, we must keep clearly in mind that the idealistic aesthetics that had ascribed a special significance to the work of art as the organon of a nonconceptual understanding of absolute truth had long since been eclipsed by Neo-Kantian philosophy. This dominant philosophical movement had renewed the Kantian foundation of scientific cognition without regaining the metaphysical horizon that lay at the basis of Kant's own description of aesthetic judgment, namely, a teleological order of being. Consequently, the Neo-Kantian conception of aesthetic problems was burdened with peculiar prejudices. The exposition of the theme in Heidegger's essay clearly reflects this state of affairs. It begins with the question of how the work of art is differentiated from the thing. The work of art is also a thing, and only by way of its being as a thing does it have the capacity to refer to something else, for instance, to function symbolically, or to give us an allegorical understanding. But this is to describe the mode of being of the work of art from the point of view of an ontological model that assumes the systematic *priority of scientific cognition*. What really "is" is thing-like in character; it is a fact, something given to the senses and developed by the natural sciences in the direction of objective cognition. The significance and value of the thing, however, are secondary forms of comprehension that have a mere subjective validity and belong neither to the original givenness itself nor to the objective truth acquired from it. The Neo-Kantians assumed that the thing alone is objective and able to support such values. For aesthetics, this assumption would have to mean that even the work of art possesses a thing-like character as its most prominent feature. This thing-like character functions as a substructure upon which the real aesthetic form rises as a superstructure. Nicolai Hartmann still describes the structure of the aesthetic object in this fashion.

Heidegger refers to this ontological prejudice when he inquires into the thing-character of the thing. He distinguishes three ways of comprehending the thing that have been developed in the tradition: it is the bearer of properties; it is the unity of a manifold of perceptions; and it is matter to which form has been imparted. The third of these forms of comprehension, in particular — the thing as form and matter — seems to be the most directly obvious, for it follows the model of production by which a thing is manufactured to serve our purposes. Heidegger calls such things "implements." Viewed theologically, from the standpoint of this model, things in their entirety appear as manufactured items, that is, as creations of God. From man's perspective, they appear as implements that have lost their implement-character. Things are *mere* things, that is, they are present without reference to serving a purpose. Now Heidegger shows that this concept of being-present-at-hand, which corresponds to the observing and calculating procedures of modern science, permits us to think neither the thing-like character of the thing nor the implement-character of the implement. In order to focus attention on the implement-character of the implement, therefore, he refers to an artistic representation — a painting by Van Gogh depicting a peasant's shoes. The implement itself is perceived in this work of art — not an entity that can be made to serve some purpose or other, but something whose very being consists in having served and in still serving the person to whom it belongs. What emerges from the painter's work and is vividly depicted in it is not an incidental pair of peasant's shoes. The emergence of truth that occurs in the work of art can be conceived from the work alone, and not at all in terms of its substructure as a thing.

These observations raise the question of what a work is that truth can emerge from it in this way. In contrast to the customary procedure of starting with the thing-character and object-character of the work of art, Heidegger contends that a work of art is characterized precisely by the fact that it is *not* an object, but rather stands in itself. By standing in itself it not only belongs to its world; its world is present in it. The work of art opens up its own world. Something is an object only when it no longer fits into the fabric of its world because the world it belongs to has disintegrated. Hence a work of art is an object when it becomes an item of commercial transaction, for then it is worldless and homeless.

The characterization of the work of art as standing-in-itself and opening up a world with which Heidegger begins his study consciously avoids going back to the concept of genius that is found in classical aesthetics. In his effort to understand the ontological structure of the work independently of the subjectivity of the creator or beholder, Heidegger now uses "earth" as a counterconcept alongside the concept of the "world" to which the work belongs and which it erects and opens up. "Earth" is a counterconcept to world insofar as it exemplifies self-concealment and concealing as opposed to self-opening. Clearly, both self-opening and self-concealing are present in the work of art. A work of art does not "mean" something or function as a sign that refers to a meaning; rather, it presents itself in its own being, so that the beholder must tarry by it. It is so very much present itself that the ingredients out of which it is composed — stone, color, tone, word — only come into a real existence of their own within the work of art itself. As long as something is mere stuff awaiting its rendering, it is not really present, that is, it has not come forth into a genuine presence. It only comes forth when it is used, when it is bound into the work.

The tones that constitute a musical masterwork are tones in a more real sense than all other sounds or tones. The colors of a painting are colors in a more genuine sense than even nature's wealth of colors. The temple column manifests the stone-like character of its being more genuinely in rising upward and supporting the temple roof than it did as an unhewn block of stone. But what comes forth in this way in the work is precisely its concealedness and self-concealing — what Heidegger calls the being of the earth. The earth, in truth, is not stuff, but that out of which everything comes forth and into which everything disappears.

At this point, form and matter, as reflective concepts, prove to be inadequate. If we can say that a world "arises" in a great work of art, then the arising of this world is at the same time its entrance into a reposing form. When the form stands there it has found its earthly existence. From this the work of art acquires its own peculiar repose. It does not first have its real being in an experiencing ego, which asserts, means, or exhibits something and whose assertions, opinions, or demonstrations would be its "meaning." Its being does not consist in its becoming an experience. Rather, by virtue of its own existence it is an event, a thrust that overthrows everything previously considered to be conventional, a thrust in which a world never there before opens itself up. But this thrust takes place in the work of art itself in such a fashion that at the same time it is sustained in an abiding [*ins Bleiben geborgen*]. That which arises and sustains itself in this way constitutes the structure of the work in its tension. It is this tension that Heidegger designates as the conflict between the world and the earth. In all of this, Heidegger not only gives a description of the mode of being of the work of art that avoids the prejudices of traditional aesthetics and the modern conception of subjectivity, he also avoids simply renewing the speculative aesthetics that defined the work of art as the sensuous manifestation of the Idea. To be sure, the Hegalian definition of beauty shares with Heidegger's own effort the fundamental transcendence of the antithesis between subject and object, I and object, and does not describe the being of the work of art in terms of the subjectivity of the subject. Nevertheless, Hegel's description of the being of the work of

art moves in this direction, for it is the sensuous manifestation of the Idea, conceived by self-conscious thought, that
constitutes the work of art. In thinking the Idea, therefore,
the entire truth of the sensuous appearance would be can-
celled. It acquires its real form in the concept. When Heidegger speaks of the conflict between world and earth and
describes the work of art as the thrust through which a truth
occurs, this truth is not taken up and perfected in the truth
of the philosophical concept. A unique manifestation of
truth occurs in the work of art. The reference to the work of
art in which truth comes forth should indicate clearly that
for Heidegger it is meaningful to speak of an *event* of truth.
Hence Heidegger's essay does not restrict itself to giving a
more suitable description of the being of the work of art.
Rather, his analysis supports his central philosophical concern to conceive being itself as an event of truth.

The objection is often made that the basic concepts of
Heidegger's later work cannot be verified. What Heidegger
intends, for example, when he speaks of being in the verbal
sense of the word, of the event of being, the clearing of
being, the revealment of being, and the forgetfulness of
being, cannot be fulfilled by an intentional act of our subjectivity. The concepts that dominate Heidegger's later philosophical works are clearly closed to subjective demonstration,
just as Hegel's dialectical process is closed to what Hegel
called representational thinking. Heidegger's concepts are the
object of a criticism similar to Marx's criticism of Hegel's
dialectic in the sense that they too are called "mythological."

The fundamental significance of the essay on the work of
art, it seems to me, is that it provides us with an indication of
the later Heidegger's real concern. No one can ignore the fact
that in the work of art, in which a world arises, not only is
something meaningful given to experience that was not
known before, but also something new comes into existence
with the work of art itself. It is not simply the manifestation
of a truth, it is itself an event. This offers us an opportunity
to pursue one step further Heidegger's critique of Western
metaphysics and its culmination in the subjectivism of the
modern age. It is well known that Heidegger renders *aletheia*,
the Greek word for truth, as *unhiddenness*. But this strong

emphasis on the privative sense of *aletheia* does not mean simply that knowledge of the truth tears truth out of the realm of the unknown or hiddenness in error by an act of robbery (*privatio* means "robbery"). It is not the only reason why truth is not open and obvious and accessible as a matter of course, though it is certainly true and the Greeks obviously wanted to express it when they designated beings as they are as unhidden. They knew that every piece of knowledge is threatened by error and falsehood, that it is a question of avoiding error and gaining the right representation of beings as they are. If knowledge depends on our leaving error behind us, truth is the pure unhiddenness of beings. This is what Greek thought had in view, and in this way it was already treading the path that modern science would eventually follow to the end, namely, to bring about the correctness of knowledge by which beings are preserved in their unhiddenness.

In opposition to all this, Heidegger holds that unhiddenness is not simply the character of beings insofar as they are correctly known. In a more primordial sense, unhiddenness "occurs," and this occurrence is what first makes it possible for beings to be unhidden and correctly known. The hiddenness that corresponds to such primordial unhiddenness is not error, but rather belongs originally to being itself. Nature, which loves to hide itself (Heraclitus), is thus characterized not only with respect to its possibility of being known, but rather with respect to its being. It is not only the emergence into the light but just as much the hiding of itself in the dark. It is not only the unfolding of the blossom in the sun, but just as much its rooting of itself in the depths of the earth. Heidegger speaks of the "clearing of being," which first represents the realm in which beings are known as disclosed in their unhiddenness. This coming forth of beings into the "there" of their Dasein obviously presupposes a realm of openness in which such a "there" can occur. And yet it is just as obvious that this realm does not exist without beings manifesting themselves in it, that is, without there being a place of openness that openness occupies. This relation is unquestionably peculiar. And yet even more remarkable is the fact that only in the "there" of this self-manifestation of

beings does the hiddenness of being first present itself. To be
sure, correct knowledge is made possible by the openness of
the there. The beings that come forth out of unhiddenness
present themselves for that which preserves them. Nevertheless, it is not an arbitrary act of revealing, an act of robbery,
by which something is torn out of hiddenness. Rather, this is
all made possible only by the fact that revealment and
hiddenness are an event of being itself. To understand this
fact helps us in our understanding of the nature of the work
of art. There is clearly a tension between the emergence and
the hiddenness that constitute the being of the work itself. It
is the power of this tension that constitutes the form-niveau
of a work of art and produces the brilliance by which it
outshines everything else. Its truth is not its simple manifestation of meaning, but rather the unfathomableness and depth
of its meaning. Thus by its very nature the work of art is a
conflict between world and earth, emergence and hiddenness.

But precisely what is exhibited in the work of art ought to
be the essence of being itself. The conflict between revealment and concealment is not the truth of the work of art
alone, but the truth of every being, for as unhiddenness,
truth is always such an *opposition of revealment and concealment.* The two belong necessarily together. This obviously
means that truth is not simply the mere presence of a being,
so that it stands, as it were, over against its correct representation. Such a concept of being unhidden would presuppose
the subjectivity of the Dasein that represents beings. But
beings are not correctly defined in their being if they are
defined merely as objects of possible representation. Rather,
it belongs just as much to their being that they withhold
themselves. As unhidden, truth has in itself an inner tension
and ambiguity. Being contains something like a hostility to
its own presentations, as Heidegger says. What Heidegger
means can be confirmed by everyone: the existing thing does
not simply offer us a recognizable and familiar surface con-
tour; it also has an inner depth of self-sufficiency that
Heidegger calls its "standing-in-itself." The complete unhiddenness of all beings, their total objectification (by means of
a representation that conceives things in their perfect state)
would negate this standing-in-itself of beings and lead to a

total leveling of them. A complete objectification of this kind would no longer represent beings that stand in their own being. Rather, it would represent nothing more than our opportunity for using beings, and what would be manifest would be the will that seizes upon and dominates things. In the work of art, we experience an absolute opposition to this will-to-control, not in the sense of a rigid resistance to the presumption of our will, which is bent on utilizing things, but in the sense of the superior and intrusive power of a being reposing in itself. Hence the closedness and concealment of the work of art is the guarantee of the universal thesis of Heidegger's philosophy, namely, that beings hold themselves back by coming forward into the openness of presence. The standing-in-itself of the work betokens at the same time the standing-in-itself of beings in general.

This analysis of the work of art opens up perspectives that point us further along the path of Heidegger's thought. Only by way of the work of art were the implement-character of the implement and, in the last analysis, the thingness of the thing able to manifest themselves. All-calculating modern science brings about the loss of things, dissolving their character of standing-in themselves, which "can be forced to do nothing," into the calculated elements of its projects and alterations, but the work of art represents an instance that guards against the universal loss of things. As Rilke poetically illuminates the innocence of the thing in the midst of the general disappearance of thingness by showing it to the angel,* so the thinker contemplates the same loss of thingness while recognizing at the same time that this very thingness is preserved in the work of art. Preservation, however, presupposes that what is preserved still truly exists. Hence the very truth of the thing is implied if this truth is still capable of coming forth in the work of art. Heidegger's essay, "What Is a Thing?" thus represents a necessary advance on the path of his thought.** The thing, which formerly did not even achieve the implement-status of being-present-to-hand,

*Gadamer is referring to the angel motif in Rilke's *Duino Elegies*.
**Cf. Heidegger, *Die Frage nach dem Ding: Zu Kants Lehre von den transzendentalen Grundsätzen*. (Tubingen: Max Niemeyer, 1962). ET: *What Is a Thing?*, trans. Barton and Deutsch (Chicago: Henry Regnery, 1967).

but was merely present-at-hand for observation and investigation, is now recognized in its "whole" being [*in seinem "heilen" Sein*] as precisely what cannot be put to use.

From this vantage point, we can recognize yet a further step on this path. Heidegger asserts that the essence of art is the process of poeticizing. What he means is that the nature of art does not consist in transforming something that is already formed or in copying something that is already in being. Rather, art is the project by which something new comes forth as true. The essence of the event of truth that is present in the work of art is that "it opens up an open place." In the ordinary and more restricted sense of the word, however, poetry is distinguished by the intrinsically linguistic character that differentiates it from all other modes of art. If the real project and the genuine artistic element in every art — even in architecture and in the plastic arts — can be called "poetry," then the project that occurs in an actual poem is bound to a course that is already marked out and cannot be projected anew simply from out of itself, the course already prepared by language. The poet is so dependent upon the language he inherits and uses that the language of his poetic work of art can only reach those who command the same language. In a certain sense, then, the "poetry" that Heidegger takes to symbolize the projective character of all artistic creation is less the project of building and shaping out of stone or color or tones than it is their secondary forms. In fact, the process of poeticizing is divided into two phases: into the project that has already occurred where a language holds sway, and another project that allows the new poetic creation to come forth from the first project. But the primacy of language is not simply a unique trait of the poetic work of art; rather, it seems to be characteristic of the very thing-being of things themselves. The work of language is the most primordial poetry of being. The thinking that conceives all art as poetry and that discloses that the work of art is language is itself still on the way to language.

13
Heidegger and the Language of Metaphysics (1967)

The tremendous power emanating from Heidegger's creative energies in the early 1920s seemed to sweep along the generation of students returning from World War I or just beginning its studies, so that a complete break with traditional academic philosophy seemed to take place with Heidegger's appearance – long before it was expressed in his own thought. It was like a new breakthrough into the unknown that posed something radically new as compared with all the mere movements and countermovements of the Christian Occident. A generation shattered by the collapse of an epoch wanted to begin completely anew; it did not want to retain anything that had formerly been held valid. Even in the intensification of the German language that took place in his concepts, Heidegger's thought seemed to defy any comparison with what philosophy had previously meant. And that was in spite of the unceasing and intensive interpretive effort that especially distinguished Heidegger's academic instruction – his immersion in Aristotle and Plato, Augustine and Thomas, Leibniz and Kant, in Hegel and Husserl.

Altogether unexpected things came to the surface and were discussed in connection with these names. Each of these great figures from our classical philosophical tradition was completely transformed and seemed to proclaim a direct, compelling truth that was perfectly fused with the thought of its resolute interpreter. The distance separating our historical consciousness from the tradition seemed to be nonexistent. The calm and confident aloofness with which the Neo-Kantian "history of philosophical problems" was accustomed to deal with the tradition, and the whole of contemporary thought that came from the academic rostrum, now suddenly seemed to be mere child's play.

In actual fact, the break with tradition that took place in Heidegger's thought represented just as much an incomparable renewal of the tradition. Only gradually did the younger students come to see both how much appropriation of the tradition was present in the criticism, as well as how profound the criticism was in the appropriation. Two great classical figures of philosophical thought, however, have long occupied an ambiguous position in Heidegger's thought, standing out as much by their affinity with Heidegger as by their radical distance from him. These two thinkers are Plato and Hegel. From the very beginning, Plato was viewed in a critical light in Heidegger's work, in that Heidegger took over and transformed the Aristotelian criticism of the Idea of the Good and stressed especially the Aristotelian concept of analogy. Yet it was Plato who provided the motto for *Being and Time*. Only after World War II, with the decisive incorporation of Plato into the history of Being, was the ambiguity in regard to Plato removed. But Heidegger's thought has revolved around Hegel until the present day in ever new attempts at delineation. In contrast to the phenomenological craftsmanship that was all too quickly forgotten by the scholarship of the time, Hegel's dialectic of pure thought asserted itself with renewed power. Hence Hegel not only continually provoked Heidegger to self-defense, but he was also the one with whom Heidegger was associated in the eyes of all those who sought to defend themselves against the claim of Heidegger's thought. Would this final form of Western metaphysics be outstripped by the radicalism with which Heidegger stirred the oldest questions of philosophy to new life? Or would the circle of the philosophy of reflection, which dashed all such hopes of freedom and liberation, force Heidegger's thought too back into its orbit?

The development of Heidegger's late philosophy has scarcely encountered a critique anywhere that does not go back in the last analysis to Hegel's position. This observation is true in the negative sense of aligning Heidegger with Hegel's abortive speculative revolution, as Gerhard Krüger[1] and countless others after him have argued. It is also valid in the positive Hegelianizing sense that Heidegger is not sufficiently aware of his own proximity to Hegel, and for this reason he does not really do justice to the radical position of speculative logic. The latter criticism has occurred basically in two problem areas. One is Heidegger's assimilation of history into his own philosophical approach, a point that he seems to share with Hegel. The second is the hidden and unnoticed dialectic that attaches to all essentially Heideggerian assertions.

If Hegel tried to penetrate the history of philosophy philosophically from the standpoint of absolute knowledge, that is, to raise it to a science, Heidegger's description of the history of being (in particular, the history of the forgetfulness of being into which European history entered in the century following Hegel) involved a similarly comprehensive claim. Indeed, there is in Heidegger nothing of that necessity of historical progress that is both the glory and the bane of Hegelian philosophy. For Heidegger, rather, the history that is remembered and taken up into the absolute present in absolute knowing is precisely an advance sign of the radical forgetfulness of being that has marked the history of Europe in the century after Hegel. But for Heidegger, it was fate, not history (remembered and penetrable by understanding), that originated in the conception of being in Greek metaphysics and that in modern science and technology carries the forgetfulness of being to the extreme. Nevertheless, no matter how much it may belong to the temporal constitution of man to be exposed to the unpredictability of fate, this does not rule out the claim continually raised and legitimated in the course of Western history to think what is. And so Heidegger too appears to claim a genuinely historical self-consciousness for himself, indeed, even an eschatological self-consciousness.

The second critical motif proceeds from the indeterminateness and undeterminableness of what Heidegger calls "being."

This criticism tries by Hegelian means to explain the alleged tautology of being — that it is itself — as a disguised second immediacy that emerges from the total mediation of the immediate. Furthermore, are there not real dialectical antitheses at work whenever Heidegger explicates himself? For instance, we find the dialectical tension of thrownness and projection, of authenticity and inauthenticity, of nothing as the veil of being, and finally, and most importantly, the inner tension and ambiguity [*Gegenwendigkeit*] of truth and error, revealment and concealment, which constitute the event of being as the event of truth. Did not Hegel's mediation of being and nothing in the truth of becoming — that is, in the truth of the concrete — already mark out the conceptual framework within which alone the Heideggerian doctrine of the inner tension of truth can exist? Hegel, by his dialectical-speculative sharpening of the antitheses in understanding, overcame a thinking dominated by the understanding. Would it be possible to get beyond this achievement, so as to overcome the logic and language of metaphysics as a whole?

Access to our problem undoubtedly lies in the problem of nothingness and its suppression by metaphysics, a theme Heidegger formulated in his inaugural address in Freiburg. From this perspective, the nothingness we find in Parmenides and in Plato, and also Aristotle's definition of the divine as *energia* without *dynamis* really constitutes a total vitiation of nothingness. Even God, as the infinite knowledge that has being from itself, is understood basically from the vantage point of the privative experience of man's being (in the experience of sleep, death, and forgetting) as the unlimited presence of everything present. But another motif seems to be at work in the history of metaphysical thinking alongside this vitiation of nothingness that extends even into Hegel and Husserl. Aristotelian metaphysics has culminated in the question, "What is the being of beings?" The question that Leibniz and Schelling asked and that Heidegger even called the basic question of metaphysics, "Why is there anything at all, and not rather nothing?" expressly continues the confrontation with the problem of nothingness. The analysis of the concept of *dynamis* in Plato, Plotinus, the tradition of negative theology, Nicolas of Cusa, and Leibniz, and all the way to Schelling — from whom Schopenhauer, Nietzsche, and the metaphysics of the will take their departure — all serve to show that the understanding of being in terms of presence [*Präsenz*] is constantly threatened by nothingness. In our own century, this situation is also found in Max Scheler's dualism of impulse and spirit and Ernst Bloch's philosophy of the not yet, as well as in such hermeneutical phenomena as the question, doubt, wonder, and so on. To this extent, Heidegger's approach has an intrinsic preparation in the subject matter of metaphysics itself.

In order to clarify the immanent necessity of the development within his own thought that led Heidegger to "the turn," and to show that it has nothing to do with a dialectical reversal, we must proceed from the fact that the transcendental-phenomenological conception of *Being and Time* is already essentially different from Husserl's conception of it. Husserl's constitutional analysis of the consciousness of time shows particularly well that the self-constitution of the primal presence (which Husserl could indeed designate as a kind of primal potentiality) is based entirely on the concept of constitutive accomplishment and is thus dependent on the being of valid objectivity. The self-constitution of the transcendental ego, a problem that can be traced back to the fifth chapter of the *Logical Investigations,* stands wholly within the traditional understanding of Being, despite — indeed, precisely because of — the absolute historicity that forms the transcendental ground of all objectivities. Now we must admit that Heidegger's transcendental point of departure from the being that has its being as an issue and the doctrine of the existentials in *Being and Time* both carry with them a transcendental appearance; as though Heidegger's thoughts were, as Oskar Becker puts it, simply the elaboration of further horizons of transcendental phenomenology that had not previously been secured and that had to do with the historicity of Dasein.[2] In reality, however, Heidegger's undertaking means something quite different. Jaspers's formulation of the border situation certainly provided Heidegger with a starting point for explicating the finitude of existence in its basic significance. But this approach served as the preparation of the question of being in a radically altered sense, and was

not the explication of a regional ontology in Husserl's sense.
The concept of "fundamental ontology" – modeled after
that of "fundamental theology" – also creates a difficulty.
The mutual interconnection of authenticity and inauthenticity, of the revealment and concealment of Dasein, which
appeared in *Being and Time* more in the sense of a rejection
of an ethicistic, affect-oriented thinking, turned out increasingly to be the real nucleus of the "question of being."
According to Heidegger's formulation in *On the Essence of
Truth*, ek-sistence and in-sistence are indeed still conceived
from the point of view of human Dasein. But when he says
that the truth of being is the *un*truth, that is, the concealment of being in "error," then the decisive change in the
concept of "essence" which follows from the destruction of
the Greek tradition of metaphysics can no longer be ignored.
For Heidegger leaves behind him both the traditional concept
of essence and that of the ground of essence.

What the interconnection of concealment and revealment
means and what it has to do with the new concept of
"essence" can be exhibited phenomenologically in Heidegger's own essential experience of thought in a number of
ways. (1) In the being of the implement that does not have
its essence in its objective obstinacy, but in its being ready-
to-hand, which allows us to concentrate on what is beyond
the implement itself. (2) In the being of the work of art,
which holds its truth within itself in such fashion that this
truth is not available in any other way but in the work. For
the beholder or receiver, "essence" corresponds here to his
tarrying alongside the work. (3) In the thing, as the one and
only reality that stands in itself, cannot be compelled to serve
our purposes, and contrasts in its irreplaceability with the
concept of the object of consumption, as found in industrial
production. (4) And finally in the word. The "essence" of
the word does not lie in being totally expressed, but rather in
what is left unsaid, as we see especially in speechlessness and
remaining silent. The common structure of essence that is
evident in all four of these experiences of thinking is a
"being-there" that encompasses being absent as well as being
present. During his early years at Freiburg, Heidegger once
said, "One cannot lose God as one loses his pocket knife."

But in fact one cannot simply lose his pocket knife in such fashion that it is no longer present. When one has lost a long familiar implement such as a pocket knife, it demonstrates its existence by the fact that one continually misses it. Hölderlin's "Fehl der Götter" or Eliot's silence of the Chinese vase are not nonexistence, but "being" in the most poetic sense because they are silent. The breach that is made by what is missing is not a place remaining empty within what is present-to-hand; rather, it belongs to the being-there of that to which it is missing, and is "present" in it. Hence "essence" is concretized, and we can demonstrate how what is present is at the same time the concealment of presence.

Problems that necessarily eluded transcendental inquiry and appeared as mere peripheral phenomena become comprehensible when we proceed from such experiences. In the first place, this holds for "nature." Becker's postulation of a paraontology is justified here insofar as nature is no longer only "a limiting case of the being of a possible inner-worldly being." But Becker himself has never recognized that his counterconcept of paraexistence, which is concerned with such essential phenomena as mathematical and dream existence, is a dialectical construction. Becker himself synthesized it with its opposite and thus marked out a third position, without noticing how this position corresponds to the Heideggerian doctrine of the "turn."

A second large complex of problems that comes into a new light in the context of Heidegger's later thought is that of the Thou and the We. We are familiar with this problem complex from Husserl's ongoing discussion of the problem of intersubjectivity; in Being and Time it is interpreted in terms of the world of concern. What constitutes the mode of being of essence is now considered from the point of view of the dialogue, that is, in terms of our capacity to listen to each other in concreto, for instance, when we perceive what governs a conversation or whenever we notice its absence in a tortured conversation. But above all, the inscrutable problem of life and corporeality presents itself in a new way. The concept of the living being [Lebe-Wesen], which Heidegger emphasized in his Letter on Humanism,* raises new ques-

*HB, pp. 15-16.

tions, especially the question of its correspondence to the nature of man [*Menschen-Wesen*] and the nature of language [*Sprach-Wesen*]. But behind this line of questioning stands the question of the being of the self, which was easy enough to define in terms of German idealism's concept of reflection. It becomes puzzling, however, the moment we no longer proceed from the self or self-consciousness, or from human Dasein, in *Being and Time,* but rather from essence. The fact that being comes to a presence in a "clearing," and that in this fashion thinking man is the guardian of being, points to a primordial interconnection of being and man. The tool, the work of art, thing, the word — in all of these, the relation to man stands forth clearly in essence itself. But in what sense? Scarcely in the sense that the Being of the human self thereby acquires its definition. The example of language has already shown us that. As Heidegger says, language speaks *us,* insofar as we do not really preside over it and control it, although, of course, no one disputes the fact that it is we who speak it. And Heidegger's assertion here is not without meaning.

If we want to raise the question of the "self" in Heidegger, we will have first to consider and reject Neo-Platonic modes of thought. For a cosmic drama consisting in the emanation out of the One and the return into it, with the self designated as the pivot of the return, lies beyond what is possible here. Or one could consider what Heidegger understands by "insistence" as the way to a solution. What Heidegger called the "insistence" of Dasein and what he called errancy are certainly to be conceived from the point of view of the forgetfulness of being. But is this forgetfulness the sole mode of coming to presence? Will this render intelligible the place-holding character of human Dasein? Can the concept of coming to presence and the "there" be maintained in exclusive relation to human Dasein, if we take the growth of plants and the living being into consideration? In his *On the Essence of Truth,* Heidegger still conceived of "insistence" from the point of view of the being that first "raised its head" [i.e., man]. But does not insistence have to be taken in a broader sense? And hence "ek-sistence" too? Certainly the confinement of the living being in its environment, discussed in the

Letter on Humanism, means that it is not open for being as is man, who is aware of his possibility of not being. But have we not learned from Heidegger that the real being of the living being is not its own individual being-there, but rather the species? And is the species not "there" for the living being, even if not in the same way that being is present for man in the insistence of the forgetfulness of being? Does it not comprise a part of the being of the species that its members "know" themselves, as the profound expression of the Lutheran Bible puts it? Indeed, *as* knowing, are they not concealed from themselves and yet in such fashion that knowing passes over into it? Is it not also characteristic of "insistence" that the animal intends only itself [*conservatio sui*] and yet precisely in this way provides for the reproduction of its kind?

Similarly, we could ask about the growth of vegetation: Is it only a coming to presence for man? Does not every form of life as such have a tendency to secure itself in its being, indeed to persist in it? Is it not precisely its finitude that it wants to tarry in this manner? And does it not hold for man as well that the Dasein in him, as Heidegger called it, is not to be thought of at all as a kind of highest self-possession that allows him to step outside the circuit of life like a god? Isn't our entire doctrine of man distorted rather than put in order by modern metaphysical subjectivism, in that we consider the essence of man to be society ($\zeta\tilde{\omega}o\nu\ \pi o\lambda\iota\tau\iota\kappa\acute{o}\nu$)? Is it not just this belief that declares the inner tension and ambiguity that is being itself? And does it not mean that it is senseless to pit "nature" against "being"?

The continuing difficulty is that of avoiding the language of metaphysics, which conceives of all these matters in terms of the "power of reflection". But what do we mean when we speak of the "language of metaphysics"? It is obvious that the experience of "essence" is not that of manipulating thinking. If we keep this distinction in mind, we can see that the concept of "re-collection" has something natural about it. It is true that recollection itself is something and that in it history has its reality, not that history is simply remembered through it. But what takes place in "recollection"? Is it really tenable to expect something like a reversal in it – like the abruptness of fate? Whatever the case may be, the important thing in the phenomenon of recollection, it seems to me, is that something is secured and preserved in the "there," so that it can never not be, as long as recollection remains alive. Yet recollection is not something that clutches tenaciously at what is vanishing; the nonexistence of what disappears is not at all concealed or obstinately disputed by it. Rather, something like consent takes place in it (of which Rilke's *Duino Elegies* tell us something). There is nothing of what we have called "insistence" in it.

Conversely, what we may call "fascination" arises through the constructive capacity and technological power of "insistence," that is, of human forgetfulness of Being. There is essentially no limit to the experience of being, which, since Nietzsche, we call nihilism. But if this fascination proceeds from such a constantly intensifying obstinacy, does it not find its own ultimate end in itself, precisely by virtue of the fact that the constantly new becomes something left behind, and that this happens *without* a special event intervening or a reversal taking place? Does not the natural weight of things remain perceptible and make itself felt the more monotonously the noise of the constantly new may sound forth? To be sure, Hegel's idea of knowledge, conceived as absolute self-transparency, has something fantastic about it if it is supposed to restore complete at-homeness in being. But could not a restoration of at-homeness come about in the sense that the process of making-oneself-at-home in the world has never ceased to take place, and has never ceased to be the better reality that is not deafened by the madness of technology? Does this restoration not occur when the illusory character of the technocracy, the paralyzing sameness of everything man can make, becomes perceptible, and man is released again into the really astonishing character of his own finite being? This freedom is certainly not gained in the sense of an absolute transparency, or a being-at-home that is no longer endangered. But just as the thinking of what cannot be preconceived [*das Denken des Unvordenklichen*] preserves what is its own, for example, the homeland, what cannot be preconceived regarding our finitude is reunited with itself in the constant process of the coming to language of our Dasein.

In the up and down movement, in coming into being and passing away, it is "there."

Is this the old metaphysics? Is it the language of metaphysics alone that achieves this continual coming-to-language of our being-in-the-world? Certainly it is the language of metaphysics, but further behind it is the language of the Indo-Germanic peoples, which makes such thinking capable of formulation. But can a language — or a family of languages — ever properly be called the language of metaphysical thinking, just because metaphysics was thought, or what would be more, anticipated in it? Is not language always the language of the homeland and the process of becoming-at-home in the world? And does this fact not mean that language knows no restrictions and never breaks down, because it holds infinite possibilities of utterance in readiness? It seems to me that the hermeneutical dimension enters here and demonstrates its inner infinity in the speaking that takes place in the dialogue. To be sure, the technical language of philosophy is preformed by the grammatical structure of the Greek language, and its usages in Graeco-Latin times established ontological implications whose prejudiced character Heidegger uncovered. But we must ask: are the universality of objectifying reason and the eidetic structure of linguistic meanings really bound to these particular historically developed interpretations of *subjectum* and *species* and *actus* that the West has produced? Or do they hold true for all languages? It cannot be denied that there are certain structural aspects of the Greek language and a grammatical self-consciousness, particularly in Latin, that fix in a definite direction of interpretation the hierarchy of genus and species, the relation of substance and accident, the structure of predication and the verb as an action word. But is there no rising above such a preschematizing of thought? For instance, if one contrasts the Western predicative judgment with the Eastern figurative expression, which acquires its expressive power from the reciprocal reflection of what is meant and what is said, are these two not in truth only different modes of utterance within one and the same universal, namely within the essence of language and reason? Do concept and judgment not remain embedded within the life of meaning of the language we speak and in which we know how to say what it is we mean? And conversely, cannot the connotative aspect of such Oriental reflective expressions always be drawn into the hermeneutical movement that creates common understanding, just as the expression of the work of art can? Language always arises within such a movement. Can anyone really contend that there has ever been language in any other sense than in the fulfilling of such a movement? Hegel's doctrine of the speculative proposition too seems to me to have its place here, and always takes up into itself its own sharpening into the dialectic of contradiction. For in speaking, there always remains the possibility of cancelling the objectifying tendency of language, just as Hegel cancels the logic of understanding, Heidegger the language of metaphysics, the Orientals the diversity of realms of being, and the poet everything given. But to cancel [*aufheben*] means to take up and use.

NOTES

1. Cf. Gerhard Krüger, "Martin Heidegger und der Humanismus," *Theologische Rundschau,* XVIII (1950), pp. 148-178.

2. Cf. Oskar Becker, "Von der Hinfälligkeit des Schönen und der Abenteuerlichkeit des Künstlers," published originally in the *Festschrift für Husserl* (1929), pp. 27-52.

Index

Adorno, Theodor, 147, 178
Aeschylus, 52
Aquinas, St. Thomas, 229
Aristophanes, 22
Aristotle, xix, xxiv, xxxii, xxxvii, 14, 21, 34, 59, 63 f., 68, 78, 119 f., 123, 155, 177, 178, 181, 196, 200-202, 204, 211, 212, 229, 232
Augustine, St., 46, 55, 176, 200, 206, 229
Avenarius, Richard, 146, 186

Bacon, Francis, 70
Barth, Karl, 137
Baumgarten, Alexander, 219
Becker, Oskar, 157, 177, 179, 181, 195, 212, 233, 235, 240
Bergson, Henri, xlii, 116, 172, 214
Berkeley, George, 165
Biel, Gabriel, 200
Bloch, Ernst, 233
Boeckh, August, 45
Brentano, Franz, 35, 123, 144, 145, 155 f., 175, 178, 203
Bultmann, Rudolf, 44, 199, 200, 206 f.

Cassirer, Ernst, 76, 199, 211
Chamberlin, Houston Stewart, 107
Chladenius, xii, 212
Cicero, 43
Cohen, Hermann, 201
Conrad-Martius, Hedwig, 150, 166, 178

Descartes, Rene, xvi, xlii, xlix, li, 24, 153, 155, 160, 185, 192, 200
Dilthey, Wilhelm, xiii-xiv, xx, xlii, 4, 18, 48, 115 f., 117, 214
Dionysus, 116
Dockhorn, Klaus, 43
Dostoevsky, Fyodor, 140
Droysen, Friedrich, 28, 47 f., 99 f., 114

Ebeling, Gerhard, xxvi, 43
Ebner, Ferdinand, 65
Eliot, T. S., 235
Ernst, Paul, 213
Euclid, 47

241